P9-CCC-267

Montana

NORMA TIRRELL
Photography by John Reddy

COMPASS AMERICAN GUIDES
An Imprint of Fodor's Travel Publications

Montana

Fifth Edition

ISBN 0-676-90133-6

Copyright © 2002 Fodor's Travel Publications
Maps Copyright © 2002 Fodor's Travel Publications

Compass American Guides and colophon are trademarks of Random House, Inc.
Fodor's is a registered trademark of Random House, Inc.

All rights reserved. No part of this publication may be translated, reproduced, or transmitted in any form or by any means, electronic or mechanical, including photocopying and recording, or by any information storage and retrieval system, without the written permission of the Publisher, except brief extracts by a reviewer for inclusion in critical articles or reviews.

Although the Publishers and the Author of this book have made every effort to ensure the information was correct at the time of going to press, the Publishers and the Author do not assume and hereby disclaim any liability to any party for any loss or damage caused by errors, omissions, misleading information, or any potential travel disruption due to labor or financial difficulty, whether such errors or omissions result from negligence, accident, or any other cause.

Editors: Julia Dillon, Barry Parr
Designers: Christopher Burt, Julia Dillon
Managing Editor: Kit Duane

Cover Design: Siobhan O'Hare
Map Design: Mark Stroud, Moon Street Cartography

Compass American Guides, Inc., 5332 College Ave., Suite 201, Oakland, CA 94618, USA

10 9 8 7 6 5 4 3 2 1   Manufactured in China

ACKNOWLEDGMENTS

THANKS ARE DUE FIRST TO **STAN MEYER**, for his vote of confidence, and to **Barry Parr**, for his encouragement and unyielding demands as an editor and writing coach. Grateful recognition goes to my technical advisers: historians **David Walter** and **Vivian Paladin**; geologist **Ray Breuninger**; wildlife and conservation pro **Jim Posewitz**; economist **Phil Brooks**; census and economic research specialists **Patricia Roberts** and **Jan Clack**; arts advocates **David Nelson**, **Jo-Anne Mussulman**, and **Julia Smith**; and photo archivists **Becca Kohl** and **Lory Morrow**. Thanks are also due my informal council of advisers: backroads buffs **Rick Rogne**, **Ken Walchek**, **Doug Monger**, and **Tom Palmer**; community insiders **Sally Mullen**, **Mick Mills**, **Becky Tirrell**, **Shirley Zupan**, **Dale Herbert**, **Patty Rambo Short**, **Victor Bjornberg**, and **Deirdre Boggs**. I am grateful, as always, to **Sherryl Vaughn** for proofreading. And I salute **John Reddy** for his photographic eye.

The publisher wishes to thank the following institutions and individuals for the use of their illustrations: **Montana Historical Society, Helena**, pp. 9, 31, 32, 34, 37, 63, 70, 81, 85, 93, 95, 101, 153, 163, 171, 192, 202, 221; **Bancroft Library, University of California at Berkeley**, pp. 30, 126; **C.M. Russell Museum, Great Falls**, 129, 243; **Independence National Historic Park, Philadelphia**, p. 42; **Travel Montana**, pp. 109, 255; **Douglas O'Looney**, pp. 38, 71, 72, 111, 215; **Galen Rowell**, p. 53; **Greg Vaughn** p. 79; and **Mark Zimmerer and the Yellowstone Art Museum**, p. 243. The quote on pages 148-149 by **Richard Ford** from *Rock Springs*, copyright 1987 is reprinted by permission of Atlantic Monthly Press. The quote on page 135 by **Mildred Walker** from *Winter Wheat* is reprinted by permission of the University of Nebraska Press; © 1944 by Harcourt Brace, © 1971 renewed by Mildred Walker. Excerpts from *The Book of Yaak* by Rick Bass, © 1996 by Rick Bass. Reprinted by permission of Houghton Mifflin Company. All rights reserved.

*For Bennett, with whom I share Montana's mountains and headwaters,
and for Janet, with whom I walked its deepest valley.*

C O N T E N T S

Literary Extracts

Topical Essays

Maps

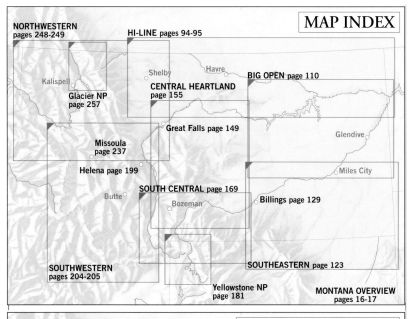

MAP INDEX

NORTHWESTERN
pages 248-249

HI-LINE pages 94-95

Kalispell

Shelby

Havre

BIG OPEN page 110

Glacier NP
page 257

CENTRAL HEARTLAND
page 155

Great Falls page 149

Glendive

Missoula
page 237

Helena page 199

Miles City

Butte

SOUTH CENTRAL page 169

Billings page 129

Bozeman

SOUTHWESTERN
pages 204-205

SOUTHEASTERN page 123

Yellowstone NP
page 181

MONTANA OVERVIEW
pages 16-17

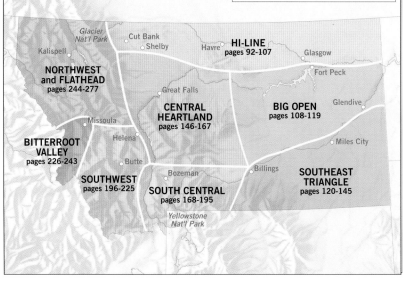

CHAPTER DIVISION

Glacier
Nat'l Park

Cut Bank

Shelby

Havre

HI-LINE
pages 92-107

Glasgow

Kalispell

NORTHWEST
and FLATHEAD
pages 244-277

Fort Peck

Great Falls

CENTRAL
HEARTLAND
pages 146-167

BIG OPEN
pages 108-119

Glendive

Missoula

Helena

BITTERROOT
VALLEY
pages 226-243

Butte

Billings

Miles City

Bozeman

SOUTHWEST
pages 196-225

SOUTH CENTRAL
pages 168-195

SOUTHEAST
TRIANGLE
pages 120-145

Yellowstone
Nat'l Park

AUTHOR'S PREFACE

LIKE MOST GUIDEBOOKS, THIS ONE is a personal reflection of its author. If I dwell on rivers and mountains, it is because that is where I spend much of my time. What will it be this weekend, Ten Lakes or the Missouri River? Bighorn Canyon or the Big Hole River? Cross-country skiing in Glacier or Yellowstone? These are the hard, year-round choices a Montanan faces. All national treasures, they are but a handful of gold nuggets in Montana's outdoor recreation bonanza.

If history keeps bobbing up, it is because the past is never out of reach in a state so young you can still sit at the knees of wranglers, homesteaders, miners, and tribal elders who keep it alive. Visit old Jake Hoover's sod-roof cabin in the Judith River country, and you'll see where cowboy artist Charlie Russell spent his early years and derived the inspiration to create his inimitable Western landscapes. Or take a walking tour of uptown Butte to sense the magnitude of the rivalry that existed between William Clark and Marcus Daly in their quest for dominance of the copper industry and the statehouse. Clark may have built the most ostentatious mansion, but it wasn't long before Daly blocked his view with a massive apartment house next door.

No longer boss of Montana's economy and politics, copper remains the symbol of a colonial state, historically driven by outside interests. After more than 150 years of long-distance promises about beaver pelts, gold, copper, silver, oil, coal, cattle, wheat, and timber, the nation's fourth-largest state still can't muster sufficient economic vitality to support more than one-third of one percent of the U.S. population—902,000 souls in all, scattered across nearly 150,000 square miles (388,500 sq. km).

But it is the resilience and diversity of its meager population that give Montana its fresh face and big heart. Smoke rising from Crow Indian sweat lodges beside Interstate 90 and cornucopian displays of fresh produce at Montana's Hutterite colonies hint at the cultural mix. Full-tilt Western blowouts, like the Miles City Bucking Horse Sale and Lewistown's Cowboy Poetry Gathering, are brassy statements about Montana's overriding cowboy culture and its attendant mythology.

In one of his essays, Wallace Stegner spoke of the importance of "placeness" in an increasingly "placeless" society. "If you don't know where you are," he said, "you don't know who you are." Montanans may be uncertain of their future, but they have never entertained doubts about their sense of place. It means more to them than money in the bank.

Through my own subjective mix of places, people, and events, I have tried to familiarize you with this addictive place. Mine is the view of a native who loves her state, and a journalist with no formal training in history, economics, or any of the isms or ologies that would lend this text the weight of authority. With any luck, it will send you searching for many of the titles that distinguish Montana nationally as a literary heavyweight. Good reading and happy travels.

Homesteaders were told of the mild winters, prodigious crop yields, and unlimited opportunity that awaited them in Montana; what many found was isolation, dust, drought, and drudgery. (Montana Historical Society)

(following pages) A perfect rainbow crowns Walton Mountain in Glacier National Park.

O V E R V I E W

MONTANA

The name *Montana* is derived from the Spanish word for mountain—yet only a third of the state is mountanous. In the west, more than two dozen distinct ranges comprise Montana's share of the Rockies. Elevations swing from valley floors at 3,500 feet to the 12,000-foot peaks of the Beartooth Plateau.

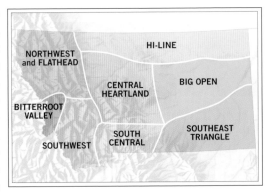

THE HI-LINE: MONTANA'S NORTHERN TIER   *pages 92–107*

The Hi-Line is the moniker given to the vast flat expanse of northern Montana running along the Canadian border from North Dakota to the foothills of the Rockies, near Cut Bank. It is a lonely stretch of land populated by ranchers, Native Americans, and Hutterites. The weather is as extreme as it gets in this nation, with a record temperatures of 60ºF below 0 in winter and 117° in summer.

THE BIG OPEN: EAST CENTRAL MONTANA   *pages 108–119*

East central Montana—the lonely, sparsely populated expanse of land between the Yellowstone River to the south and the Missouri to the north—is known as the Big Open. The largest town in its 12,000 square miles is the village of Circle, with only 700 inhabitants. Fort Peck Reservoir is the region's most notable natural feature.

SOUTHEAST TRIANGLE

pages 120–145

Like the Big Open, south-eastern Montana is Big Sky country. A land of canyons, buttes, and badlands, it is also home to Billings, one of the state's largest cities, and to major attractions, incuding the Big Horn Canyon and the Little Big Horn Battlefield Monument.

CENTRAL HEARTLAND *pages 146–167*

Central Montana marks the transition from plains to mountains and rangeland to wheat land. The foothills and front range of the Rockies run north to south through this area and provide some of Montana's lovliest scenery and recreation possiblities. In the city of Great Falls is the famous C. M. Russell Museum.

SOUTH CENTRAL: YELLOWSTONE COUNTRY *pages 168–195*

The Greater Yellowstone Ecosystem (which contains the eponymous national park) is an immense wilderness plateau straddling the Continental Divide and shaping the landscape of Wyoming, Idaho, and Montana. Montana's Yellowstone Country extends north from the park—home to elk, grizzly bears, buffalo, geese,

and swans—to Bozeman, Livingston, and Big Timber. It stretches west to the Madison River and beyond to the Gravelly Range and the Tobacco Root Mountains; and it reaches east to the mountain town of Red Lodge, at the base of the 12,000-foot-high Beartooth Plateau. Within are stunning natural wonders:

the Grand Canyon of the Yellowstone, 12,799-foot-high Granite Peak, trout-rich Madison River, and Red Rock Lakes, a wildlife sanctuary for the trumpeter swan. Even driving is a pleasure when the road follows a sparkling river and promises glimpses of golden eagles, elk, and bighorn sheep along the way.

SOUTHWEST MONTANA   *pages 196–225*

Livestock and high-tech mining operations are the bones and sinew of this corner of the state. While the prospector mining spirit lives on in weathered ghost towns and Victorian mansions, today visitors "mine" the area not just for its colorful history but also for its natural beauty and recreational opportunities—its trout streams and forested mountains. Georgetown Lake, the Anaconda-Pintler Wilderness, the Big Hole River, and Gates of the Mountains are just some of the getaways that make this part of the state so attractive to sightseers and sportsmen.

MISSOULA AND BITTERROOT COUNTRY   *pages 226–243*

The Bitterroot Valley takes its name from the river that flows its length and the mountain range that forms its western wall—and both are named for the diminu-

tive wildflower that grows in the ponderosa forests here. This distinctive valley, which resembles a snout on the face of western Montana, appears isolated from the rest of the state but is central to its history. Here too is Missoula, the state's most sophisticated city.

NORTHWEST MONTANA AND THE FLATHEAD
pages 244–277

Bordered by wilderness, encircled by mountains, watered generously by lakes and rivers, and soothed by a Pacific Northwest climate, the Flathead Valley makes its living hosting visitors. The raw materials are Flathead Lake and a stockpile of nationally protected recreational resources: Glacier National Park; the adjacent Bob Marshall Wilderness; the National Bison Range; Jewel Basin Hiking Area; Mission Mountains Wilderness; and Flathead National Wild and Scenic River. Add The

Big Mountain ski resort and a chain of lakes called the Seeley Swan, and you have a year-round playground of immense proportions. streams, and small, friendly towns. It's an addictive landscape for both residents and visitors, but not for those who thrive on the infinite sky and open spaces of eastern Montana.

Unlike the thirsty, windswept plains of eastern Montana, the northwest woods fill up with snow each winter, yielding roughly double the moisture of the Big Open. Here, the trees grow so thick that there isn't space to graze a cow. David Thompson, the first non-native explorer to chart these woods and waters, noted that the area's isolation left its timber "without the possibility of being brought to market."

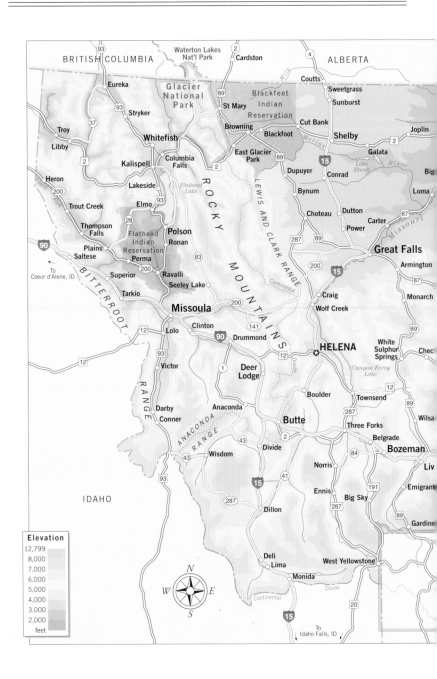

Elevation

12,799
8,000
7,000
6,000
5,000
4,000
3,000
2,000
feet

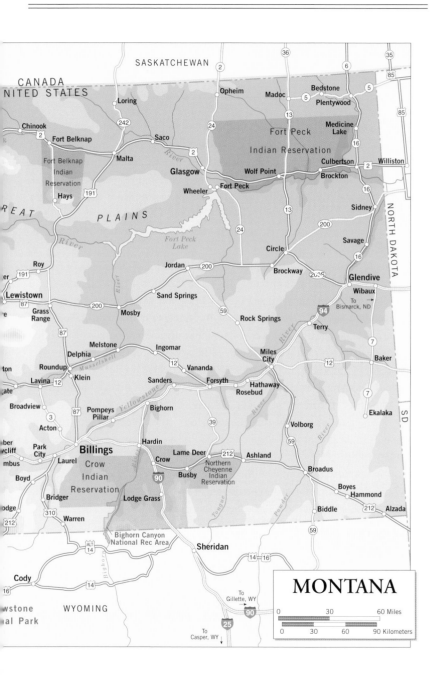

MONTANA

0   30   60 Miles

0   30   60   90 Kilometers

INTRODUCTION

■ LAND AND SPACE, MOUNTAINS AND SKY

DRIVING ACROSS EASTERN MONTANA—from, say, Sidney to Lewistown—can be either an uneasy or an exhilarating experience. Uneasy if you find comfort in crowds; exhilarating if space is what you seek. The trip will take the better part of a day, and still you will be only halfway across the state. You will travel through all or part of five counties (roughly the equivalent of driving from Maine to New York) with a total population of fewer than 30,000. Of those counties, Garfield has 1,280 residents scattered over an area about the same size as Connecticut, with its 3.4 million people.

If you are open to a new perception of beauty, the lunar landscapes of eastern Montana can be endlessly absorbing. This is the Earth itself speaking, but if you have been conditioned to the babel of humanity, you may not hear it. So pack along a cassette tape of *High Plains Music* by Montana native, Phil Aaberg. His high-spirited and haunting piano celebrates the landscape and beckons you to the uninterrupted stretch of highway ahead. Soon, you will realize that you are surrounded not by emptiness, but by *space*. In Montana, there is a difference.

Eastern Montana space is filled with the subtlest forms of beauty. Shifting light and shadow play on coulees, badlands, and breaks. Western meadowlarks remind you with one astonishing trill that it's good to be alive. Neutral earth tones of ocher and sage magnify a 180-degree backdrop of sky that broods and shimmers in primary colors.

Driving south from Lewistown, the space becomes more immediate, more dramatic. It is defined by solitary mountain ranges that appear as islands in an ocean of grass—the Big Snowies, the Little Belts, the Castles, and the Crazies. Keeping to themselves in the distance, these isolated ranges are your signal that the landscape is about to change dramatically.

■ FROM PLAINS TO MOUNTAINS

Turning west at Big Timber, you might as well be in a different state. In fact, you have reached Montana's mid-point. Yet to come are the mountains that gave Montana its name. First, the Absarokas and the Bridgers, then the Madison Range, the

Tobacco Roots, the Pioneers, the Sapphires, and on and on, range after range, until they meld into one hazy ridge floating on the horizon. These views need no introduction; you've seen them on movie screens and travel posters. This is the Montana that outsiders know about: the mountains and trout streams, guest ranches and ski resorts, national parks and wilderness areas. You may have missed where the Dakota plains ended and the plains of eastern Montana began, but the imprint of the Northern Rockies will stay with you forever.

Scooped out of each range of mountains is a glaciated valley fed by rivers and streams that begin as snowfall on peaks that range from 7,000 to 12,000 feet above sea level. But for an occasional town or small city, these timbered valleys and granite ranges are the domain of wildlife—abundant populations of elk, deer, moose, mountain goats, bighorn sheep, waterfowl, upland birds, and trout. The roster includes endangered and threatened species like the bald eagle, gray wolf, and grizzly bear. A popular Montana guest ranch offers this comparison to illustrate the company Montanans keep and the space they enjoy:

PER SQUARE MILE IN MONTANA

3.3 deer ❧ 1.4 elk or antelope ❧ 896 catchable-size trout ❧ 6 people

The conventional view of a remote, sparsely populated state like Montana is that there is nothing going on out here. Just land and space. In his *Montana: High, Wide, and Handsome,* Joseph Kinsey Howard wrote: "Montana is a remote hinterland about as well known to the average eastern seaboard citizen as East or West Africa. But it is this space that defines Montana and shapes the outlook of its residents." The newsman and historian also said of this place:

> This sums up what I want in life—room to swing my arms and to swing my mind. Where is there more opportunity than in Montana for creation of these broad margins, physical and intellectual? Where is there more opportunity to enjoy the elemental values of living, bright sun and clean air and space? We have room. We can be neighbors without getting in each other's hair. We can be individuals.

The fact that there is still a place like Montana, where humanity does not dominate the landscape, is immensely important in a world that is overrun with people and their impact. Space and an unspoiled landscape are increasingly hard to come by, and herein lies Montana's appeal.

■ LIFESTYLE

Montanans treasure their space and the lifestyle it allows. Residents of even the largest cities can be skiing, hiking, fishing, or hunting in less than an hour. The Rattlesnake Wilderness is only a mile from the city limits of Missoula, western Montana's largest city. The people of Kalispell regard Glacier National Park as their own backyard. Bozeman skiers can choose between two of Montana's premier downhill areas—Bridger Bowl is 15 miles north, Big Sky 30 miles south. And one of Montana's finest floating and fishing rivers, the Missouri, is a half-hour drive from Bozeman, Helena, and Great Falls.

Isolation, a harsh climate, and a fickle, historically resource-based economy over which they have little control are the trade-offs Montanans are willing to make for this lifestyle. Global markets control the commodities that come from Montana: grain, livestock, minerals, energy fuels, and timber. Because of Montana's isolation from the nation's commercial centers, most of these are shipped out of the state as raw materials. It is cheaper to refine them near the markets where they will be used. The result back home is what one newspaperman has described as a "niche-poor" economy that cannot provide enough good-paying jobs to keep people, especially young people, in the state.

Montana's history has been marked by uneven growth and decline. Following nearly three decades of prosperity starting in the 1950s, Montana's population reached a peak of 824,000 in 1985. In the 1980s, Montanans were shaken by upheavals in the state's oil and gas, transportation, and timber industries. The clincher was a persistent drought that damaged the agriculture industry in much of eastern Montana, and kindled massive forest fires in the west. In this decade Montana's economy shrunk by one percent, and by 1990, the population had slipped to just under 800,000. The 1990s were a period of growth. Population increased to 902,000 by the year 2000. The economy was also strong, with gross state output (adjusted for inflation) increasing about 29 percent. The outlook for the 21st century is bright as Montana shifts from a cyclical, resource-based economy to a more diversified and sustainable economy built on small business and the service and construction industries. Between 1991 and 1996, the number of jobs in Montana increased by 15 percent—the biggest jump in two decades. The downside is that Montana consistently ranks towards the bottom in state-by-state comparisons of per capita income, and currently holds the title of lowest wages in the nation. Still, fewer than 10 percent say they would move out of state for higher

paying jobs. Some time ago, *Newsweek* presented a pessimistic forecast for the upper Great Plains and northern Rocky Mountain region, including Montana, in an article entitled "America's Outback." Describing the area as a "lost frontier" prone to chronic recession and decline, the magazine pronounced it, for all intents and purposes, dead. Montanans had mixed reactions to the article, rejecting the death sentence but warming up to a new nickname. America's Outback. They liked it. In two words, it sized up what they love about their state.

No one ever said it was easy to live in Montana. But for those who have staked their claim here, it is the *only* place to live.

■ A LAND AT ODDS WITH ITSELF

From the high plains of eastern Montana to the Rocky Mountain west, Montana has never made much sense as one state. Physically, economically, politically, and socially, it has always been at odds with itself. Back in 1880, when Montana was still a territory, the vast majority of its residents lived in the west, as a majority do today. According to the late historian K. Ross Toole, no one gave much thought to the plains at that time. In his 1959 history of the state, *Montana: An Uncommon Land,* he theorized that in 1889, when it came time to draw state boundaries, the plains were "simply marked off and drawn in."

The result is a sprawling state that is pulled in opposite directions. Endowed with adequate rainfall, minerals, timber, rivers, and abundant wildlife, the mountains and valleys of western Montana support a diversified economy of government and education, mining, wood products, tourism, and recreation. Most of Montana's population live in these stream-fed western valleys. (Even so, the region's largest city, Missoula, has a population of just under 57,000.)

While western Montana is considered an extension of the Pacific Northwest, it is hard to tell where eastern Montana ends and the Dakotas begin. Eastern Montana is the heart and soul of the northern Great Plains, and it has nothing to do with western Montana. Residents of Montana's extreme eastern corners travel regularly to nearby Williston, North Dakota, and Belle Fourche, South Dakota, for shopping and entertainment, and are oriented toward the Dakotas' media and public affairs. To compound this east-west schism, Montanans living along the sparsely populated northern tier are as much at home in the western Canadian cities of Regina, Moose Jaw, and Lethbridge as they are in Glasgow, Havre, and Great Falls.

The Pryor Mountains are a remote, highland junction of desert and ice west of Bighorn Canyon, on Montana's southern border.

H I S T O R Y

■ NATURAL HISTORY AND GEOLOGY

MONTANA'S MOST SCENIC FEATURES were born in violent natural acts that place the exploits of humanity in the realm of light comedy. Fire and ice, wind and water—in the form of rivers of molten lava, massive glaciers, vast shallow seas, scorching heat: these are the ancient forces that sculpted the mountains, scoured the plains, chiseled river canyons, scooped out great basins, and nurtured a prehistoric kingdom of dinosaurs.

While the "basement" rocks that underlie the northern Rockies can be traced back 2.5 to 3 billion years, the Rockies themselves did not begin forming until some 100 million years ago. Before that, Montana was a flat plain, flooded periodically by shallow water. The action that created the dramatic landscape we know today began when giant masses of molten rock deep within the Earth began rising to the surface. Pushing and heaving, they broke the surface to create some of the peaks that distinguish the Western mountain ranges. The action was compounded by tectonic pressure that pushed, folded, and thrust the soft sedimentary surface rock eastward. Further tension stretched the Earth's crust east and west, forcing north-south blocks to tilt upward. The result was a massive jumble of mountains ranges, whose peaks and valleys have been further defined by rivers and glaciers over millions of years. As the mountains grew from the plain, surrounding seas drained away, but not all at once. Episodic floods engendered periods of lush plant growth followed by drought, leaving carbon-rich dessicated plant life to accumulate between successive layers of marine sediment. Millions of years of pressure cooked and compacted these deposits into thick beds containing petroleum, gas, and coal, all of which lie beneath the plains of central and eastern Montana.

Once formed, the peaks of the Rockies spent several ice ages buried under glaciers, rivers of ice that flowed and slid down mountains, gouging valleys and carving the details of today's landscape. Vestiges of these ice ages are most visible in northwestern Montana's **Glacier National Park,** which gets its name not from the glistening white snow patches that cling to its mountains today, but from the ancient ice sheets that molded this magnificent park. Glacier's photogenic vistas, its sculptured peaks, chiseled valleys, dazzling lakes, waterfalls, and cascades are all testimony to the last great glaciers that melted about 10,000 years ago.

The interdendent artistry of fire and ice is especially evident in Yellowstone National Park; in fact, the twins forces are still at work, performing their act to this day. Yellowstone was created by a series of volcanic eruptions, the most recent of which began more than a million years ago and culminated in a blast 600,000 years ago, larger than any other that can be detected today in the geologic record today. The explosion spewed tons of gases and hot ash across North America, with fragments landing more than a thousand miles away. Estimates rank this cataclysmic blowout anywhere from 1,000 to 10,000 times greater than the Mount St. Helens blast of 1980. More recently, receding glaciers and diminishing seas carved out the majestic Grand Canyon of the Yellowstone. But fire and water are not finished with Yellowstone yet, and we can thank the Earth's thin crust here for enabling the awesome duet they perform today—and for making Yellowstone the busiest hot spot on the globe. Intense geothermal heat forces water from the area's many underground springs, and as it flows through complicated volcanic "plumbing," the water superheats, building up pressure until it finally erupts in the form of spouting geysers, bubbling mud caldrons, hot springs, and steaming fumaroles.

■ THE AGE OF DINOSAURS

For 140 million years—more than twice as long as mammals have dominated the Earth—dinosaurs ruled the world, and the evidence of their domain is plentiful in Montana. As the Rockies were forming and dinosaurs were dying, sediment sloughed off the rising slopes and formed a layer over their remains. In later epochs glaciers scoured the plains, removing layers of sedimentation that had long buried dinosaur remains. Today, fossils are found on or near the surface of a land that has been largely undisturbed by industrial or residential development. Thanks its prehistory, Montana is a naturally perfect laboratory for the study of dinosaurs, and not surprisingly, the state attracts (as well as produces) some of the world's leading dinosaur paleontologists.

In recent years, a few of those experts are challenging long-held views about the physiology, and by extension the behavior, of these prehistoric creatures. Fossil discoveries by Montana paleontologist Jack Horner have forced scientists to rethink old theories about dinosaurs, long presumed to be solitary, cold-blooded beasts more dependent upon brawn than brains for survival. Horner, who presides over the paleontology wing of Montana's Museum of the Rockies, made one of his field's most important discoveries in 1978. Following a tip from an amateur paleontologist, he unearthed a nest of dinosaur eggs and hatchlings on the eastern slope of the Rocky Mountains near Choteau. Later digs revealed more nests and a huge bone bed that lend credence to an emerging theory that dinosaurs were less like reptiles and more like birds: warm-blooded creatures that traveled in herds and cared for their young.

A must-see attraction for dinosaur lovers of all ages is the **Museum of the Rockies,** located on the campus of Montana State University in Bozeman. In addition to lifelike displays, exhibits, and a fossil preparation room where visitors can watch scientists at work, the museum sponsors summer field trips that enable visitors to participate in dinosaur digs with knowledgeable "bone hunters." Field training in fossil location and identification is also available at the **Old Trail Museum** in Choteau, near the site where dinosaur nests were first discovered. Visitors to

A robotic Triceratops family greets visitors at the Museum of the Rockies in Bozeman.

southeastern Montana will be surprised by the **Carter County Museum** in the tiny town of Ekalaka. Developed by local amateur paleontologists, the museum houses an impressive collection of bones and fossils, including the 35-foot-long skeleton of a duck-billed dinosaur named *Anatosaurus.* Long recognized as an important paleontological site, this area has also turned up some of the oldest evidence of humanity in North America.

■ THE FIRST "MONTANANS"

◆ PALEO-INDIANS

Montana's human record is but a millisecond on the geologic timetable. It is believed that Asiatic peoples first entered North America between 10,000 and 30,000 years ago during a period of glaciation when sea levels dropped enough to form a land bridge across the Bering Strait. These Asian migrants traveled south from Alaska along the eastern slope of the Rockies on what has become known as the "Great North Trail." Some wandered all the way to South America.

Those who remained in the north left evidence indicating they hunted big game animals, including the now extinct mammoth. Following a major climatic change that turned the Great Plains into a desert, both the hunters and the hunted disappeared. Beginning about 6,000 to 7,000 years ago, a different crowd moved north from the desert southwest. More foragers than hunters, these migrants occupied the western valleys. About 2,000 years later, the last wave of prehistoric migrants—the so-called "late hunters"—entered Montana from the south and west. Historians believe they were the direct ancestors of today's Indian tribes. Evidence of their culture lingers in the tepee rings and buffalo jumps that still exist on the plains of eastern and central Montana.

◆ NATIVE AMERICANS OF THE MODERN ERA

The ancestors of Montana's present-day Indian tribes roamed the plains as hunters, relying on vast herds of bison that once ranged throughout the American West. Plains Indians as we think of them today did not arrive in Montana until after 1620. (Flathead Indians, the only Montana tribe living west of the Continental Divide, had come about a century earlier.) For a period of about 250 years following the arrival of the first Plains Indians, several tribes flourished on the plains and in the western valleys before being displaced by non-native expansionism.

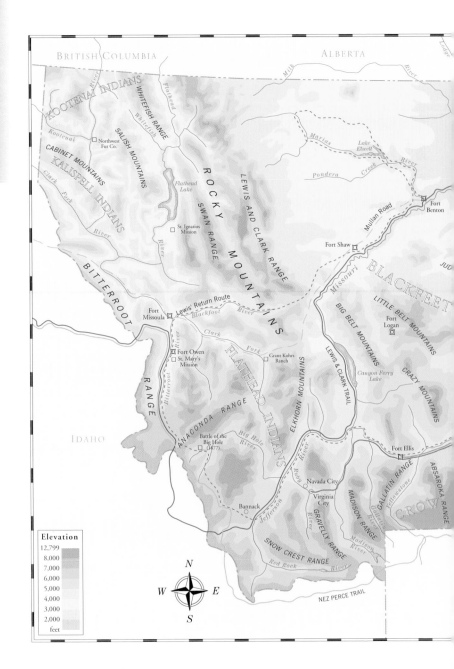

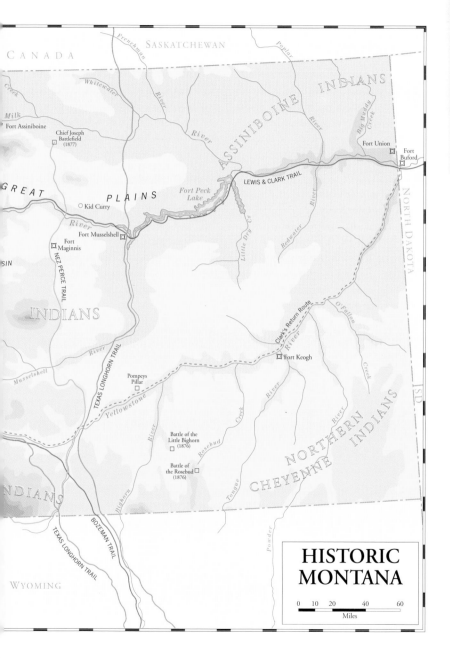

CANADA

SASKATCHEWAN

Frenchman

Poplar

Whitewater

Creek

River

Milk

River

Fort Assiniboine

Chief Joseph
Battlefield
(1877)

ASSINIBOINE INDIANS

River

Big Muddy Creek

Fort Union

Fort
Buford

GREAT PLAINS

Fort Peck
Lake

LEWIS & CLARK TRAIL

NORTH DAKOTA

Kid Curry

River

River

Redwater

Little Dry Cr.

Fort Musselshell

Fort
Maginnis

'SIN

NEZ PERCE TRAIL

Clark's Return Route

O'Fallon

INDIANS

River

TEXAS LONGHORN TRAIL

Fort Keogh

River

S.D.

Musselshell

Pompeys
Pillar

River

Creek

River

Creek

NORTHERN CHEYENNE INDIANS

Yellowstone

River

Battle of the
Little Bighorn
(1876)

Rosebud

Battle of
the Rosebud
(1876)

Tongue

NDIANS

Bighorn

BOZEMAN TRAIL

Powder

TEXAS LONGHORN TRAIL

HISTORIC
MONTANA

WYOMING

0 10 20   40   60

Miles

Blackfeet

Moving into Montana from the north and east were the powerful Blackfeet Indians, whose fierce war parties dominated north-central Montana and whose influence reached as far south as present-day Yellowstone National Park. Montana's largest Indian tribe, they now live on the Blackfeet Indian Reservation at the eastern edge of Glacier National Park.

Gros Ventre, Assiniboine, and Yanktonai Sioux

To the east of the Blackfeet were the Atsinas, who came to be known as the Gros Ventres, or "Big Bellies." Once allies of the Blackfeet, the Gros Ventres later aligned themselves with the Assiniboine and now live with them on the Fort Belknap Indian Reservation between the Milk River and the Little Rocky Mountains in north-central Montana. Another band of Assiniboine Indians aligned themselves with the Yanktonai Sioux; the two tribes now live together on northeastern Montana's Fort Peck Indian Reservation.

Crow

Moving into the Yellowstone River valley from the east were the Crows, enemies of the Blackfeet. Once ranging over a broad area that stretched from the upper Yellowstone River into the Big Horn and Wind River mountains of Wyoming, they now live on the Crow Indian Reservation, covering most of Big Horn County in south-central Montana.

Northern Cheyenne

Between the Crow reservation and the Tongue River to the east is the Northern Cheyenne Indian Reservation. The Northern Cheyenne arrived in Montana later than most other Plains Indians but were here in time to join forces with the Sioux to defeat Lt. Col. George Armstrong Custer in 1876 at the Battle of the Little Bighorn.

Chippewa and Cree

The last Plains Indians to arrive were the Chippewas and Crees of Algonquin heritage, and the Metis, or "Mixed Bloods," who were a racial mixture of Cree, Assiniboine, Chippewa, and French. Rocky Boy's Indian Reservation lies northwest of the Bear Paw Mountains in north-central Montana.

Salish and Kootenai

To the west of the Continental Divide were the tribes of the Columbia Plateau, which clustered in villages and relied on plants and fish. Plateau Indians living in Montana, most notably the Salish and Kootenai, combined the two lifestyles, crossing the mountains to hunt buffalo in the summer and returning to their villages in the winter. Today, the Salish and Kootenai live together on Montana's westernmost Flathead Indian Reservation. Once dominant, these native peoples now comprise only six per cent of the population. They live on seven semi-sovereign reservations. Although they coalesce on some issues, they are, in essence, seven separate nations living within the borders of Montana.

In their *Montana: A History of Two Centuries,* historians Michael Malone, Richard Roeder, and William Lang describe Montana's native peoples as a "highly diversified group, combining plateau-mountain peoples from the west, Great Basin Indians from the south, hardy plainsmen from the north and east." They sum up the brief rise and fall of recent Indian culture in Montana this way:

> *P*rior to 1800, Montana was the eye of a cultural hurricane, where Indians migrating from all directions, bringing horses and guns with them, met to create new and unusual societies. These Indians would share a common fate in the years following 1800, as Americans and Canadians drove them from their lands, reduced them by war, disease, and alcohol, and shattered their native cultures.

In most of Montana, all that remains of these native cultures are the place names—Chinook, Ekalaka, Charlo, Kalispell, Yaak—with which Montana's native tribes long ago honored their land and their home.

■ LEWIS AND CLARK AND THE CORPS OF DISCOVERY

The nation's third president, Thomas Jefferson, saw westward expansion as the key not only to inland commerce but also to control of a growing trade with China via the Pacific. With a single real estate deal, Jefferson doubled the size of the United States when he bought Louisiana Territory from France in 1803 for a sum of $16 million. The Louisiana Purchase reached from the Gulf of Mexico to the Canadian border through what is now the nation's mid-section; its width stretched from the Mississippi to the Rockies.

To explore this vast and uncharted land, Jefferson appointed a "Corps of Discovery," headed by his private secretary—Meriwether Lewis— and William Clark, younger brother of Gen. George Rogers Clark.

On May 14, 1804, their party of 45 soldiers, guides, interpreters, and others set out from St. Louis, poling up the Missouri by flatboat and keelboat. They spent that winter in a North Dakota Mandan village, and continued upriver in canoes and keelboats the following spring.

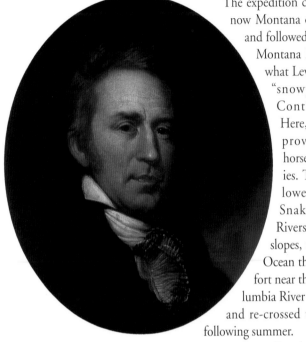

The expedition crossed into what is now Montana on April 27, 1805, and followed the Missouri to its Montana headwaters, and to what Lewis described as the "snowy barrier" of the Continental Divide. Here, Shoshone Indians provided guides and horses to cross the Rockies. The party then followed the Clearwater, Snake, and Columbia Rivers down the western slopes, reaching the Pacific Ocean that fall. They built a fort near the mouth of the Columbia River for winter quarters, and re-crossed the mountains the following summer.

William Clark (Independence National Historic Park, Philadelphia)

On the return trip east, Lewis and Clark split the expedition into two parties near what is now Lolo, Montana. Lewis and his detachment went northeast to explore the Blackfoot, Sun, and Marias rivers; Clark and his group headed southeast to explore the Yellowstone River. Six weeks later, they reached their rendezvous, near the mouth of the Yellowstone River, within nine days of one another. In the words of Robert Fletcher, popularizer of Montana history: "Considering distance and unexplored terrain, they were tolerably punctual."

On September 23, 1806, the expedition finally arrived back in St. Louis, long after everyone but President Jefferson had given them up for dead. The trip proved a vital step in bringing the Northwest under the U.S. flag, and in revealing the great wealth of this land to those back east. In just over 28 months, the expedition had traveled more than 8,000 miles by foot, horseback, and boat. Well over a quarter of that distance encompassed what is now Montana.

At the same time, international interest in the North American fur trade was threatening a cultural showdown between natives and newcomers. Not surprisingly, among the goals of the Lewis and Clark expedition was an inventory of the West's fur-trade potential.

Shortly after Meriwether Lewis reported that "that portion of the continent watered by the Missouri and all its branches… is richer in beaver and otter than any country on earth," trappers and traders arrived in great numbers, and the West, as the Indians knew it, was changed forever. By the early 1880s, hide hunters had shot the buffalo to virtual extinction, and similarly rubbed out the lifestyle and culture of the Indians who relied on it for their food, shelter, clothing, and tools.

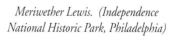

Meriwether Lewis. (Independence National Historic Park, Philadelphia)

HISTORY

FOLLOWING THE CORPS OF DISCOVERY

Retracing the Path of Lewis and Clark

Travelers in Montana can visit several spots along the Lewis and Clark National Historic Trail.

SELF-GUIDED TOURS

Developed sites accessible by car are:

Giant Springs State Park, Great Falls   *map page 149*
Here Clark discovered a huge "fountain or spring" during a formidable, 18-mile portage around a series of waterfalls, now altered by dams and development).

Lewis and Clark National Historic Trail Interpretive Center   *map page 155, A-2*
This spectacular edifice opened in 1998 on the banks of the Missouri River next to Giant Springs State Park. Exhibits inside detail every imaginable aspect of the expedition;

Missouri Headwaters State Park, near Three Forks   *map page 155, A-4*
This is where the expedition traced the "heretofore conceived boundless Missouri" to its birthplace at the confluence of the Jefferson, Gallatin, and Madison Rivers.

Lolo Pass Visitor Center   *map page 204, A-2*
on US 12 at the Montana-Idaho border, which explains the significance of both the Lewis and Clark Expedition and the Nez Perce Indians in this part of the state, on US12 near Idaho border.

BOAT TOURS

One of the most enjoyable ways to retrace Lewis and Clark's journey is by boat. Commercial boat tours operate on the Missouri at the places listed below. Call the **Bureau of Land Management** in **Lewistown** for outfitters; 406-538-7461.

Gates of the Mountains, where the river flows through a narrow canyon flanked by what Lewis described as "the most remarkable clifts that we have yet seen.

Upper Missouri National Wild and Scenic River, at the white cliffs area, guided canoe trips are available, as well as rentals and shuttle service for those who want to explore the river on their own.

MAPS

Several maps provide detailed information on the paths of Lewis and Clark. These include the following:

Lewis and Clark Trail.
  A National Park Service map available from Travel Montana; call 800-847-4868.

Lewis and Clark in the Rocky Mountains.
  A map of the expedition's route through western Montana, available from the U.S. Forest Service, Missoula; 406-329-3511.

The Explorers at the Portage.
  A map of the expedition's portage route around the Great Falls of the Missouri. Contact the Great Falls Chamber of Commerce, Great Falls ; 406-761-4434

Floater's Guide to the Upper Missouri National Wild and Scenic River.
  From Bureau of Land Management, Airport Rd., Lewistown; 406-538-7461.

Lewis and Clark hold a council with some of the Indians they met on their transcontinental trek. (Bancroft Library, University of California at Berkeley)

■ ANGLO AND EUROPEAN SETTLERS

As states go, Montana is just a kid. A little more than a century old, it is a state where you can learn history at the knee of an elder who has lived it. Among Montana's native peoples, the "Old Ones" sustain a rich oral tradition with songs and stories about the buffalo and coyote, the seasons, "Sun Chief," and the "Above Ones." Homesteaders recount the isolation, dust, drought, and drudgery that awaited them in Montana after they swallowed the railroads' claims of mild winters, prodigious crop yields, and unlimited opportunity. Old-timers in the stock-growers industry heard first-hand accounts of the brutal winter of 1886–87 which, together with overgrazing and barbed wire, brought an end to Montana's legendary open-range era.

The contrary values of independence and neighborliness define the character of a Montanan. This dual personality can be traced more than a century back to the explorers, fur traders, prospectors, miners, laborers, stockmen, and homesteaders who abandoned all that was familiar to them for the promise of freedom and independence in the American West. They came, one by one and family by family, from the East and Midwest, and from ancestral neighborhoods—the Piedmont region of northern Italy, the Volga River valley of Russia, the Pyrenees, Croatia, Scandinavia, and other European enclaves. Together with relatives and friends, they brought Old World place names that still remain in the neighborhoods and towns they built. Finn Town, Caledonia, Scotch Coulee, Dublin Gulch, Belgrade, Glasgow, Frenchtown, and Amsterdam, to name just a few in Montana.

While the state's European ethnic heritage has been diluted over four and five generations as it has elsewhere in America, remnant populations of these clannish settlements still exist in the once-booming mining and smelter towns of Butte, Anaconda, Red Lodge, East Helena, and Black Eagle. The colorful mining city of Butte, which erupted in the 1880s as the greatest mining camp in the West, has the most visible ethnic mix. St. Patrick's Day is the biggest day of the year here, drawing thousands of Butte Irish and would-be Irish from throughout the state. But Serbian Christmas and Chinese New Year are also observed in Butte, where as many as 60 different nationalities once lived and worked together.

Scandinavian immigrants left their imprint on farming communities and lumber towns, and Scot names are still prevalent in ranching communities, like Miles City. Germans were the largest, single ethnic group to settle in Montana. They came as homesteaders and their descendants still farm near small communities throughout northern and eastern Montana. Farther south the Yellowstone River Valley attracted Russian Germans who became successful sugar beet producers.

Retired miners can pinpoint the hour of the Smith Mine disaster in Bearcreek, when 74 coal miners were killed in an underground explosion, or the night radical labor leader Frank Little was hanged in Butte after delivering a fiery speech against U.S. involvement in World War I. All significant in the development of the West, these legends and events are still within reach in Montana, where history is a hands-on affair.

■ AN ERA OF EXPLOITATION

The ultimate victor of the so-called "war of the copper kings" was Marcus Daly's original mining company, the Anaconda Copper Mining Company, which gradually absorbed the interests of all three men. At one time controlled by Standard Oil and William Rockefeller, Anaconda's Montana empire held mines, smelters, lumber and railroad operations, coal fields, and most of the state's major daily newspapers in the snakelike grip for which the company was named. The loser was Montana, which was dominated for years by one corporation.

The colossal fortunes created by Butte's concentrated deposits of metal ores never remained in Butte long enough to mitigate the damage created by their extraction. Instead, they wound up in the hands of three principal entrepreneurs, who came to be known as Montana's "copper kings," and the Wall Street investors who backed them in their mining ventures. s after building a mining fortune in Butte and buying a seat in the U.S. Senate. Driven by political and financial ambitions, Clark had barely won election to the Senate in 1899 before he was derailed by rival copper king Marcus Daly, who engineered a Senate investigation of alleged campaign fraud and bribery. Earlier, the two went head to head and pocketbook to pocketbook over Clark's campaign to become a territorial delegate to Congress and his successful drive to make Helena the permanent state capital. Following the Daly-inspired investigation into Montana politics, Clark was found guilty of bribery and was promptly unseated. Clark then formed an alliance with Butte's third rising star, Augustus Heinze, who built his mining empire by bribing the courts to settle property ownership disputes in his favor. Together, Clark and Heinze set out to discredit Daly and elect a pro-Clark legislature, which they did.

Marcus Daly, founder of Anaconda Copper and one of Butte's famous "copper kings." (Montana Historical Society)

Because U.S. senators were still elected by state legislatures at that time, Clark soon regained the Senate seat he had so long desired.

Following a single, undistinguished term in the Senate, Clark took his Montana-made fortune to New York City, where he built an elegant mansion on Fifth Avenue and filled it with one of America's major turn-of-the-century art collections, consisting of approximately 800 works of original art. Thought to be one of the world's eight richest men at the time, Clark is said to have left an estate valued at

Montanans had an opportunity to re-examine this chapter in their state's history of exploitation in 1989, the year they celebrated their statehood centennial. Residents got a glimpse of the fabulous wealth one of those copper kings amassed when the Corcoran Gallery of Art in Washington, D.C., agreed to lend a portion of its priceless William A. Clark art collection to Montana for temporary display at the Yellowstone Art Center in Billings. Clark assembled his collection of European paintings, Renaissance ceramics, sculpture, and antiquities $150 million upon his death in 1925.

Heinze reaped $10 million from the sale of his Butte mining interests in 1906. He, too, was drawn to New York. But unlike Clark, who built his fortune over a lifetime of studied and shrewd investments, Heinze engaged in some madcap ventures on Wall Street and lost his millions almost as soon as he arrived. Daly, who died in 1900, divided his assets between the town of Anaconda, where he built a huge smelter to process his ore, and southwestern Montana's scenic Bitterroot Valley, where he built a 42-room mansion and pursued his passion for breeding and racing fine horses on a baronial country estate.

Surely the most colorful story of conquest and development of Montana's vast resources, the story of the copper kings is not unique in Montana history. The importation of capital, exploitation of resources, and exportation of profits has been a recurring pattern since the fur-trade era, when beaver pelts left Montana by the boatload. Later in the century, Montana's "free grass" and "free water" gave rise to a cattle boom that was financed largely by British capitalists and East Coast investors, the same crowd that developed the mining frontier and stretched railroad tracks across the continent.

In his *Montana: An Uncommon Land,* historian K. Ross Toole captured Montana's historic dilemma: "Distance meant cost, cost meant capital, capital meant

Once the "richest hill on Earth," the copper-mining town of Butte is still known for its scarred landscape and spirited people. (Montana Historical Society)

OWNING THE EARTH

*T*he earth was created by the assistance of the sun, and it should be left as it was... The country was made without lines of demarcation, and it is no man's business to divide it... I see the whites all over the country gaining wealth, and see their desire to give us lands which are worthless... The earth and myself are of one mind. The measure of the land and the measure of our bodies are the same. Say to us if you can say it, that you were sent by the Creative Power to talk to us. Perhaps you think the Creator sent you here to dispose of us as you see fit. If I thought you were sent by the Creator I might be induced to think you had a right to dispose of me. Do not misunderstand me, but understand me fully with reference to my affection for the land. I never said the land was mine to do with it as I chose. The one who has the right to dispose of it is the one who has created it. I claim a right to live on my land, and accord you the privilege to live on yours.

—Chief Joseph, 1832–1904

Chief Joseph of the Nez Perce Indians. (Haynes
Foundation Collection, Montana Historical Society)

absentee ownership, absentee ownership meant absentee control, and absentee control meant operation in the essential interest of outsiders with local interests a very secondary consideration. And so it was with beaver, beef, sheep, silver, copper, oil, and, to a lesser extent, even with lumber and wheat."

■ SAVING THE LAND

True to its genre, the romance of the West is a highly idealized account of great deeds and adventures, conquest, and fortune. Indeed, great fortunes were made in Montana, but always at the expense of the state and its residents. The fresh face of Montana that greets visitors today belies a past of abuse and exploitation. Since 1805, when Lewis and Clark unlocked the West for the fur traders, prospectors, miners, loggers, stockmen, and sodbusters who followed, Montana's history has been that of an isolated colony held captive by outside interests. Armed with capital to develop the riches of this sprawling land, they trapped its beaver, slaughtered its buffalo, plowed its virgin grasslands, fenced its plains, logged its timber, mined its precious metals, removed tons of earth to expose its thick seams of coal, and most recently, used toxic cyanide to leach scant ounces of gold from tons of ore deposits.

Nowhere is the legacy of Montana's extractive economy more apparent than in Butte, where the environmental wreckage that began a century ago still blights the landscape. In its heyday, Butte was known as "the richest hill on Earth." The hill that produced more than $2 billion worth of gold, silver, copper, and zinc is now a crater. Underground mines were gradually replaced by a huge open-pit mine that opened in 1955. Until it was closed in 1983, the Berkeley Pit ate away at the city like a beast that feeds on its own flesh. Butte now has the distinction of being one of the nation's largest Superfund sites.

During an unusual period of prosperity, urbanization, and political activism in the 1970s, Montanans began to write a new chapter of history by fighting back to save the land they loved. Fueled by a global energy crisis, large out-of-state coal companies were sending their lease hounds into the cattle country of southeastern Montana to secure mineral rights to the low-sulfur coal that lay in thick seams beneath prairie grasslands. In 1971 the federal government released a study calling for construction of 42 new coal-fired generating plants in the northern Plains states, half of them targeted for Montana. In addition to threatening eastern

Montana's agricultural values and diverting enormous quantities of precious water from the Yellowstone River, the power plants would have obscured Montana's open spaces with a network of high-voltage transmission lines designed to carry electricity from the mines to urban markets. Determined not to repeat their history, Montanans pulled together to keep their state from becoming what some described as a "national sacrifice area." In the end, the energy crisis dissipated and the North Central Power Study was shelved. Although millions of tons of coal were stripped from the plains of southeastern Montana, the boom gave rise to a burst of landmark environmental legislation. Some of the nation's most stringent conservation laws can be traced two decades back to Montana's legislative halls and courtrooms.

Inevitably, as the recession in the 1908s gave way to the budget-cutting and conservatism of the '90s, environmental concerns lost ground and cutting government spending, including oversight agencies, became the paramount issue of the day. Daily newspaper headlines focus attention on disputes between Montana's conservation community and the state's industrial giants over forest and mining practices, wilderness classification, cleanup of hazardous wastes, subdivision development, water and air pollution, exploration and development of energy resources, grizzly bears, bald eagles, gray wolves, and a seemingly endless array of issues that won't go away. But if Montanans are torn, they also know that Montana simply wouldn't be Montana without its open spaces, great trout streams, and abundant wildlife.

■ MONTANANS TODAY

With just over 900,000 residents, Montana has been likened to a mid-size American city, each town representing a different neighborhood with a distinct personality. Helena is the government town, Miles City the cowboy town, Billings the business town, and Missoula the university town. Each of these larger cities appears in bold type on the map of Montana and is, in itself, a bold expression of what Montana is about. But to understand what it's like to live in a rural Western state, it makes sense to look to the smaller towns—like Libby, Browning, Wolf Point, Roundup.

Small-town America is in decline nationally, and so it is in Montana. But don't be fooled by sleepy-looking towns like Malta and Big Timber, and so many others with populations of less than 2,500. Compared with America's urban centers and mid-size cities, these small communities look like the end of the line. What do they do here, you will wonder. Not to worry. Between kids, sports, church, and local government, most residents are busy every night of the week. There are 4-H programs, basketball practices, choir rehearsals, and fund-raisers for the volunteer fire department, the senior citizens' center, and the family whose budget has been ravaged by a medical crisis. Somehow, though, there always seems to be half an hour to catch up with friends over coffee, or half a day to help a neighboring farm family with harvest.

Because Montana is so sparsely settled, neighbors are valued. Without asking, neighbors rely on one another to watch their homes while they are away or fill in when help is needed at critical times of the year, like calving and branding. Here is how one rancher describes relations in the low-lying Bull Mountains of south-central Montana: "We've worked together so long, we know what needs to be done without being told. If something happens to one of our families, our neighbors know our business better than we do and the work just goes on." This is what community is all about, and it is engendered by Montana's rural demography. Montanans rely on the entire state to provide the network of friends and business contacts most Americans find in the cities where they live and work.

The difference between commuting across the state in Montana and across town in one of America's major metro areas is that in Montana, there is nothing between Point A and Point B. Nothing manmade, that is, except an occasional gas station or roadside saloon. Montanans become intimately familiar with the look of the land as they drive to Helena to testify at legislative hearings, Miles City to place a bid at a livestock auction, or Great Falls to do some shopping. And they are all too familiar with ground blizzards, black ice, and snow-packed mountain passes. As soon as they learn to drive a car or handle a rifle, Montanans learn self-sufficiency. Neighbors are to be trusted, but it is this ability to take care of one's self that defines the Montana spirit.

WILD MONTANA
WILDLIFE, BIRDS & FISH

IF HOME IS WHERE THE HEART IS, then the soul of a Montanan resides in the great outdoors. Here, it is still possible to retreat to the woods or the plains and never see another person.

Not all states were created equal. Montana boasts two national parks and a national recreation area, 10 national forests, 15 wilderness areas, eight national wildlife refuges, 370 miles of national wild and scenic river, and several national scenic trails, including the Continental Divide Trail. Complementing these federal holdings are 60 state parks, seven state forests, and roughly 600 miles of prized, blue-ribbon trout streams.

These natural areas are the result of visionary Montanans who fought to preserve their state's rivers, forests, and open spaces. A vigilant conservation community continues this tradition by keeping watch on many fronts, ranging from forest practices and mined land reclamation to streambed protection and cleanup of toxic wastes. Priceless resources like the free-flowing Yellowstone River and the trout-rich Madison, the northern Yellowstone elk herd, and the lower 48's largest populations of grizzly bears and bighorn sheep are the reward for these efforts.

In Montana, hunting and fishing are inalienable, if not divine, rights. Montanans worship at holy places like the Big Hole River, Freezeout Lake, and the C. M. Russell Game Range. They celebrate holy days like the salmon fly hatch and the opening day of antelope season. Beyond the need to feed their souls and fill their freezers, Montanans are just plain in love with wildlife. Fishing and hunting news is reported regularly in most newspapers, and a wolf sighting or the results of a new grizzly bear study merit front-page coverage. A reporter for Kalispell's *Daily Inter Lake,* published next door to Glacier National Park and the Bob Marshall Wilderness, once told a fellow journalist, "Every time a grizzly farts, we're expected to be there."

The harmony and perfect grace of trumpeter swans in flight, the soulful song of coyotes calling, or the tonic sleep that follows a day outdoors will verify the ancient doctrine that the best things in life are free. If you have forgotten that lesson and allowed your priorities to shift in accordance with the demands of careers, possessions, and other false idols, Montana outdoors is a good place to get a fix on the planet and your place in it.

■ WILDLIFE WATCHING

To see wildlife native to the northern Rockies, you're best off visiting the parks, refuges, and wilderness areas established for the protection of those animals. In addition to the famous (or infamous) grizzly bear, bighorn sheep, mountain goats, buffalo, pronghorn antelope, wild horses, elk, deer, and coyotes live here in great numbers as well.

Glacier National Park   *map page 257*
This park, on Montana's northern border, hosts a diversity of wildlife ranging from the tiny five-ounce pika to the Lower 48's largest carnivore, the grizzly bear. Glacier is probably best known for the bighorn sheep and mountain goats that grace its rocky outcrops and mountaintop perches, far removed from predators. Bands of bighorns are readily seen in the Many Glacier and Haystack Butte areas. *See page 256.*

Wildhorse Island State Park
   map page 248, C-3
Surrounded by Flathead Lake, is another good place to view bighorn sheep. Bighorns have flourished on this 2,165-acre island since they were transplanted here in 1940. Other wildlife include deer, coyotes, waterfowl, raptors, and songbirds. Boats depart for the island from Bigfork. *See page 247.*

The National Bison Range
   map page 248, C-5
South of Flathead Lake, these 19,000 acres of grassland are shared by deer, elk, bighorn sheep, pronghorn antelope, and well over 400 buffalo—but a vestige of the estimated 13 million buffalo that once roamed Montana's plains. The herd was established in 1908, and the refuge, one of the nation's oldest wildlife preserves, soon afterward.

The range can be explored by car on a self-guided tour which offers stunning views of the Flathead Valley and the Mission Mountains. In spring, newborn calves can be seen. The annual buffalo roundup in early October may be the most dramatic time to visit: as cowboy rangers thin the herd, thick clouds of dust fill the air and the rumble of stampeding hooves grows to a dull thunder. *See page 254.*

**Charles M. Russell National
   Wildlife Refuge**   *map page 110, A/B-1*
On the grasslands of northeastern Montana, once the buffalo's domain, elk, pronghorns, bighorn sheep, deer, waterfowl, and upland game are protected on this sprawling, million-acre refuge. Together with the **UL Bend Wilderness,** which it encompasses, the C. M. Russell refuge is the only area in Montana where elk still occupy their native prairie year-round. The refuge surrounds enormous **Fort Peck Lake,** home to trout, sauger, bass, catfish, perch, pike, and paddlefish. *See page 118.*

Pryor Mountains Wild Horse Range
   map page 123, A-2
Near Bighorn Canyon in south-central Montana, this was the nation's first wild horse range. The highland desert here supports about 130 free-roaming mustangs,

(following pages) Southeast of Livingston, the Absaroka Range runs through the Absaroka-Beartooth Wilderness, which is home to bighorn sheep, bear, elk, and moose.

some of which may have descended from those ridden by the Spanish explorers. In this rugged country, birding, hiking, and fossil hunting are possible year-round. *Bighorn Canyon National Recreation Area: 307-548-2251. See page 138.*

Yellowstone National Park   *map page 181*
Although primarily within Wyoming, Yellowstone National Park is a major drawing card for Montana visitors. Elk, moose, and bison regularly graze alongside highways, causing traffic to back up while otherwise responsible motorists simply abandon their vehicles for a better view. September is an especially good time to visit the park, when bull elk are challenging one another for possession of harems numbering as high as 30 cows each. There are usually one or two harems lolling around National Park Service headquarters at Mammoth under the jealous gaze of the bulls. *See page 180.*

■ WILD COUNTRY: GRIZZLIES AND WOLVES

◆ GRIZZLY BEARS

Of all the animals that inhabit the northern Rockies and Great Plains, the one that keeps Montana truly wild is the grizzly bear. Indeed, many biologists regard the presence of the grizzly as an indicator of the quality of wilderness: where there are grizzlies, there is wilderness; where there are none, there is no wilderness.

Ever since Lewis and Clark crossed what is now Montana in 1805–06, there's been trouble between people and bears.

Red Rock Falls in the Many Glacier area of Glacier National Park.

TROUBLE ON THE RANGE

Montanans are happy to share their space with the kinds of animals most people see only in zoos. Most will never meet a grizzly bear or a mountain lion in the wild, but knowing they could is a source of pride. They may well be in love with the idea of wildlife, but their love is not unconditional. Livestock producers, in particular, live in perpetual tension with wildlife. While ranchers are accustomed to sharing their haystacks and grain fields with deer and antelope, they draw the line on predators that threaten their cash crop of newborn lambs and calves.

Recently, grizzly bears have begun wandering out of the mountains and onto the plains near Choteau, Dupuyer, and other ranching communities along the Rocky Mountain Front. Actual depredation along the Front has been limited to a few sheep and commercial beehives, but fear of depredation has marshalled the livestock industry against the grizzly. Troublesome bears are usually trapped and transplanted to remote mountain areas. If they stay in the mountains, chances are good that they will survive their brief encounter with humanity. But if they are tempted back to the plains by the prospect of vegetation or the scent of a fresh carcass, they may wind up as what most ranchers would call "good bears"—dead bears, that is.

Grizzlies once numbered as high as 50,000, with a range extending east to the Mississippi. Unfortunately, rapid settlement of the region decimated grizzly numbers and pushed them into remote Western wilderness areas, where today they are protected under the federal Threatened and Endangered Species Act. Gradual recovery of bear populations, especially in Montana, has stirred debate over whether the grizzly should be "delisted" as a threatened species. Of the thousand or so grizzlies living in the American West, most survive in two major ecosystems: the Northern Continental Divide Ecosystem, which includes **Glacier National Park** and the **Bob Marshall Wilderness;** and the **Greater Yellowstone Ecosystem** which, in Montana, includes the **Lee Metcalf** and the **Absaroka-Beartooth Wilderness Areas** and surrounding forests.

Outside of Glacier and Yellowstone National Parks, chances of seeing a grizzly in the wild are slim. Bears do not seek human encounters. Indeed, grizzlies are so elusive that even frequent visitors to bear country believe it's a privilege to see one. As the number of hikers visiting these wild places grows, however, there are bound to be conflicts. By 1997 the number of visitors to Glacier National Park—which, together with Waterton, the adjoining Canadian park, is regarded as one of North America's premier hiking destinations—had reached nearly two million a year.

THE "TREMENDUOUS" BEAR

A little before dark McNeal returned with his musquet broken off at the breach, and informed me that on his arrival at willow run [on the portage] he had approached a white bear within ten feet without discover[ing] him, the bear being in the thick brush. The horse took the alarm and turning short threw him immediately under the bear. This animal raised himself on his hinder feet for battle, and gave him time to recover from his fall which he did in an instant, and with his clubbed musquet he struck the bear over the head and cut him with the guard of the gun and broke off the breech. The bear, stunned with the stroke, fell to the ground and began to scratch his head with his feet; this gave McNeal time to climb a willow tree which was near at hand and thus fortunately made his escape. The bear waited at the foot of the tree until late in the evening before he left him, when McNeal ventured down and caught his horse which had by this time strayed off to the distance of 2 Ms. and returned to camp. These bear are a most tremenduous animal; it seems that the hand of providence has been most wonderfully in our favor with rispict to them, or some of us would long since have fallen a sacrifice to their farosity. There seems to be a sertain fatality attached to the neighbourhood of these falls, for there is always a chapter of accedents prepared for us during our residence at them.

—Meriwether Lewis, journal entry from the Marias River on July 15, 1806

(photo by Galen Rowell)

At 10,000 feet above sea level, the rugged Centennial Mountains capture winter's snowfall, replenishing the lakes and marshes of southwestern Montana's Red Rock Lakes National Wildlife Refuge.

Bear attacks are not always fatal to people; more often the bear is the loser. If a bear becomes conditioned to human food or cannot be successfully relocated from popular trails and campgrounds, park officials may have no choice but to destroy it.

◆ WOLVES

Montana's reputation got wilder when wolves were reintroduced in Yellowstone National Park. Crates containing 14 gray wolves from Canada were released inside the park in 1995; another 17 were introduced in 1996. By January 2001, nearly 170 wolves in an estimated 16 packs were thriving in and around park forests.

In the 1970s, wolves started showing up naturally—without reintroduction—in northwestern Montana near Glacier National Park. Nonetheless, it was the reintroduction of wolves in Yellowstone that captured the nation's imagination.

First of all, wild wolves had never been captured and reintroduced in this country. Furthermore, the experiment has been extremely successful: Yellowstone is now the best place in the world to observe wolves in the wild.

Wolves were introduced in an effort to restore balance to an ecosystem which, since exposure to people in large numbers, was widely believed to have grown imbalanced by overpopulations of ungulates, especially elk and deer. That wolves are now flourishing confirms they have had plenty to eat. Interestingly, since the wolf reintroduction, coyote populations have declined by as much as 50 percent; red foxes are making a comeback; and grizzly bears are holding their own. According to wildlife officials, wolves and grizzlies are more or less tolerating one another.

Livestock producers ranching on the edges of Yellowstonewere less tolerant of the idea; however, livestock depredation has been lower than anticipated, and producers are reimbursed for any livestock killed by wolves.

One of the best places to view wolves is the Lamar Valley in Yelowstone's northeast corner, where the Druid Peak Pack often roams and hunts within range of spotting scopes. You'll know you've arrived at "Club Wolf" when you reach a spot along the highway with enough cameras—film, video, and still—for a Capitol Hill press converence, and more spotting scopes than you've ever seen outside an optics shop. Dawn and dusk are the best times to be there.

■ BIRDWATCHING

Montana's best birding opportunities are the refuges for the state's many songbirds, raptors, and waterfowl at Freezeout, Medicine, and Red Rock Lakes.

Freezeout Lake   *map page 249, F-4*
During peak migration periods, up to a million waterfowl can be observed at this state-managed refuge in north-central Montana, about 40 miles northwest of Great Falls. Snow geese and tundra swans arrive by the thousands. Other resident and migratory birds include Canadian geese, mallards, teal, pintails, eagles, hawks, owls, sandhill cranes, egrets, and ibis.

Medicine Lake National Wildlife Refuge
   map page 95, F-1
Spring and fall migrations each bring up to 250,000 waterfowl to this refuge on Medicine Lake, which lies between Culbertson and Plentywood in Montana's far northeast corner. Especially important for white pelicans (and for whooping cranes in smaller numbers), the refuge also attracts great blue herons, cormorants, gulls, and most species of North American ducks.

In addition, Medicine Lake National Wildlife Refuge encompasses Medicine Lake Wilderness, Montana's smallest designated wilderness, which contains a small parcel of mixed-grass prairie and a large population of white-tailed deer.

A wildlife biologist near Ringling, with a quizzical bald eagle.

Red Rock Lakes National Wildlife Refuge
map page 205, D-6

This refuge in the remote Centennial Valley is one of North America's most important nesting sites for the majestic trumpeter swan. Here in southwestern Montana, this largest of all North American waterfowl made an extraordinary comeback.

When the refuge was established in 1935, fewer than 100 swans were known to exist in the entire nation; two-thirds of them lived in this valley. Today, about 500 nesting swans in the Greater Yellowstone area are joined by 1,000 more on their winter migrations from Canada and Alaska. *406-276-3536.*

The refuge's lakes, marshes, and creeks sustain 23 different species of waterfowl. Other residents and visitors include sandhill cranes, sage grouse, hawks, falcons, moose, elk, deer, and pronghorn antelope.

■ NATURE STUDY VACATIONS AND TOURS

Elderhostel.
777 Grandview Dr., Kalispell;
877-426-8056
Field study courses in and around Glacier National Park for people age 55 and over; April through October.

Fort Belknap Buffalo Tours.
Harlem; 406-353-2205
Since 1974, the Gros Ventres and Assiniboine tribes of Fort Belknap have worked to rebuild a buffalo herd as part of their wildlife mangement program; the herd now numbers 300. Tours depart from the Buffalo Reserve Visitor Center in Harlem May through September and can be scheduled by phone or upon arrival. Several excellent wildlife viewing sites.

Glacier Institute.
137 Main St., Kalispell; 406-755-1211
One-to-seven day field seminars on Glacier National Park geology, botany, wildlife, history, and photography.
www.glacierinstitute.org

Museum of the Rockies.
Montana State University, Bozeman;
406-994-6618
One-day to two-week paleontology and archaeology field trips with professional scientists. College credit available.

Pine Butte Guest Ranch.
Choteau; 406-466-2158
Week-long workshops on birding, mammal tracking, photography, paleontology, and back-country horsepacking at this Nature Conservancy property along the Rocky Mountain Front.

Yellowstone Institute.
Yellowstone National Park, WY
307-344-2294
Wilderness writing and photography, llama trekking, catch-and-release fly fishing, horse packing and backpacking are just some of the more than 80 field courses conducted each year in Yellowstone. *www.yellowstoneassociation.org*

Yellowstone Safari Company.
Bozeman; 406-586-1155
Year-round wildlife, natural and cultural history field tours led by a wildlife biologist. Wolf and bear watching safaris in Yellowstone Park. Trips are geared to guests' interests and budgets.

FLY-FISHING THE SEA OF GALILEE

*I*n our family, there was no clear line between religion and fly fishing. We lived at the junction of great trout rivers in western Montana, and our father was a Presbyterian minister and a fly fisherman who tied his own flies and taught others. He told us about Christ's disciples being fisherman, and we were left to assume, as my brother and I did, that all first-class fishermen on the Sea of Galilee were fly fishermen and that John, the favorite, was a dry-fly fisherman.

—Norman MacLean, *A River Runs Through It and Other Stories,* 1976

■ FLY FISHING

There's nothing quite like the action of a 16-inch rainbow trout cart wheeling at the end of an invisible line surgically knotted to a tiny, hand-tied morning dun or an even tinier *Tricorythodes*, a.k.a. "trico." And there are few places as perfect to experience such a rush as Montana. Beginning with the publication in 1976 of Norman MacLean's novella *A River Runs Through It* and continuing with the subsequent release in 1992 of the Robert Redford movie by the same name, the secret is out about Montana and fly-fishing. The sport has burgeoned over the past few years—no doubt with some help from Redford's visually stunning film —and the state's hallowed waters are considered the crème de la crème for anglers the world over. Among insiders though, Montana has always been the destination of choice.

What's so special about the fishing in Montana? All of the Rocky Mountain states are headwaters states, and all are endowed with icy, clear-running mountain streams—the kind that grow up to be legendary trout rivers. So why is it that only Montana ranks consistently with the upper Great Lakes states in terms of nonresident fishing license sales? And why is it that most trout fishermen, given a choice, would rather fish the Madison, the Gallatin, or the Yellowstone than any other river in the continental United States?

The answer lies in the cooperation of visionary sportsmen's and conservation groups, and an aggressive state fish and game agency that gets high marks among its peers for fisheries management. While other states still stock their streams and rivers with hatchery-reared trout, Montana manages its thousands of miles of streams and rivers for *wild* trout. And that means taking care of the land and water that support trout.

The importance of habitat was recognized by state lawmakers in 1963 with passage of the nation's first stream preservation law. What followed over the next 20 years was a series of laws designed to protect water quality, instream flows, streambank cover, and streambed integrity. These laws provide a solid framework for the conservation of Montana's streams and rivers. Together with aggressive regulations and a growing catch-and-release ethic, they have enhanced a sport fishery of national, if not international, significance.

The rivers of southwestern Montana are the heavyweights in a statewide lineup of champions. Premier trout streams include the upper Missouri and its headwaters—the Madison, Jefferson, Gallatin, Beaverhead, and Big Hole—and the waters in and around Yellowstone National Park, including the Yellowstone itself, the Firehole, Gibbon, Lamar, Gardner, and Lewis Rivers, plus Slough Creek and, just over the Idaho border, the Henry's Fork of the Snake. To the northwest are the Clark Fork and Bitterroot; to the east is the Bighorn. And in between are the countless smaller streams that feed these rivers and reward the anglers who seek them out with the promise of a day well spent.

Trouble came to paradise though in 1994, when biologists discovered the presence of whirling disease in the Madison River. Large numbers of rainbow trout were dying as a result of a microscopic parasite that damages its host's cartilage, causing the symptomatic whirling or tail-chasing behavior in infected trout. Since the onset of the disease, more than 85 individual waters in Montana, mostly in the western part of the state, have been infected with the parasite.

Fishing remains world-class on most of these streams since the infections are light to moderate. While there is no known cure for the parasite, researchers are exploring a number of variables to find ways to help trout survive the disease. As a precaution, anglers are encouraged to clean and dry their equipment when moving from one body of water to another and to remove mud from their boats and trailers to avoid further spreading of the disease.

Lunkers like this chunky rainbow trout are plentiful in Montana, especially in stocked lakes and reservoirs. But a growing number of river and stream fishermen prefer to release their catch for future enjoyment.

Fly-fishing is one of those passions that takes a lifetime to learn. Most anglers never learn it all, and therein lies a good part of its appeal. Wild trout are incredibly deft creatures, and catching one is a scholarly challenge as well as a test of wits. For those who'd like a crash course in the finer points of the art of casting, reading water, understanding aquatic ecology, tying leaders, selecting and tying flies, and putting it all together on the water to catch fish successfully, there are plenty of experts in Montana. Following is a list of the state's most highly regarded fly-fishing outfitters, fly shops, and schools and instructors.

FLY FISHING OUTFITTERS

Billings Area

Bighorn Angler.
Fort Smith; 406-666-2233
Fly shop, guide service, boat rental/shuttle, restaurant and motel on the Bighorn.

Bighorn Fly & Tackle Shop.
Billings; 406-656-8257
Full service outposts in Hardin: 406-665-1321 and Fort Smith: 406-666-2253.

Bighorn Trout Shop.
Fort Smith; 406-666-2375
Guide/instruction, fly shop, motel units, situated along the Bighorn.

Rainbow Run Fly Shop.
Billings; 406-656-3455
Full-service fly shop with friendly and knowledgeable staff.

Bozeman Area

Bozeman Angler.
Bozeman; 406-587-9111
Guide service, fly shop, excellent fishing school, including ladies-only classes.

Fins & Feathers of Bozeman.
Bozeman; 406-586-2188
Orvis dealer, guides, classes, instruction.

Madison River Fishing Co. Ennis;
406-682-4293
Excellent fly shop; mail order catalog.

Montana Troutfitters.
Bozeman; 406-587-4707
Bozeman's oldest fly shop offers knowledgeable staff and top-notch guides.

The River's Edge.
Bozeman; 406-586-5373
Fly shop, guides, instructors, gear rental.

The Tackle Shop.
Ennis; 406-682-4263
Fly shop and guide service on the Madison River.

Butte Area

Complete Fly Fisher.
Wise River; 406-832-3175
This all-inclusive resort lives up to its name—just show up and they'll take care of food, lodging, gear, instruction.

Four Rivers Fishing Co.
Twin Bridges; 406-684-5651
Full-service fly shop with helpful staff.

(FLY FISHING OUTFITTERS continues page 58)

(FLY FISHING OUTFITTERS continued from page 57, continues page 60)

Helena/Great Falls Area

Cross Currents.
Helena; 406-449-2292
Full fly shop, knowledgeable guides and instructors, and quality gear for rent.

Montana Board of Outfitters.
111 North Jackson, Helena;
406-444-3738
Directory of licensed outfitters who provide hunting and fishing trips, trail rides, whitewater raft trips, scenic floats, and other guided outdoor trips.

Montana River Outfitters.
Great Falls; 406-761-1677

Two shops and top-notch guides specializing in the Missouri and Smith Rivers.

Paul Roos Outfitters.
Helena; 406-442-5489
Rustic lodging on the Blackfoot River; experienced guides and instructors included. Day trips on the Missouri, extended trips on the Smith.

The Terminal Tackle.
Wolf Creek; 406-235-9000
Missouri River shop, guide service, shuttle service, boat rentals.

The Trout Shop.
Craig; 406-235-4474
Missouri River shop, guide service, shuttle service, boat rentals.

(above) Thanks to the efforts of fishing and conservation groups and an aggressive state fisheries management program—not to mention a spectacular natural setting—Montana is one of the most revered fly-fishing destinations in the world. (opposite) Montana is a headwaters state. Countless rivers are born in the snowmelt that cascades down Montana's mountain ranges.

(*FLY FISHING OUTFITTERS continued from page 58*)

Livingston Area

George Anderson's Yellowstone Angler.
Livingston; 406-222-7130
Instruction, guides, shop, gear rental.

Dan Bailey Fly Shop.
Livingston; 406-222-1673
Since 1938, Dan Baily's has been selling top-of-the-line gear and dispensing valuable info. They also have some of the best guides around.

Federation of Fly-Fishers, International Fly Fishing Center.
Livingston; 406-222-9369
Offers summer casting clinics taught by topnotch instructors.

Park's Fly Shop.
Gardiner; 406-848-7314
Full-service fly shop with guide service.

Sweet Cast Angler.
Big Timber; 406-932-4469
Guide service and instruction on the Yellowstone and Boulder Rivers.

Missoula Area

Grizzly Hackle Outfitting.
Missoula; 406-721-8996
Pro shop, guides, and five-room lodge on Butler Creek 12 miles west of town.

West Yellowstone

Blue Ribbon Flies.
West Yellowstone; 406-646-7643
Well-stocked shop and outfitter services.

Bud Lilly's Trout Shop.
West Yellowstone; 406-646-7801
Great fly shop and knowledgeable and entertaining guides.

Jacklin's Outfitters.
West Yellowstone; 406-646-7336
Extensive fly shop, gear rental, and experienced and lovable guides.

Madison River Outfitters.
West Yellowstone; 406-646-9644
All-around outdoor store with large fly shop, guide services, and rental gear.

■ OUTDOOR GUIDES AND PLANNERS

Austin-Lehman Adventures.
Billings; 800-575-1540
Montana-based adventure travel company that specializes in guided biking, hiking, horseback riding, rafting and ski tours nationwide. Montana tours include Glacier, Yellowstone, and Bozeman–Big Sky. Singles, groups, and families welcome

Montana Outfitters & Guides Association. Helena; 406-449-3578
Another organization to contact for guiding information.

Montana Wilderness Association.
Helena; 406-443-7350
One-day and extended hikes led by Wilderness Association members into Montana's roadless backcountry.

Off the Beaten Path.
27 E. Main St., Bozeman;
406-586-1311, 800-445-2995
Personalized itineraries by travel consultants who match clients' interests with outfitters, guest ranches, ski resorts, and tour operators.

WINTER RECREATION

ALTHOUGH MONTANA IS GENERALLY VIEWED as a summer destination, winter is an attraction in its own right. The difference between the two seasons is in the way people travel. While summer travel is geared to the open road, the goal in winter is to ditch the car as soon as possible. Snow and ice take the pleasure out of exploring Montana's vast and diverse landscape, so winter travel is generally confined to a single destination. A number of attractive resorts and winter services in nearby Yellowstone National Park make Montana an increasingly popular winter destination.

The mountains of western Montana begin filling up with snow in September and October, and by December the winter season is in full swing. Because of Montana's dry climate, snow piles up as deep, dry powder—perfect for skiing and snowmobiling. Each year, a growing number of skiers abandons the congestion and long lift lines of better-known ski areas in Colorado and Utah for the uncrowded, easygoing, and more affordable atmosphere of Montana's downhill ski areas. There are also a number of cross-country ski resorts within gliding distance of national forest and wilderness trailheads.

■ DOWNHILL SKIING

Montana's downhill areas range from destination resorts to locally popular day-use areas. The 12 areas below are listed in order by size, with the largest listed first.

The Big Mountain.
8 miles north of Whitefish;
406-862-1900 or 800-858-3930
This destination resort draws heavily on the western Canadian market as well as skiers from the Pacific Northwest who arrive by Amtrak. The area has 81 marked runs, two quads, one gondola, one double chair, four triple chairs, and one quad chairlift. The resort offers a variety of lodging options, several restaurants and bars, ski shop, ski school, day care, and Nordic center.

Big Sky.
43 miles south of Bozeman, Gallatin Canyon; 406-995-5000 or 800-548-4486
One of Montana's top destination resorts, Big Sky boasts the highest vertical drop (4,350 feet) in the nation. Three mountains with 122 runs, one gondola, a two-car tram, three high-speed quads, four triple chairs, four double chairs, and one quad. More than 1,000 rooms and 100 condo units, restaurants, bars, and shops, ski shop, day care, and superb cross-country skiing at nearby Lone Mountain Guest Ranch.

Bridger Bowl.

16 miles northeast of Bozeman;
406-586-1518 or 800-223-9609

Primarily a day-use area: lots of powder and challenging runs. Limited lodging on the slope, but full services in nearby Bozeman make this a popular area for serious skiers. With 69 runs, one quad, five double chairs, and one quad chair. Limited condo units and private home rentals, day lodge with cafeteria and bar, ski shop, and day care.

Discovery Basin.

20 miles west of Anaconda;
406-563-2184

Located near Georgetown Lake and the Anaconda Pintler Wilderness, this is a popular day-use area for skiers in the Butte-Anaconda area. There are 40 runs, three double chairs, and one triple chair. Facilities include a day lodge with cafeteria, ski shop, and nearby cross-country ski trails. Lodging is available at Fairmont Hot Springs, 32 miles east, and in Anaconda and Butte.

Great Divide.

22 miles northwest of Helena;
406-449-3746

Near the ghost town of Marysville, this is the capital city's neighborhood ski area. There are 100 runs and five double chairs. Facilities include a day lodge with restaurant and bar, a ski shop, and instruction. Full services in Helena.

Lost Trail Powder Mountain.

90 miles south of Missoula on US 93;
406-821-3508

Straddling the Montana-Idaho border, this day-use area is known for its reliable snow

and long season. There are 21 runs and three double chairs. Facilities include a day lodge with cafeteria and a ski shop. Limited lodging in Darby and nearby resorts; full services in Hamilton, 45 miles north, and Salmon, ID, 45 miles south.

Red Lodge Mountain.

Just outside Red Lodge, 60 miles south-west of Billings; 406-446-2610 or
800-444-8977

This popular day-use area in the Beartooth Mountains has lots of intermediate slopes and great spring skiing. As Montana's east-ernmost ski area, it draws heavily on skiers from the upper Midwest. There are 70 runs, two high-speed quads, one triple chair, and four double chairs. Restaurant, cafeteria, a few bars, ski shop, kids' ski program, and gift shop. Full lodging, food, and services available in nearby Red Lodge.

Marshall Mountain.

6 miles northeast of Missoula;
406-258-6000

A beginner and intermediate day-use area with 29 runs and one triple chair; night skiing. On-site are a day lodge, snack bar, pub, and ski shop. Full services in Missoula.

Maverick Mountain.

In Beaverhead National Forest;
35 miles west of Dillon 406-834-3454

Located in the Pioneer Mountains, this locally popular day-use area can be rented by groups for private skiing three days a week. There are 18 trails and one double chair. Day lodge with food and beverage service and ski shop. No lodging; limited lodging at nearby resorts; full services in Dillon.

Red Lodge Mountain is famous for its spring skiing. (courtesy Travel Montana)

Montana Snowbowl.

12 miles northwest of Missoula;
406-549-9777

Home of the annual National Gelande Jump Championship. Steep slopes and deep bowls make this day-use area especially popular with extreme skiers. There are 35 runs and two double chairs. On-site are a cafeteria, saloon, ski shop, and nursery. Full lodging, food, and services in Missoula.

Showdown Ski Area.

8 miles south of Neihart and
60 miles southeast of Great Falls;
406-236-5522 or 800-433-0022

Part of the Kings Hill Winter Sports complex in the Little Belt Mountains of central Montana, this popular family area draws heavily on the Great Falls market. There are 34 runs, one triple chair, and one double chair. On-site are a cafeteria, saloon, ski shop and nursery. Fine Nordic skiing and snowmobiling nearby. Limited lodging and food available in nearby Neihart and White Sulphur Springs; full services in Great Falls.

Teton Pass.

60 miles north of Great Falls and
30 miles west of Choteau on the Rocky
Mountain Front, 406-466-2209

This locally popular, family-oriented day-use area offers 26 trails and one double chair. On-site is a day lodge with cafeteria and bar, ski shop, and day care. Lodging is available in Choteau.

■ CROSS-COUNTRY SKIING

Montana has several one-of-a-kind cross-country ski resorts, plus some excellent day-use Nordic centers and trail systems. Following are brief descriptions of the foremost resorts and areas:

Big Mountain Nordic Center.

8 miles north of Whitefish;
406-862-1900 or 800-859-3526

An international training and racing center for cross-country and biathlon teams. Open to the public are six miles of groomed and tracked trails, plus instruction, rentals, and guided tours of nearby Glacier Park and other backcountry areas.

**Bohart Ranch Cross Country
Ski Center.**

16 miles northeast of Bozeman;
406-586-9070

Adjacent to Bridger Bowl, the center has 18 miles of groomed and tracked trails suitable for diagonal stride skiing and skating, plus rentals, lessons, and a warming cabin. Biathlon range for year-round training and competition. Full services in Bozeman.

Holland Lake Lodge.

In Seeley Swan Valley, off MT 83;
406-754-2282 or 877-925-6343

A comfortable lodge with 15 miles of groomed trails. Rooms start at about $170 per night for two in the lodge to $200 for four in cabins, gourmet meals included.

Skiers can rent a caboose for overnight stays at the Izaak Walton Inn, a popular cross-country ski lodge near Glacier Park.

Izaak Walton Inn.

At Essex, just off US 2,
between East and West Glacier;
406-888-5700

Close to Glacier National Park and the Great Bear Wilderness, this historic railroad inn wins raves from everyone. About 23 miles of groomed and tracked trails are augmented by a network of backcountry trails. Amtrak stops at the back door. Rentals, instruction, and tours of Glacier Park are available. Packages are offered for up to seven days. Reservations recommended. Trail system open to day skiers.

Lone Mountain Ranch.

40 miles south of Bozeman; 20 miles
northwest of Yellowstone National Park;
406-995-4644 or 800-514-4644

Montana's finest Nordic resort, this guest ranch is within skiing distance of the Big Sky downhill ski resort. The ranch offers 47 miles of groomed and tracked trails for skiers and skaters, plus guided tours into Yellowstone, instruction and rentals, sleigh ride dinners, on-the-trail gourmet lunches, excellent food and lodging. Most trips are booked on a week-long, package basis at a rate of around $1,900 for the first person and $1,100 for the second person, double occupancy. Reservations are required. The trail system is open to day skiers for a fee.

Red Lodge Nordic Ski Area.
Just outside Red Lodge, 60 mi. southwest of Billings.; 406-446-9191 or
800-425-0076
This trail system has nine miles of groomed
trails for skiers, plus instruction, rentals, a
skiathlon course, guided backcountry tours,
and shuttle service to nearby Red Lodge
Mountain downhill ski area. Full lodging,
food, and services in town.

Yellowstone Rendezvous Trail System.
Next to Yellowstone National Park;
406-646-7701
The town of West Yellowstone maintains
15 miles of groomed and tracked trails that
are used for early-season training by the
U.S. Nordic and Biathlon teams. Full lodging, food, and services, plus rentals, instruction, and guided tours of the park, in town.

■ GLACIER AND YELLOWSTONE NATIONAL PARKS

Yellowstone and Glacier dazzle winter visitors with their quiet beauty and abundant wildlife. Of the two, Yellowstone is far more developed for winter visitors,
with its many miles of groomed cross-country ski and snowmobile trails, ski and
snowmobile rentals, guided ski and snowcoach tours, plus lodging and food service inside the park. Plenty of lodging awaits visitors just outside the park, in West
Yellowstone, Gardiner, and Cooke City. No visitor services are open inside Glacier
Park during winter, but the Park Service does maintain about a dozen cross-country ski trails. Lodging, food, and services are available just outside the park at West
Glacier, East Glacier, and Essex. For more information about winter in the parks:
    Yellowstone National Park. Superintendent, WY 82190; 307-344-7381.
    Glacier National Park. Superintendent, West Glacier, MT 59936; 406-888-7800.

■ SNOWMOBILING

Since 1977, when Montana set aside a portion of its gasoline tax for development
of snowmobile recreation, nearly 3,000 miles of trails have been designated for
snowmobiling, most of them in national forests. Each year they are marked and
groomed through cooperative agreements between local snowmobile clubs, the
Montana Department of Fish, Wildlife and Parks, and the U.S. Forest Service.
The most popular place for snowmobilers is West Yellowstone, which up until recently billed itself as the "snowmobile capital of the world" because of access to
hundreds of miles of groomed snowmobile trails both inside and outside Yellowstone National Park. A new ruling on winter use may ban snowmobiles at some

Cross-country skiing at Lolo Pass, near Missoula.

point in the future, however, West Yellowstone still accesses a vast trail system that begins right in town, where snowmobilers share city streets with motorists. Snowmobile sales, service, rentals, instruction, and guide service, as well as complete lodging and food service, are all available in town. Other locally popular snowmobile areas in Montana are Cooke City, Lolo Pass, Seeley Lake, Lincoln, Kings Hill, Polaris-Wise River, and Georgetown Lake. For more information about snowmobiling, write:

Montana Snowmobile Association. Box 4714, Missoula, MT 59806.

Montana Department of Fish, Wildlife & Parks. 1420 Sixth Ave.,
Helena, MT 59620; 406-444-2535.

Holland Lake in the Seeley Swan Range.

■ GUIDED WINTER TOURS

Amfac Parks and Resorts.

Yellowstone National Park, WY;
307-344-7311

The major concessioner in Yellowstone National Park provides guided ski and snowcoach tours of the park, plus ski and snowmobile rentals, lodging; and meals.

Off the Beaten Path.

Bozeman; 406-586-1311

This Bozeman-based travel consulting service designs personalized itineraries. You let them know what you're interested in seeing and doing, and they put the trip together using your guidelines. Emphasis is on high-quality facilities and services.

Yellowstone Alpen Guides.

West Yellowstone; 406-646-9591

Also based in West Yellowstone, this company provides snowcoach tours of Yellowstone National Park as well as guided ski tours inside and out of the park, skier drop-offs, and charters.

Yellowstone Safari Company.

Bozeman; 406-586-1155

The owner of this company is a wildlife biologist who guides his guests year-round in and around Yellowstone on personalized half-, full-, and multi-day tours. Winter tours are geared to snowshoeing and cross-country skiing.

T H E   A R T S

MOST VISITORS ARE SURPRISED BY the vitality and diversity of the arts in Montana. Those who expect to see quality Western art will not be disappointed. Montana's Western art museums are among the finest. But those who view contem- porary art, literature, and the performing arts as strictly East Coast or urban attractions will be astonished. Montanans—all 900,000 of them—can boast:

- More professional, non-profit art museums, per capita, than any other state
- Eight symphony orchestras, plus the New World Symphony of Miami, whose summer residence is in Big Sky
- More resident visual artists with fellowships, per capita, than any other state

While these declarations come as a surprise to most non-residents, they make perfect sense to Montana artists and art lovers. Because the state's small rural communities are so widely dispersed, each looks to itself for cultural survival. Sheer distance keeps one community from living off another's culture. It is not unusual to find an art center, symphony, and theater group in towns with fewer than 15,000 residents. And the relatively low cost of living in Montana appeals to artists, as does a natural environment that feeds the soul.

■ WESTERN ART

The genre "Western art" may first call to mind, say, a painting by Charles M. Russell, but the category also includes 19th-century frontier photographs and Blackfeet ceremonial objects, and the following list (arranged by city) covers that range.

◆ BOZEMAN

The permanent collection at the **Museum of the Rockies** includes works by Edgar S. Paxson, C. M. Russell, R. E. DeCamp, Olaf Seltzer, and William Standing, as well as a fine collection of traditional objects made by Plains Indian tribes, including bead-and-quillwork, clothing, toys, weapons, and ceremonial items. *Kagy Boulevard and Greek Way on the Montana State University campus; 406-994-2251.*

    Coffrin's Old West Gallery is a commercial gallery which shows and sells the prints of L. A. Huffman, the Army photographer who came to Montana Territory in 1878 and recorded the last of the great buffalo herds, the final Indian wars, and the arrival of railroads and ranchers. *8118 Rolling Hills Drive; 406-586-0170.*

THE ARTS

"The Jerkline," by Charles M. Russell. (C. M. Russell Museum)

In nearby Livingston, **The Depot Center** shows the works of Charles Russell, Frederic Remington, Edward Borein, Thomas Moran, Karl Bodmer, and others. *200 West Park; 406-222-2300.*

◆ BROWNING

The Museum of the Plains Indian on the Flathead Indian Reservation houses a comprehensive collection of Blackfeet Indian artifacts. **The Bob Scriver Studio** features the Western and wildlife sculptures of C. M. Russell. *Junction of Highways 2 and 89W; 406-338-2230.*

◆ GREAT FALLS

The C. M. Russell Museum Complex houses the world's largest collection of Russell's work. Original oils, bronzes, watercolors, and illustrated letters are shown in a gallery next door to the cowboy artist's original log-cabin studio. Also exhibited are works by many of Russell's contemporaries. *400 13th Street North; 406-727-8787.*

◆ HELENA

The Montana Historical Society has many Russell works as well as a large permanent collection of photographs by F. Jay Haynes, official photographer for the Northern Pacific Railroad and Yellowstone National Park circa 1900. At the state capitol are murals by early Western artist Edgar S. Paxson—and more Russells. *225 North Roberts; 406-444-2694.*

◆ MISSOULA

Likewise, adorning the foyer of the **Missoula County Courthouse** are Edgar S. Paxson's large murals depicting Lewis and Clark and groups of Flathead Indians.

■ CONTEMPORARY ART

Although Montana is known for its many Western painters, the state also claims many prominent contemporary artists, among them Livingston resident Russell Chatham, whose landscapes come alive with the spirit of this spacious land.

◆ BILLINGS

The Yellowstone Art Museum has the most significant contemporary collection in Montana, and its annual art auction is said to be the best of its kind in the nation. *401 North 27th Street; 406-256-6804.*

◆ BOZEMAN

Beall Park Art Center is a showcase for the city's vital arts community, with its exhibits, workshops, lectures, concerts, and performances. *409 North Bozeman; 406-586-3970.*

◆ BUTTE

Arts Chateau is housed in the old **Charles Clark Mansion,** where parlors and a second-floor kitchen have been transformed into art galleries, and the rest of the 26-room mansion has retained its elegance as a period museum. *321 West Broadway; 406-723-7600.*

Pequest, a signature stoneware "stack" by Montana native and Archie Bray alumnus Peter Voulkos, stands four feet tall. (photo by Schopplein studio, courtesy Peter Voulkos)

In a state known for its Western art, Billings' Yellowstone Art Museum has built an impressive collection of contemporary art. Shown here are sculptures by Deborah Butterfield (background) and Clarice Dryer (foreground). (photo by Mark Zimmerer, courtesy Yellowstone Art Museum)

◆ GREAT FALLS

Paris Gibson Square Museum of Art rotates exhibits in three galleries and conducts classes, seminars, and tours. *1400 First Avenue North; 406-727-8255.*

◆ HELENA

The **Montana Historical Society** houses the **Poindexter Gallery,** with its important collection of original works by artists of the New York School of modern art, including Franz Kline, Willem DeKooning, and Jackson Pollock. *225 North Roberts; 406-444-2694.*

The Archie Bray Foundation offers one of the world's finest residency programs for ceramic artists. Past directors and distinguished alumni include Rudy Autio, Peter Voulkos, Kurt Weiser, David Shaner, Ken Ferguson, and Akio Takamari. *Call 406-443-3502 for more information.*

Holter Museum of Art has just completed a $2 million capital campaign to expand its exhibition space and educational programs, which are considered the best in Montana. *12 East Lawrence; 406-442-6400.*

THE ARTS

◆ KALISPELL

Hockaday Museum of Art has a permanent collection of regional works, plus rotating exhibits in three galleries, tours, and classes for students and adults. *302 Second Ave. East; 406-755-5268.*

◆ MILES CITY

Custer County Art Center in Miles City is housed in the city's old water works plant, which provides spacious display areas for changing exhibits and a growing collection of vintage photographs by L. A. Huffman and Evelyn Cameron. *Waterplant Road half a mile west of town on Route 12; 406-232-0635.*

◆ MISSOULA

The Art Museum of Missoula features rotating exhibits, gallery talks, and an annual art auction. *335 North Pattee; 406-728-0447.*

■ THE PERFORMING ARTS

The performing arts in Montana run from opera and Shakespeare to recitations by some of the top cowboy poets in the West. Eight Montana communities support symphony orchestras, ranging from the state's largest—and the only one that pays all of its musicians—in Billings, to an act of love called the **Prairie Symphonette,** in the shrinking northeastern farm town of Scobey, population 1,131. In between are orchestras in Bozeman, Missoula, Great Falls, Kalispell, Helena, and Butte.

◆ BOZEMAN

Bozeman has the distinction of sustaining Montana's only opera company, the **Intermountain Opera,** founded by the late Metropolitan Opera baritone Pablo Elvira, who lived in Bozeman during the off-season.

Bozeman is also the home of **Shakespeare in the Parks,** a professional touring company that performs the Bard's comedies for audiences in Montana and nearby states during the summer months. (The company grew out of Montana State University's media and theater arts department.) Other Bozeman "don't miss" performers are **Montana Ballet,** as well as renowned classical guitarist **Stuart Weber.**

◆ MISSOULA

Montana's other university town also nurtures an active community of performing artists. Theater groups include the **Montana Repertory Theatre,** a professional touring company based in the university's drama-dance department; the **Missoula**

Children's Theatre, which tours nearly 300 communities annually; and the **Missoula Community Theatre,** which performs year-round. In addition to its symphony orchestra and chorale, Missoula is the home of the **Garden City Ballet.**

◆ SUMMER STOCK

Three communities have made a specialty of summer theater. **The Bigfork Summer Playhouse,** the **Fort Peck Summer Theatre,** and the **Virginia City Players** draw large crowds for their rotating schedules of comedy, vaudeville, and musicals.

■ THE LITERARY LANDSCAPE

In 1984, half a dozen Montana writers and historians hatched the idea of assembling an anthology of Montana literature as a birthday present to the state on the occasion of its 1989 statehood centennial. The result, four years later, was a five-pound, 1,161-page tome entitled *The Last Best Place,* reprinted many times since. Acclaimed coast to coast as a literary milestone, the bestseller secured Montana's standing as an important, if remote, enclave for writers. As one reviewer put it, "There's something about Montana that makes Montanans write and makes other people arrive here with notebook in hand and typewriter in the back seat." Visitors have been recording their images of Montana ever since Lewis and Clark traveled up the Missouri River in 1804. Native peoples had developed a strong oral tradition long before that. Much of the appeal of *The Last Best Place* is in the re-telling of these native stories, many of which appear in print for the first time. Side by side traditional myths of Napi, the Ghost Owl, and Lodge-Boy are the contemporary observations of best-selling Montana authors like Ivan Doig, A. B. Guthrie, Jr., Tom McGuane, and James Welch.

The *Los Angeles Times* once described Montana as "the literary capital of the country." How did that happen? The University of Montana's creative writing program (consistently rated one of the top 10 writing programs in the nation), a seductive landscape, the "get-away" factor, and a low-rent lifestyle are often given as the reasons for the state's abundance of writers. Bozeman poet Greg Keeler narrows it down to the basics: "Some of us were born here, and some of us came for the trout." For whatever reason, Montana's writing tradition is firmly entrenched and now grows on its own strength. The university town of Missoula is the unrivaled capital of Montana's statewide literary community, supporting a surprising number of published authors, poets, and playwrights, and somewhere between 15 and 20 bookstores, many of them independent and locally owned. *(See "RECOMMENDED READING" on pages 293-295 for a selected bibliography of Montana books.)*

OLD WEST MONTANA
RODEOS, POWWOWS & DUDE RANCHES

—by Don Pitcher and Norma Tirrell

MONTANA CAN CERTAINLY JUSTLY CLAIM its cultural sophistication, but that doesn't mean we've disavowed our Old West history. Native American powwows, rodeos and bucking horse contests, cowboy poetry readings—these events are all widely performed and heavily attended by Montana residents. And lest we neglect our visitor population, dozens of dude and guest ranches—from family-oriented working cattle ranches to ultra-deluxe resorts with stables *and* spas—offer access to "Wild West" activities such as horseback riding, cattle round-ups, sleigh rides, square dances, and cook-outs.

■ RODEOS

The Western sport of rodeo grew out of cowboys' passion for their occupation. When they weren't movin', sortin', and brandin' cows, or breakin', buyin', and sellin' horses, cowboys were testing their day-to-day skills against one another to see who was the best calf roper or bronc rider. Before long, these barnyard contests were attracting kids and neighbors, and a professional sport was born. Cowboys began traveling from rodeo to rodeo, and the good ones won enough prize money to finance next year's circuit. Few actually make a living as rodeo cowboys, but most come away with something; if not a cash prize or a new belt buckle, often a busted jaw and a crooked grin. Some have even died doing what they loved best. But all have been lassoed by a sport that requires skill, courage, a good deal of luck, and a love of livestock. From Thompson Falls in timber country to Brockway on the plains, cities and towns across Montana celebrate their Western heritage with a weekend of rodeo, usually in summer.

◆ RODEO EVENTS: RIDING AND ROPING

Most rodeo events fall into two categories: riding and roping. Riding events include saddle bronc riding, bareback bronc riding, and bull riding, while roping events include steer wrestling and calf roping. Women's barrel racing, along with various other sports, complete the roundup. In most events, luck has a lot to do with who wins. Much of the scoring is based on the difficulty of the ride (the toughest broncs or bulls are favorites because they mean higher scores), and times for ropers are dependent upon the speed and behavior of the calf or steer they are trying to tackle.

Steer Wrestling

Steer wrestling, or bulldogging, involves leaping from a quarter horse onto the back of a 700-pound Mexican steer running at 25 miles an hour, grabbing his horns and wrestling him to the ground. If you think that sounds easy, try it some time! The sport originated in 1903 when Bill Pickett, a black Texas cowboy (many early cowboys were black), jumped on the back of an ornery steer, grabbed its horns, bent over its head and bit the steer's lower lip like an attacking bulldog. Soon he was repeating the stunt for the 101 Ranch Wild West Show. Others copied this feat, and though the lip-biting part has long since disappeared, the name bulldogging has stuck.

Steer wrestling today involves two men: a dogger and a hazer. When the steer hurtles into the arena, the two spur their horses in quick pursuit, with the hazer trying to force the steer to run straight ahead while the dogger gets into position to leap onto the steer's horns, wrestling him to the ground with his feet and head facing the same direction. Since they are competing with other doggers on time, every second counts. Good doggers can get a steer down in less than seven seconds.

Calf Roping

Calf roping originated in the Old West when ropers would pull down a calf and quickly tie it up for branding. Today, this is the most competitive of all rodeo events, and there is often big money for the winners. Calf ropers chase a 200- to 350-pound calf on their expertly trained horses, roping it and then quickly throwing it on its side. After a quick wrap of the piggin'

string around three ankles, followed by a half hoitch knot, the calf is allowed to try to break free. If it can't within six seconds, the time stands and an untie man rides in to free the calf.

Saddle Bronc Riding

The oldest of all rodeo sports, saddle bronc riding originated from cowboys' attempts to train wild horses. Broncs are saddled up in the chutes (fenced-in enclosures along the edge of the arena) and riders climb on, grabbing a thick hemp rope in one hand and sinking their boots into the stirrups. When the gate opens, the bronc goes wild, trying to throw the rider off. The smooth back and forth motion of a good saddle bronc rider makes it appear that he is atop a rocking chair. Rides only last eight seconds; when the horn sounds, a pickup man rides alongside the bronc and the rider slides onto the other horse.

Bareback Bronc Riding

Bareback riding is similar to saddle bronc riding, but the cowboy rides with only a minimum of equipment—no stirrups and no reins. A small leather rigging held on by a leather strap around the horse is topped with a suitcase-like handle. A second wool-lined strap goes around the flank of the horse to act as an irritant so that the bronc bucks more. The cowboy holds on with one hand and bounces back and forth in a rocking motion, an effort akin to trying to juggle bowling pins while surfing a big wave. Eight seconds later it's over and a pickup man comes in to rescue the rider (if he hasn't been thrown to the ground).

Bull Riding and Rodeo Clowns

Bull riding is in a class of danger all its own. Unlike broncs who just want that man off their back, bulls want to get even. When a bull rider is thrown off (and this is most of the time, even with the best riders), the bull immediately goes on the attack, trying to gore or trample him. Many bull riders are seriously injured and some die when hit by this 2,000 pounds of brute force. There are no saddles in bull riding, just a piece of thick rope wrapped around the bull's chest with the free end wrapped tightly around the bull rider's hand. A cowbell hangs at the bottom of this contraption to annoy the bull even more. When the chute opens, all hell breaks loose as the bull does everything it possibly can to throw his rider off—spinning, kicking, jumping, and running against the fence.

If the rider hangs on for the required eight seconds (style isn't very important), the next battle begins, getting out of the way of one very angry bull. Here the rodeo clown comes in. Dressed in baggy pants and bright red and white shirts, clowns look like human Raggedy Andy dolls. In reality they are moving targets. Clowns use every trick in the book—climbing into padded barrels that the bulls butt against, weaving across the arena, mocking the bulls with matador capes, and simply running for their lives to reach the fence ahead of the bull. Frequently, two clowns work in tandem to create confusion, one acting as the barrel man, and the other as a roving target. Rodeo clowns also play another role, that of entertainer between events. Their stock of supplies includes rubber chickens, trick mules, a series of pantomimed jokes with the announcers, and anything else that might keep folks from getting restless.

Barrel Racing

One of the only female-dominated events, barrel racing is found at nearly every rodeo, and consists of a triangular course of three barrels arranged a hundred feet apart. The event requires riding a fast horse in a set pattern around these barrels, trying not to knock any over.

◆ CALENDAR OF RODEOS AND BUCKING HORSE EVENTS

JANUARY

Montana Professional Rodeo Cowboys Association Circuit Finals.
Late January or early February
Great Falls; 406-727-8115
This national organization is divided into 12 competitive regions, or circuits. This rodeo is the final round of competition for the Montana circuit.

MAY

Miles City Bucking Horse Sale. *Late May*
Miles City; 406-232-6585
This cowboy classic features three days of bucking horse action, pari-mutuel horse racing, wild horse races, dances, parade.

Bull riding is one of rodeo's most exciting and dangerous events. (photo by Greg Vaughn)

JUNE

American Legion Rodeo. *Late June*
 Augusta; 406-562-3448
One of the big-time small-town rodeos.

JULY

Livingston Roundup.
 Fourth of July weekend
 Livingston; 406-222-0850
This PRCA rodeo features three days of rodeo competition, plus a parade, skits, fireworks, and other entertainment.

Arlee Powwow. *Fourth of July weekend*
 Arlee; 406-675-2700
On the Flathead Indian Reservation. Combined celebration of the Salish and Kootenai tribes, with horse races and rodeo. *See page 83 for more.*

Home of Champions Rodeo.
 Fourth of July weekend
 Red Lodge; 406-446-1718
This three-day PRCA event occurs at the base of the Beartooth Highway.

Fourth of July Rodeo.
 Fourth of July weekend
 Ennis; 406-682-4700
Another popular Fourth of July weekend rodeo, this one is organized by the National Rodeo Association.

Wild Horse Stampede. *Early July*
 Wolf Point; 406-653-2220
On the Fort Peck Indian Reservation. This event grew out of traditional Indian powwows and bucking contests. Wild horse races and other events draw a crowds to the "granddaddy" of all Montana rodeos.

Bannack Days. *Mid July*
 Bannack State Park; 406-834-3413
Horse and buggy rides, black powder rifle shooting, gold panning, frontier arts, crafts, music, and food at one of Montana's foremost historic parks.

North American Indian Days. *Mid-July*
 Browning; 406-338-7276
On the Blackfeet Indian Reservation. Highlights of this major celebration include a large rodeo. *See page 83 for more.*

AUGUST

Crow Fair. *Mid-August*
 Crow Agency; 406-638-2601
On the Crow Indian Reservation. One of the nation's premier native cultural celebrations, Crow Fair draws Native Americans and spectators from throughout North America. Parades, rodeos, dancing, and horse races. *See page 83 for more.*

SEPTEMBER

Jaycee Rodeo. *Labor Day weekend*
 Dillon; 406-683-5511
Montana's largest Labor Day rodeo features top national and Montana cowboys and cowgirls in two days of competition, plus dances, a parade, and barbecue.

OCTOBER

Northern International Livestock Exposition. *Mid-October*
 Billings; 406-256-2495
Indoor rodeo at season's end brings some of the nation's top contestants to this growing event, which also features a stock show and commercial exhibits.

(above and opposite) Scenes from Montana powwows.

■ POWWOWS

Powwow is a time of pageantry and celebration on Montana's seven Indian reservations, and there is nothing quite like it in the state's dominant white culture. For three to five days, tribal members abandon the day-to-day challenge of reservation life and come together for renewal and reunion. They perform traditional ceremonies and compete in dancing and games. They race prized horses and parade in beautifully beaded buckskins and feathered headdresses. They call on spirits, give gifts, and look to tribal elders to keep ancient stories alive. Through it all, they fortify the bonds that tie Indian families and clans so closely together.

Non-Indian visitors are welcome as spectators, but don't expect these events to conform to the schedules and comforts of the American middle class. Leave your own cultural trappings behind and go to powwow with the expectation of enriching your understanding of the West by learning about its native culture. Some of Montana's best-known powwows are included in the list that follows.

*J*UNE

Red Bottom Celebration.

Late June Frazer

On the Fort Peck Indian Reservation. Traditional Indian celebration commemorating the Lower Band of the Assiniboine; dancing, contests, hand games.

*J*ULY

Arlee Powwow. *Fourth of July weekend*

Arlee; 406-675-2700

Combined celebration of the Salish and Kootenai tribes held on the Flathead Indian Reservation. Rodeo, horse racing, stick games, competitive dancing, stick games.

Wild Horse Stampede.

Early July

Wolf Point; 406-653-2220

This event on the Fort Peck Indian Reservation grew out of traditional Indian powwows and bucking contests. Wild horse races and other events draw a crowds to the "granddaddy" of all Montana rodeos.

North American Indian Days.

Mid-July

Browning; 406-338-7276

On the Blackfeet Indian Reservation. Highlights of this major, authentic celebration are dancing, singing, rodeo, and drumming competitions, parade, and games.

*A*UGUST

Crow Fair. *Mid-August*

Crow Agency

On the Crow Indian Reservation. One of the nation's premier native cultural celebrations, Crow Fair draws Native Americans and spectators from all over North America. Hundreds of tepees rise from the banks of the Little Bighorn River, making this the "Tepee Capital of the World" for five days of parades, rodeos, dancing, singing, feasting, gambling, horse races, and relays.

COWBOY POETRY

Cowboy poetry is a genre unto itself, and its popularity continues to grow. Mid-August Lewistown; 406-538-8278Three days of rhymes and recitations, jam sessions, music, and dance. This is no ersatz imitation or goopy reminiscence: this is the real thing.

The Bucking Horse Moon

A kiss for luck, then we'd let 'er buck—
  I'd spur electric on adrenaline and lust.
She'd figure-8 those barrels
  on her Crimson Missile sorrel—
we'd make the night air swirl with hair and dust.

At some sagebrushed wayside, 3 A.M.,
  we'd water, grain, and ground-tie Missile.
Zip our sleeping bags together,
  make love in any weather,
amid the cactus, rattlers, and thistle.

Seems the moon was always full for us—
  its high-diving shadow kicking hard.
We'd play kid games on the big night sky,
  she'd say "that bronco's Blue-Tail Fly,
and ain't that ol' J. T. spurrin' off its stars?"

We knew sweet youth's no easy keeper.
  It's spent like winnings, all too soon.
So we'd revel every minute in the music of our Buick
  running smooth, two rodeoin' lovers cruising to another—
beneath Montana's blue roan bucking horse moon.

The Augusta perf* at 2, we'd place again,
  then sneak off to our secret Dearborn River spot.
We'd take some chips and beer and cheese,
  skinny-dip, dry off in the breeze,
build a fire, fry the trout we caught.

*the American Legion rodeo, in Augusta

Down moonlit gravel back to blacktop,
    she'd laugh and kill those beams for fun.
That old wagon road was ours to own—
    30 shows since I'd been thrown
and 87 barrels since she'd tipped one.

We knew that youth won't keep for rainy days.
    It burns and turns to ash too soon.
So we'd revel every minute in the music of our Buick
    running smooth, two rodeoin' lovers cruising to another—
beneath Montana's blue roan bucking horse moon.

                                    —Paul Zarzyski, 1988

Cowboy poet reciting at the annual Lewistown, Montana event.

■ GUEST RANCHES

Montana's most distinctive accommodations are its many guest ranches, where hosts offer vacations with a Western flair and rooms with a view. No two ranches are alike, and rates vary widely, but most include lodging, meals, and activities. Many take guests only on a weekly basis. The ranches listed below represent but few of Montana's many guest ranches. Go to "Trip Planner" at www.visitmt.com for a full listing of ranch vacations, and for more information on the ranches listed here.

◆ EASTERN MONTANA

Double Spear Ranch.
Pryor; 406-259-8291
Located on the Crow Indian reservation, the Blackmore family offers a "real ranch experience, not an upscale vacation." Guests can join in on ranch operations, nearly all of which take place on horseback, and tour nearby Little Bighorn Battlefield and Bighorn Canyon Recreation Area.

Hell Creek Guest Ranch.
Jordan; 406-557-2224
Working cattle ranch in the heart of the Big Open, near Fort Peck Lake and the C. M. Russell National Wildlife Refuge. Aside from ranch chores, there's fossil hunting and seasonal big-game hunting.

Montana River Ranch.
Bainville; 877-277-4084
Working farm-ranch operation in Montana's northeast corner, near the confluence of the Yellowstone and Missouri rivers. Easy access to Forts Union and Buford historic sites. Warmwater fishing, float trips, canoe rentals, bird watching, wildlife viewing, and closeup views of ranch operations.

Schively Ranch.
Lovell; 406-259-8866
(winter: 307-548-6688)
Working cattle ranch near the Pryor Mountains and Bighorn Canyon National Recreation Area. Serious horseback riding; cattle drives and roundups.

Seventh Ranch.
Garryowen; 800-371-7963
Working ranch two miles from Little Bighorn Battlefield. Guided tours, horseback riding, cattle drives, fishing.

The Wald Ranch.
Lodge Grass; 406-639-2457
Family ranch in the Bighorn Mountains; takes one family or group at a time. Take part in unstructured activities or just relax.

Wolff Farms.
Circle; 406-485-2633, 888-900-2985
The Big Open at its best. A working ranch where you can learn to ride and rope from a leading rodeo competitor, help doctor some cattle, or simply lose yourself to the sights and sounds of eastern Montana's wide open spaces. Activities include bird watching, wildlife viewing, hiking, horseback riding, and seasonal hunting.

◆ CENTRAL MONTANA

Blacktail Ranch.
Wolf Creek; 406-235-4330
Working paint horse ranch in the mountains between Helena and Great Falls. Horseback riding, great fishing on private trout stream, hiking, and wildlife viewing.

Bonanza Creek Ranch.
Martinsdale; 800-476-6045
In the foothills of the Castle Mountains, with views of the Crazy Mounains. This is cattle country, and you are invited to help with ranch chores, fish for wild trout, or catch wildlife on camera. Recently listed in *Travel & Leisure* as one of Montana's great guest ranches.

Careless Creek Ranch.
Shawmut; 888-832-4140
Get a taste of ranch living on a 48,000-acre sheep and cattle ranch just souh of the Big Snowy Mountains. In addition to horseback riding, enjoy hiking, fishing, and wildlife viewing. In addition to the main lodge, accommodations include an original sheepherder's wagon, which sleeps two.

Circle Bar Ranch.
Utica; 888-570-0227
In the beautiful Judith River Valley, where Charlie Russell fell in love with the state. Horseback riding, fishing, hunting, cross-country skiing, snowmobiling.

G Bar M Ranch.
Clyde Park; 406-686-4423
In the foothills of the Bridger Mountains north of Livingston. This 3,200-acre, working cattle ranch has been taking in guests (10 to 15 at a time) since 1900. Horseback riding, horsemanship, and fishing.

JJJ Wilderness Ranch.
Augusta; 406-562-3653
Near the Sun River Canyon and Bob Marshall Wilderness. Horseback riding, fishing, hiking.

Klick's K Bar L Ranch.
Augusta; 406-467-2771
or 406-562-3589
Stunning location near Bob Marshall Wilderness and Sun River Game Preserve. Horseback riding, fishing, hiking, hunting, hot springs pools.

Pine Butte Ranch.
Choteau; 406-466-2158
A Nature Conservancy property on the east slope of the Rockies near the Bob Marshall Wilderness. Horseback riding, fishing, hiking, naturalist-guided tours. An environmental education in the ecology of the Rocky Mountain Front.

Rocking Z Guest Ranch.
Wolf Creek; 406-458-3890
Outside Helena and minutes from great fishing on the Missouri River. Working cattle ranch with lots of additional activities, including guided trail rides, guided fly fishing trips, and boat tours of the Gates of the Mountains, an important landmark on the Lewis and Clark Trail. Consider reserving the entire ranch for your family Christmas vacation.

Seven Lazy P Ranch.
Choteau; 406-466-2044
On the Teton River and next door to the Bob Marshall Wilderness. Horseback riding, fishing, hunting, cross-country skiing.

OLD WEST
MONTANA

◆ YELLOWSTONE AREA

B Bar Guest Ranch.
Emigrant; 406-848-7523
Cabins and a nicely furnished lodge in the Paradise Valley. Eat organic beef from cattle raised at the ranch, enjoy the garden's produce, and live the good life.

Boulder River Ranch.
McLeod; 406-932-5926
South of Big Timber, near Absaroka-Beartooth Wilderness. Horseback riding, fly fishing, hiking.

CB Ranch.
Cameron; 406-682-4954
Madison River Valley near Ennis. Horseback riding; fly fishing.

Diamond J Ranch.
Ennis; 406-682-4867
Madison River Valley near Ennis. Horseback riding, fly fishing, hiking, trap and skeet shooting.

Hawley Mountain Guest Ranch.
McLeod; 877-496-7848
Near Absaroka-Beartooth Wilderness. Horseback riding, fishing, hiking, hunting.

Lazy K Bar Ranch.
Big Timber; 406-537-4404
Working 22,000-acre ranch in the foothills of the Crazy Mountains. Hiking, horseback riding, fishing, square dancing.

Lone Mountain Ranch.
Big Sky; 800-514-4644
Near the Gallatin River, the Spanish Peaks, Big Sky ski resort, Yellowstone. Horseback riding, fly fishing, Yellowstone visits, nordic skiing. Great food. It's all done just right.

Mountain Meadows Guest Ranch.
Big Sky 6; 888-644-6647
Upscale guest ranch just south of Big Sky Ski Resort. Luxurious guest rooms, gourmet food, year-round activities. In summer:

(opposite) A split rail fence frames the sky at this Mission Valley Ranch. (above) A beautiful fall in the Swan Range in the Bigfork-Flathead Valley.

horseback riding, hiking, mountain biking, fly fishing, whitewater rafting, golf, tennis, and trips into Yellowstone. In winter: skiing (nordic and alpine), snowshoeing, sleigh rides, and snowcoach tours of Yellowstone.

Mountain Sky Guest Ranch.
  Emigrant; 800-548-3392
In the Paradise Valley. Hiking, horseback riding, swimming, fishing, and tennis.

Nine Quarter Circle Ranch.
  Gallatin Gateway; 406-995-4276
In the Gallatin Canyon, north of Yellowstone National Park. Horseback riding, fly fishing. Lots of family activities; childcare.

Parade Rest Ranch.
  West Yellowstone; 800-753-5934
Near Yellowstone National Park's West Entrance. Fly fishing, horseback riding.

63 Ranch.
  Livingston; 406-222-0570
Near the Absaroka-Beartooth Wilderness. Hiking, fly fishing, horseback riding, photography workshops. Owned by a family who love the lifestyle and the place.

Sweet Grass Ranch.
  Big Timber; 406-537-4477
In the Crazy Mountains north of Big Timber. All you'd expect on a working cattle ranch, plus rodeos, square dancing, cattle roundups, and fly-fishing.

320 Ranch.
  Gallatin Gateway; 406-995-4283
Year-round resort between Yellowstone and Big Sky. Trail rides, fishing, hiking, skiing, sleigh rides, cook-outs, square dancing.

OLD WEST MONTANA

◆ WESTERN MONTANA

Blue Spruce Lodge and Guest Ranch.
   Trout Creek; 800-831-4797
In the foothills of the Bitterroot Mountains and near Noxon Reservoir in northwestern Montana. Trail rides, float fishing, boating, hunting, cross-country skiing, and snow-mobiling. All wheelchair accessible.

Divide Wilderness Ranch.
   Lima; 888 764-3300
Sited in one of Montana's most beautiful valleys, this remote ranch lies between the Centennial Mountains and Red Rock Lakes. Wildlife and birds are abundant; people, few and far between. Red Rocks is home to the trumpeter swan and many other water-fowl and shorebirds. Unsurpassed fall beauty.

Flathead Lake Lodge.
   Bigfork; 406-837-4391
Western living and water sports, all in one gorgeous location on the northeast shore of Flathead Lake. Horseback riding and tennis are available too.

Hargrave Guest Ranch.
   Marion; 406-858-2284
Working cattle ranch in the Thompson River Valley west of Kalispell. Horseback riding, cross-country skiing, fishing, hiking.

Horse Prairie Ranch.
   Dillon, 888-726-2454
Located in the heart of cattle country and one of Montana's oldest cattle ranches. Traditional activities: cattle drives, pack trips, barbecues, Dutch oven cookouts. Great fishing in Big Hole River and Clark Canyon Reservoir. Geared to families and groups.

Laughing Water Guest Ranch.
   Fortine; 406-882-4680
   or 800-847-5095
Between Glacier National Park and Lake Koocanusa. Hiking, horseback riding, fishing, swimming.

Triple Creek Guest Ranch.
   Darby; 406-821-4600
An ultra-deluxe lodging and dining "hide-away" in the Bitterroots. Horseback riding, hiking, swimming, tennis, mountain-bike riding, snow-mobiling, spa, cross-country skiing, and hot tubs everywhere.

West Fork Meadows Ranch.
   Darby; 406-349-2030
Deluxe cabins and fine dining on the West Fork of the Bitterroot River. Horseback riding, floating, biking, fishing, hiking.

White Tail Ranch.
   Ovando; 888-987-2624
With the Bob Marshall Wilderness to he north and the Blackfoot River Valley to the south, there's no shortage of gorgeous country and great fishing to explore. Famous for its horsepacking trips; also hiking, fly fishing and mountain bike riding. Professional fly fishing guides and wranglers will help as much or as little as you like.

■ CATTLE DRIVES AND WAGON TRIPS

If you're looking for a cowboy-style tour through part of Montana and you're not planning on staying at a guest or dude ranch, all is not lost. The following tour guides offer cattle drives and wagon trips in different parts of the state; just be sure to book ahead.

Beartooth Travel Service.
Roberts; 406-445-2303
or 800-554-2303
Booking agent for several cattle drives and wagon trips in the state.

Montana High Country Cattle Drive.
Townsend; 800-345-9423
Three authentic cattle drives each year in June and August. Space limited.

Powder River Wagon Trains & Cattle Drives.
Broadus; 406-436-2350.
Another look at southeastern Montana's cattle country.

A driver takes a break during one of the several wagon train rides that rolled across Montana in 1989 during the statehood centennial celebrations.

OLD WEST
MONTANA

T H E   H I - L I N E
M O N T A N A ' S   N O R T H E R N   T I E R

Map pages 94-95

Havre
Chief Joseph Battlefield

THE SO-CALLED "HI-LINE" is Montana's northern tier, an immense land of cattle and grain, wildlife, waterfowl, and open space. The region's few people meet for coffee in small towns and cities along US 2—also known as the Hi-Line—which links the high plains of eastern Montana with the Rockies to the west. Sparsely populated as it is, the sociology of northern Montana is as diverse as any you will find in the state. Scattered across this broad landscape are the descendants of immigrant farmers, ranchers, and railroad workers, the members of six Indian tribes living on four reservations, and the German-speaking residents of nearly two dozen Hutterite colonies. Adding to the mix is a regular flow of traffic to and from the Canadian provinces of Alberta and Saskatchewan, Montana's closest neighbors to the north.

■ A RESILIENT PEOPLE

The communities that dot the Hi-Line bespeak the resilience of their founders and residents. Appealing as Montana is, no one ever said it was easy to live here, and life on the Hi-Line can be especially challenging. In addition to extremes in weather that scour the plains with arctic winds in winter and scorch them in summer, the Hi-Line has ridden out all manner of ups and downs, including the collapse both of the open range cattle industry and the homestead movement, the changing fortunes of the Great Northern Railway, cyclical drought, dust, and grasshoppers, boom and bust in the northern oil fields, and the vagaries of federal farm legislation and global grain markets. Ever since the massive farm foreclosures of the twenties, when half the state's farmers lost their land and Montana lost 60,000 residents, population along the Hi-Line has declined, due primarily to a steady out-migration from the eastern counties.

Yet, it is in the face of hardship and decline that the character of the Hi-Line reveals itself. Because people are so scarce, people matter. Neighbors are valued, and visitors frequently make the pages of the weekly newspaper. The bygone traits of compassion, good will, and humor are still palpable in communities like Malta and Glasgow. As one Hi-Liner put it: "You have to value people as the main thing when you live up here." In addition to the county fairs, church suppers, rodeos, and bull sales that bring area residents together, school sports draw passionate crowds from one end of the Hi-Line to another. It is not unusual for a Hi-Liner to drive 300 miles from, say, Cut Bank to Wolf Point, in the dead of winter, to see a closely contested high school basketball game.

Much of the Hi-Line was settled in the late 1880s, when Jim Hill's Great Northern Railway laid tracks across the northern Great Plains to link the Great Lakes with the Pacific Coast. (Montana Historical Society)

Many of the settlements along US 2 got their start as railroad towns in 1887. Later, the Great Northern Railway Company continued west through Shelby and Cut Bank, crossed the Continental Divide at Marias Pass on Glacier National Park's southern border, and reached Seattle in 1893. Linked to the Great Lakes and the Pacific Coast by rail, these brand new towns became important storage and shipping centers for grain and livestock. **Havre** and **Shelby** are still important railroad towns along the track, now owned by the Burlington Northern Railroad. Since the discovery of oil and gas fields in north-central Montana in the 1920s and '30s, energy fuels have also been important, if fickle, partners in the local economies of Shelby and **Cut Bank.** Farther east, Fort Peck Dam and the now-defunct Glasgow Air Force Base both significantly added to—then just as significantly subtracted from—the population of **Glasgow.** Smaller towns almost wholly dependent on farming and ranching are Malta, Harlem, Chinook, Chester, and, in the northeast corner, Scobey and Plentywood.

The Canadian border is less than an hour's drive north of US 2 in most places. Ever since the 1920s, when bootleggers wore ruts into these and other "whiskey roads" hauling cargoes of smuggled booze into the states in defiance of Prohibition, there has been a steady flow of traffic between Canada and Montana. More than a dozen border stations are spaced along the 570-mile international border

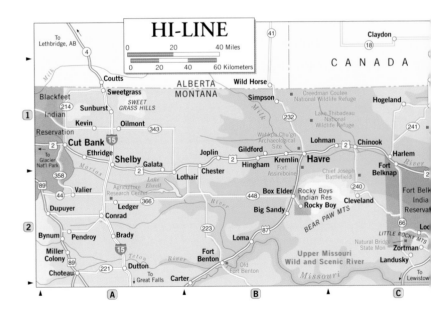

Montana shares with Canada. The busiest border crossing between Seattle and Minneapolis is at Sweetgrass, north of Shelby on Interstate 15, which funnels traffic into the United States from the Alaska and MacKenzie Highways and the province of Alberta.

■ DRIVING THROUGH

US Highway 2 is a relentless double lane of "oil"—in the local vernacular—that follows the Missouri and the Milk Rivers from the North Dakota state line to Havre, then highballs west through Shelby and Cut Bank to Glacier National Park. The accommodations and cafés are few and far between in this remote country, but most of the small towns have all-American food and homey motels; the **West Prairie B&B** in Havre is a 1920s home with broad views of the plains. And in Glasgow, Sam's, at 307 First Avenue North, has earned a reputation for fine steaks and local walleye.

Just when you think the plains will never end, the Sweet Grass Hills, the Bear Paw Mountains, and the Little Rockies appear like ghosts on the horizon. Amtrak's *Empire Builder*—named after 19th-century railroad magnate James J. Hill, whose Great Northern Railway stretched from Minneapolis to Seattle—follows a similar route across northern Montana.

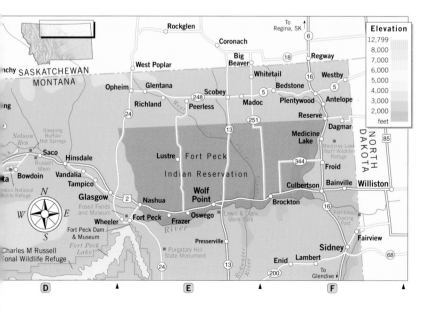

■ WILDLIFE ALONG THE MISSOURI RIVER

Earlier visitors did it the hard way, pushing upstream against the Missouri River, original highway of the West. Lewis and Clark made numerous diary entries about the "uncommonly large" and "excessively tormenting" mosquitoes they endured as they made their way up the Missouri and past its tributaries, including the Milk. Like so many other aspects of the Lewis and Clark Trail in Montana, this one has not changed. Mosquitoes are still a summertime nuisance in the Milk River valley, especially around Malta and Saco in a wet year.

Other wildlife, however, would prove less resistant to settlement. Upon entering what is now Montana at the confluence of the Missouri and Yellowstone Rivers, Meriwether Lewis wrote: "We can scarcely cast our eyes in any direction without perceiving deer Elk Buffaloe or Antelopes." The date was April 29, 1805. By the end of the century, the buffalo had been shot to near extinction by hide hunters and the elk had been forced to higher ground. But the vast plains, rivers, and reservoirs of northern Montana are still home to a great variety of wildlife. Clouds of ducks and geese eclipse the moon during spring and fall migrations.

◆ MEDICINE LAKE NATIONAL WILDLIFE REFUGE   *map page 95, F-1*

Motorists commonly spot big game and birds from the road throughout Montana, but several refuges and reservoirs along the Hi-Line assure more intimate views. One of North America's largest nesting colonies of white pelicans returns to Medicine Lake National Wildlife Refuge each spring, along with about 100,000 ducks and geese. Get here via a paved-then-gravel road that turns east from scenic Montana State Highway 16, halfway between Culbertson and Plentywood. Medicine Lake also provides sanctuary for the threatened piping plover and an occasional endangered whooping crane. This isolated refuge in Montana's extreme northeast corner encompasses Montana's smallest classified wilderness, also called Medicine Lake, which preserves the lake's islands and waters, a small parcel of mixed-grass prairie, and a prehistoric tepee ring.

◆ BOWDOIN NATIONAL WILDLIFE REFUGE   *map page 95, D-2*

Another bird sanctuary, Bowdoin National Wildlife Refuge lies about a half-day's drive west on US 2. Spring is a busy time at Bowdoin. Starting in late March, bald eagles arrive to feast on winter-kill fish. Male sharp-tailed grouse bow and strut, coo and cackle, as they compete for mates on traditional dancing grounds in April and May. The best months to view waterfowl are May and June, as migration winds down and nesting begins. More than 200 species of birds in all, in addition to deer and antelope, make Bowdoin a favorite spot for wildlife watchers.

Just across the highway, **Nelson Reservoir** is best known for its walleye, northern pike, and perch fishing, but birders visit, too, for views of its abundant waterfowl and shorebirds. Fresno Lake, Lake Elwell, and Lake Frances are also popular oases along US 2 for fishing and hunting, wildlife viewing, and water sports.

■ THE FUR TRADE

Of all the wildlife reported by Lewis and Clark along the Missouri, none had more immediate impact on Montana's history than the beaver. The West presented a brand new frontier for the expanding fur trade, and eastern and European entrepreneurs lost no time in exploiting it. In 1828, John Jacob Astor's powerful American Fur Company established what was to become the preeminent fur-trading post on the Missouri River. From its strategic location at the mouth of the Yellowstone River, Fort Union dominated the northern plains and Rocky Mountain fur trade from the 1830s to the Civil War. A colorful cast of characters enlivened this lonely outpost—eastern capitalists and Plains Indians, boorish mountain men, Jesuit missionaries, artists, scientists, and European royalty anxious to glimpse America's exotic new frontier. Untold thousands of beaver pelts were floated downriver from Fort Union to St. Louis. The demand for beaver fur declined when men switched from fur to silk hats.

Fort Union Trading Post, (*map page 95, F-2*) on the Montana–North Dakota border just south of US 2, has been preserved by the National Park Service as a historic site. Here, in this unlikely location, visitors can explore the fort's Bourgoise House, once the setting of elegant dinners for distinguished guests like the German explorer Prince Maximilian, naturalist John James Audubon, and artists Karl Bodmer and George Catlin. Newly restored to its 19th-century glory, Fort Union reflects one of the most colorful eras of the nation's westward expansion.

A lively chapter in Western history, this era brought death and disease to the native culture. Once nomadic, self-sufficient buffalo hunters, many Plains Indians grew dependent on the whiskey and guns they received in exchange for furs. Trappers and traders also brought smallpox, a disease that proved fatal to Indians who had no immunity. The Mandan tribe of North Dakota was almost entirely wiped out by the smallpox virus, and throughout Montana, thousands more Plains Indians died. The *coup de grâce* was the wholesale extermination of buffalo in the mid-1870s, when buffalo hides replaced beaver pelts as the West's most profitable

A GRASSY CLEAN WIND

*A*cross its empty miles pours the pushing and shouldering wind, a thing you tighten into as a trout tightens into fast water. It is a grassy, clean, exciting wind, with the smell of distance in it, and in its search for whatever it is looking for it turns over every wheat blade and head, every pale primrose, even the ground-hugging grass. It blows yellow-headed blackbirds and hawks and prairie sparrows around the air and ruffles the short tails of meadowlarks on fence posts. In collaboration with the light, it makes lovely and changeful what might otherwise be characterless.

It is a long way from characterless; "overpowering" would be a better word. For over the segmented circle of earth is domed the biggest sky anywhere, which on days like this sheds down on range and wheat and summer fallow a light to set a painter wild, a light pure, glareless, and transparent. The horizon a dozen miles away is as clean a line as the nearest fence. There is no haze, neither the woolly gray of humid countries nor the blue atmosphere of the mountain West. Across the immense sky move navies of cumuli, fair-weather clouds, their bottoms as even as if they had scraped themselves flat against the flat earth.

The drama of this landscape is in the sky, pouring with light and always moving. The earth is passive. And yet the beauty I am struck by, both as present fact and as revived memory, is a fusion: this sky would not be so spectacular without this earth to change and glow and darken under it. And whatever the sky may do, however the earth is shaken or darkened, the Euclidean perfection abides. The very scale, the hugeness of simple forms, emphasizes stability. It is not hills and mountains which we shall call eternal. Nature abhors an elevation as much as it abhors a vacuum; a hill is no sooner elevated than the forces of erosion begin tearing it down. These prairies are quiescent, close to static; looked at for any length of time, they begin to impose their awful perfection on the observer's mind. Eternity is a peneplain.

—Wallace Stegner, *Wolf Willow*, 1962

Northern Montana is an immense land of cattle and grain, space and sky.

commodity. By 1883, the buffalo was gone and so was the Plains Indian culture it supported. Unable to provide for themselves and defend their way of life, the tribes were vulnerable to the federal government, which confined them to reservations. Even these limited reservations diminished as settlers demanded more land for farming, ranching, mining, and railroads.

■ INDIAN RESERVATIONS

The present boundaries of the Fort Peck, Fort Belknap, and Blackfeet reservations were established by the Sweetgrass Hills Treaty of 1888. The federal government created the Hi-Line's fourth reservation—**Rocky Boy's**—in 1916. Like Indian reservations throughout America, these four offer a bleak insight into the conquest of one culture by another. Unemployment runs as high as 80 percent on some, and all have been ravaged by poverty and alcoholism. Cultural leaders trace a loss of pride and purpose to federal policies at the beginning of this century that out-

Assiniboine Indians at Glasgow awaiting the arrival of President Franklin Roosevelt in 1934 to launch construction of Fort Peck Dam. (Montana Historical Society)

CHIEF JOSEPH AND THE NEZ PERCE

One of the last major battles of the United States' campaign to win control of the plains took place about 16 miles south of the Hi-Line town of **Chinook.** In 1877, the federal government tried to force the Nez Perce Indians of Oregon's Wallowa Valley onto an Idaho reservation so that white ranchers could have their lands. The Nez Perce stubbornly refused. A few drunk young men killed four whites, and subsequent raids led to the deaths of at least 14 more. The U.S. Army retaliated, but was turned back by the Indians.

Rather than face government reinforcements and certain defeat, more than a thousand Nez Perce began an 1,800-mile flight in a desperate bid to reach safety in Canada. A series of running battles followed as the Indians used their geographic knowledge and battle skills to confound the inept Army. Finally, just 45 miles from the international border with Canada, the Army of Gen. Nelson A. Miles caught up with the Nez Perce. After the fierce, four-day Battle of the Bears Paw, Chief Joseph is remembered for closing one of the great speeches in the history of the West with these words: "Hear me, my chiefs, I am tired; my heart is sick and sad. From where the sun now stands, I will fight no more forever." The Nez Perce were forced to surrender, though 300 made good their escape to Canada. Despite promises that they would be allowed to return home, the Nez Perce were hustled onto a reservation in Oklahoma, while whites remained on their ancestral lands farther west. Chief Joseph died in 1904, reportedly of a broken heart.

Now managed as a state park, **Chief Joseph Battlefield** has been proposed as part of a new Nez Perce National Historic Park.

lawed traditional ceremonies like the Sun Dance and prohibited Indians from speaking their native tongues. On reservations across Montana, these people are now working with missionary zeal to heal the wounds of cultural deprivation by rescuing the language, songs, stories, and spiritual traditions of their ancestors.

Visitors can witness this cultural revival at any of the Indian powwows, where traditional dancing, drumming, singing, and games blend spirit and spectacle, reverence and revelry. The excellent **Museum of the Plains Indian** in Browning uses Blackfeet Indian tribal artifacts and other exhibits to explain the culture and history of the tribes that inhabited northern Montana. *For information, call 406-338-2230.*

(following pages) Costumes are elaborate and spirits are high as native dancers from throughout the country compete at Crow Fair. (photos by Douglas O'Looney)

■ ISLAND MOUNTAIN RANGES

Whether traveling north-south or east-west through Montana's northern tier, you will be struck by the sheer size of the landscape. With the exception of three small but surprising mountain ranges, there is nothing to interrupt the view for miles in every direction. Mere suggestions of the mountain landscape that lies to the west, the Little Rockies, Bear Paw Mountains, and Sweet Grass Hills add welcome dimension to the linear geometry of the plains. The Buckhorn store, cabins, and cafe (see page 298 for specifics) in Zortman provide a pleasant stopping place at the base of the Little Rockies.

◆ LITTLE ROCKY MOUNTAINS   *map page 94, C-2*

The Little Rocky Mountains are nearly as rich in Old West romance as they are in precious metals. Surrounded by a sea of grass and the rugged breaks of the Missouri River, these mountains provided refuge for outlaws, whiskey traders, and assorted scamps and scoundrels with names like Kid Curry, Butch Cassidy, Pike Landusky, Jew Jake, and the Sundance Kid. Tales of their Christmas shoot-outs, train robberies, and other carryings-on are as colorful as the gold that glittered in the gulches. Gold was first discovered here in 1884, and by World War II, the Little Rockies are said to have yielded $25 million of the precious metal. Mining resumed in 1979 when the Pegasus Gold Co. developed a huge cyanide heap-leach mine above the historic mining camp of Zortman. After peak annual production of 70,000 to 100,000 ounces of gold in the early 1990s, Pegasus filed for bankruptcy in January 1998, leaving taxpayers responsible for millions of dollars worth of water quality reclamation.

Zortman and Landusky once fell within the borders of the adjoining Fort Belknap Indian Reservation. After the discovery of gold, however, agents of the federal government persuaded the Assiniboine and Gros Ventre Indians to give up this mineral-rich chunk of land for a mere $350,000. This land grab shows up clearly on the map as a big bite taken from the reservation's southern border.

◆ SWEET GRASS HILLS   *map page 94, A-1*

Similarly, the Blackfeet Indians lost a precious piece of their traditional homeland in the Sweet Grass Hills, north of Chester, after gold was discovered there in 1885. The gold in these hills never amounted to a major strike. Nonetheless, this area, historically a sacred place for the Blackfeet, is still held privately by non-Indians.

◆ BEAR PAW MOUNTAINS   *map page 94, B/C-2*

The Bear Paw Mountains rise invitingly behind Havre—the Hi-Line's largest city—and Rocky Boy's Indian Reservation—Montana's smallest Indian reservation. Said to resemble a giant paw print from a distance, the grassy buttes and rounded peaks of the Bear Paws offer cool refuge from summer's sun-scorched plains. Hill County maintains a 10,000-acre public park along Beaver Creek leading into the Bear Paws, south of Havre. Billed as the largest county park in the nation, Beaver Creek Park offers ready access to fishing, camping, swimming, and wildlife watching for local sportsmen and outdoor lovers.

Chief Joseph Battlefield (*map page 94, C-2)* lies south of Chinook along MT 240. The battlefield is well marked but otherwise undeveloped, allowing visitors to use their imagination in re-creating the last battle of the Nez Perce Indian War. *(See page 71.)*

Like portents in a well-crafted novel, these isolated mountain ranges foreshadow a dramatic plot turn, when the plains run headlong into the wall of the Rockies.

THE HUTTERITES

Montana's cloistered Hutterites are conspicuous to the outside world by the homespun skirts, scarves, and black, Western-cut suits they wear when they come to town. These German-speaking exiles are masters of the soil and devout servants of God.

The plains of Montana, the Dakotas, and Canada provided the isolation and productive land that the Hutterite Brethren sought when they fled from intolerance and religious persecution in Russia after 1870. Firm in their insistence on adult baptism, communal living, and their refusal to bear arms or participate in prevailing social and economic institutions, these Anabaptists had already been driven from Austria, Moravia, and several eastern European countries. Between 1874 and 1877, the Hutterites established a beachhead in South Dakota, where they prospered until the patriotic fervor of World War I forced them north to Canada to avoid military conscription in the United States. Government-imposed limitations on land ownership in Canada pushed some of them back over the border after the war, and in 1937, the Hutterites established their first colony in Montana near Lewistown. About 40 colonies, each with a population of 60 to 100, now dot the plains of central and north-central Montana, where a live-and-let-live attitude has allowed the Hutterite people to flourish.

Self-sufficient and isolated by choice, Hutterites do not mix with secular society. This is not to say they are secretive or standoffish. Always willing to help non-Hutterite farmers and ranchers with repairs and chores, they are good neighbors. They visit nearby towns as necessary to pick up supplies, vote in elections, or deliver fresh produce to grocery stores.

At home and in their colonies, Hutterites speak German as a first language. English is used at school and in dealings with the outside world. Hutterite men work the land and raise the livestock; women perform all household duties. Children attend school until age 16, the minimum required by the state; then, they go to work for the colony. Hutterite women marry outside their own colony and take up residence in their husband's colony. When a colony outgrows the basic farm-ranch operation, it splits in two, with one half moving to a new site. At the heart of every colony is a philosophy of communal sharing and caring. All members work for the colony and the colony takes care of them from cradle to grave.

Visitors can get a glimpse of colony life during late summer and fall when Hutterites harvest truckloads of fresh vegetables from their large gardens. Many colonies display signs near their entrances announcing fresh tomatoes, corn, beans, potatoes, and squash. And for many Montana families, Christmas would not be Christmas without a fat, grain-fed Hutterite goose.

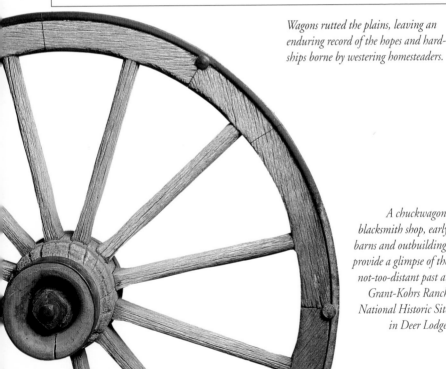

Wagons rutted the plains, leaving an enduring record of the hopes and hardships borne by westering homesteaders.

A chuckwagon, blacksmith shop, early barns and outbuildings provide a glimpse of the not-too-distant past at Grant-Kohrs Ranch National Historic Site in Deer Lodge.

THE BIG OPEN
EAST CENTRAL MONTANA

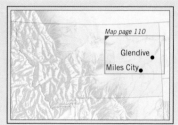

Map page 110

Glendive

Miles City

I glance higher for some hint of the weather, and the square of air broadens and broadens to become the blue expanse over the Montana rangeland, so vast and vaulting that it rears, from the foundation-line of the plains horizon, to form the walls and roof of all life's experience that my younger self could imagine, a single great house of Sky.

—Ivan Doig, *This House of Sky:
Landscapes of a Western Mind,* 1978

THE MID-SECTION OF EASTERN MONTANA—the lonely expanse of plains wedged between the Yellowstone River on the south and the Missouri on the north—has inspired many epithets over the years. While insiders have long known it as the "Big Dry Country" and "Next Year Country," visitors and newcomers can find the region's vastness awe-inspiring. Those with a writerly bent have come up with some nicknames that seem a little exotic for this place—"The American Outback," "The American Serengeti," and "Buffalo Commons," for example. But the name that stuck, coined in 1878 by frontier photographer L. A. Huffman, was a suitably straightshooting, plain English moniker: the Big Open.

◼ ABOUT THE BIG OPEN

The Big Open is exotic. Barely relevant to western Montana, it is the fulfilment of our folklore about the West. Undoubtedly the state's most unadulterated travel destination, the Big Open has no resorts, no gourmet restaurants, no shopping centers. About the closest thing to a privately developed tourist attraction is a handful of working cattle ranches that take in guests. (See "Guest Ranches" on page??? 299 for specifics.) Its largest city is **Circle** (pop. 644) which made the news some winters back when Montana State Highway 13 north of town was clogged with tumbleweeds after a November blow. The state highway department responded, as it does to most winter emergencies, by dispatching snowplows to the site. The second biggest town, **Jordan** (pop. 364), once described by a New York radio station as "the lonesomest town in the world," became notorious during an FBI standoff with the anti-government Freemen group in 1996.

With a population of roughly 4,000 scattered over 12,000 square miles, the Big Open encompasses just under 10 percent of Montana's land base but accounts for only one-half of one percent of its population. People have been quitting the Big Open ever since the failure of the homestead experiment—surely an ill-fated idea in a land that gets 12 to 13 inches of moisture in a good year.

◼ THE OPEN RANGE

Ironically, this was a land of opportunity in the glory days of the open range cattle boom. In a New Deal–era guidebook to Montana, the Federal Writers' Project reported that "a man who could ride a horse and do his share of corral work was always sure of a job here." This was a land of big cow outfits like the Texas-based XIT, which employed more than 200 cowboys to ride herd on 15,000 head, and the CK, part of a four-state, million-acre cattle empire owned by Conrad Kohrs. This was also the land that invented the rugged individualist—a way of life that survives, even though today's stockgrowers are tethered to the land, their security dependent upon the next weather report, cattle futures, global markets, and international trade policies over which they have no control.

Overgrazing, compounded by the brutal winter of 1886–87 and the arrival of plows and barbed wire, brought an end to the days of the open range. The end of an era, perhaps, but by no means the end of an industry. Numbering more than

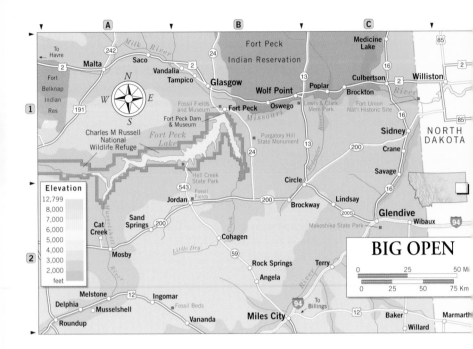

300,000 head, cattle and sheep still outnumber people nearly a hundred to one in the Big Open.

On land that requires 30 to 40 acres to support a cow and a calf, it takes a big spread and a friendly banker to build a ranch "that a cow can pay for," as the folks out here would say. This is the kind of ratio that inspires Rutgers University professors Frank and Deborah Popper to carry on their campaign to rid this and other semi-arid Western lands of cattle and give them back to grass and buffalo, creating a "Buffalo Commons." Describing the Homestead Act of 1862 as "the largest, longest-running agricultural and environmental mistake in United States history," they propose that the government buy back the land, tear down the fences, replant the shortgrass, and restock the plains with buffalo. The result would be the world's largest national park, an idea whose time has decidedly *not* arrived in the Big Open.

■ THE PEOPLE

Those who live outside the Big Open have long questioned the rationale of living inside. But for the few who remain and the occasional outsiders who yearn for the open road, there's no place like it. Let's start with those few souls who live here. Most live on a piece of land that has been under the stewardship of one family for three, four, perhaps five generations. It is all they know, but it is more than that. It has to do with ties that bind generation to generation, neighbor to neighbor, rancher to earth, earth to sky. In a land of infinite space, relations out here are skintight. Next door may mean 20 miles away, but telephone lines here are everlastingly busy—an indication that neighbors know more about one another's lives here than their counterparts do in Billings or Great Falls.

In this land of isolation, harsh winters, and cyclical droughts, people hang together. To get through the inevitable hard years, they sell off their herds or commute to Miles City or Glendive for temporary, hard-to-find jobs. They do what

Frontier photographer L.A. Huffman came west with the Army in 1878, and captured an era.
His photo of a homesteader breaking the prairie is entitled "The Honyocker."
(Montana Historical Society)

(top) A hopeful graingrower checks his barley crop before harvest.
(bottom) Rhythm and texture play their parts in the business of farming.

(top) Not everyone rides a horse in Montana, but they're not hard to come by.
(bottom) Grain bins form the skyline of many small farming communities.

they have to do to make it through this season because things are sure to be better next year. And, within this landscape of treeless plains bleached by sun, scoured by wind, and engulfed by sky, residents see unsurpassed beauty. This is the land of the long look, the unobstructed view; they wouldn't trade it for a dozen Glacier Parks.

Likewise, the inscrutable beauty of the Big Open either eludes visitors altogether or draws them back again and again. As a circuit-riding doctor from Billings describes it, "I used to think you had to have trees where you live. But pretty soon, you start seeing sunrises, sunsets, and incredible skyscapes."

It takes a good, long while to traverse the Big Open. Rolling ahead for as far as the eye can see, Montana State Highway 200 was made for those who travel for the sheer love of driving. Figure five hours of driving from Sidney to Lewistown, and that's with no stops. It will take at least that long to disengage from the world as you know it and adopt a new outlook. The view from the Big Open begins and ends with the sky. It has little to do with humanity, and so it raises fundamental questions about existence. How do they make it out here, you will wonder. Wits, humor, tolerance, and style are some helpful traits, and they are visible in the weathered faces and egalitarian dress of the locals. They are audible in the no-frills dialect of the plains. To listen up and get acquainted, stop for soda at the general store in Sand Springs, a bowl of pinto beans at the Jersey Lilly in Ingomar, or a rib steak at QD's Cafe in Jordan. In 1995, the latter served as media headquarters during an 81-day standoff between the FBI and the Freemen, a group of anti-government activists who'd holed up in a nearby ranch and were charged with tax evasion and other federal crimes. Several defendants were finally brought to trial in the summer of 1998.

The McCone County Museum in Circle is the place to go for a more formal introduction to the development of this country. It took a 6,400-square-foot building to house the artifacts and memorabilia that have been assembled by this preservation-minded community. Besides comprehensive displays of the area's homestead and cattle range eras, the museum has impressive collections of firearms, Indian artifacts, arrowheads, and fossils. *Call 406-485-2213 for hours.*

■ DINOSAUR COUNTRY   *map page 110, B-1/2*

Much of Montana east of the Rockies is dinosaur country, and one of the areas richest in fossils lies north of Jordan. Paleontologists and trained excavation crews comb these plains each summer for the fossilized remains of the plant and animal life that thrived here 65 million years ago, when the area was covered by swamps and shallow seas. The latest major find, discovered recently by two amateur fossil hunters, appears to be the most complete skeleton ever found of *Tyrannosaurus rex,* largest of the predatory dinosaurs. Standing more than 18 feet tall and weighing about seven tons, T-rex is thought to have been the most ferocious of all dinosaurs. Its six-inch-long serrated teeth prompted Montana paleontologist Jack Horner to describe this prehistoric giant as having had "a mouth full of steak knives." Of the seven other partial T-rex skeletons that have been unearthed, five were taken from this general area of Montana. The latest skeleton has been added to the already impressive paleontology collection at the Museum of the Rockies in Bozeman.

More fossils from the bone beds of the Big Open can be seen at the **Fort Peck Museum,** on the northeast end of Fort Peck Lake, where exhibits feature fossils salvaged from what is now the bottom of Fort Peck Lake during the construction of Fort Peck Dam. *For information, call 406-526-3411.*

■ DAMMING THE MISSOURI

Once free-flowing and spirited, the Missouri River has been tamed dramatically since the days when explorers and mountain men muscled their way upriver to unlock the West. Several dams now control the upper river's once-treacherous current, generating electrical power and providing irrigation and recreation in the upstream states and flood control and navigation downriver. The Missouri's largest dam in Montana is at Fort Peck. Indeed, **Fort Peck Dam** is one of the world's largest earth-fill dams, and the single greatest manmade alteration to Montana's landscape.

Today, a proposal to build a dam anywhere—let alone one on the Missouri, and one on the scale of Fort Peck at that—would spark lengthy and intense debate among politicians and public policy experts. But back in the "Dirty '30s," the only resistance to Fort Peck Dam came from the handful of ranchers whose lands were inundated by its floodwaters. America was in the grip of the Great Depression, and, though not a Dust Bowl state per se, Montana was nonetheless suffering from the same severe drought. Families across the nation were desperate for work. President Franklin Roosevelt responded with the New Deal—a highly ambitious, federally funded program of diverse public works, civic art projects, and near miracles of engineering. One of the largest in the latter category was Fort Peck Dam. When Glasgow mayor Leo Colemen learned of plans to build a dam 250 feet high and 21,000 feet across, he responded with an incredulous: "Hell, a dam like that might cost a million dollars." In fact, Fort Peck Dam cost $156 million.

Workers flocked to the site and boomtowns sprang from the plains of northeast Montana. Clusters of tents, tarpaper shacks, dance halls, and flop houses, these now-forgotten towns carried names like New Deal, Square Deal, and Wheeler. In 1936, at the height of constructio, nearly 11,000 workers were employed on the project. Despite the dust, danger, and drudgery, these were happy times in Montana. Paychecks came regularly and booze flowed again following the repeal of Prohibition. For an entertaining look back at this era, read *Bucking the Sun*, a whodunit written by one of Montana's finest historians and writers, Ivan Doig.

Fort Peck Dam remains a monument to this troubled and triumphant era in U.S. history. Travelers today are more likely to visit Fort Peck for its recreational opportunities than its historic value, but in 1936, journalists sensed a big story here. Pulitzer Prize-winning reporter Ernie Pyle visited Fort Peck that year and described the town of Wheeler as "the wildest wild-west town in North America." Also that year, *LIFE* magazine was born,

Fort Peck Dam, close to its 1938 completion. (Montana Historical Society)

and Fort Peck Dam appeared on its first cover.

Be sure to visit the museum located in the powerhouse at the dam, just south of US 2 between Wolf Point and Glasgow. Besides telling the human story behind this massive public works project, the Fort Peck Museum has an impressive collection of fossils found during construction of the dam. The government-built town of Fort Peck is smaller and much more sedate today than it was during its dam-building days, but it offers one of Montana's finest summer playhouses, the **Fort Peck Theatre**, which features lively musicals and drama every weekend during the summer.

■ FORT PECK LAKE   *map page 110, A/B--1*

Stretching 134 miles across the northern rim of the Big Open, Fort Peck Lake covers portions of six counties and draws half-a-million visitors each year to its 1,520-mile shoreline, campgrounds, and recreation areas. In recent drought years, however, drawdowns by the Army Corps of Engineers to satisfy demands by downstream users have dropped water levels and raised heck with the lake's recreation industry. Montana and the Dakotas took the federal agency to court, where they successfully defended fish, wildlife, and recreation as equal in importance to navigation and flood control.

Between the lake and the surrounding Charles M. Russell National Wildlife Refuge, visitors can choose from boating, fishing, hiking, horseback riding, wildlife watching, and hunting. Until recently, many of the roads into the area were impassable in wet weather because eastern Montana's clay soil turns into tire-grabbing muck. Today many roads are newly graveled for all-weather travel, but it is always a good idea to check weather and road conditions before leaving pavement in the Big Open. Two fine drives are the gravel roads leading from Winnett (Crooked Creek Road), and Jordan (Hell Creek Road) to Fort Peck Lake—not many people, but plenty of wildlife, along with impressive badlands topography.

Every year in July, amateur and professional anglers from throughout the nation converge on Fort Peck Lake to compete in the annual **Governor's Cup Walleye Tournament**. While walleye is Fort Peck's best known game fish, it is by no means the only fish in this inland sea. Other popular game fish are sauger, northern pike, smallmouth bass, channel catfish, lake trout, perch, and chinook salmon. Montana's largest fish, the paddlefish, is also found in these waters, but prefers the river to the lake for its spring spawning run.

■ C. M. RUSSELL WILDLIFE REFUGE   *map page 110, A-1*

Charles M. Russell Wildlife Refuge was named for cowboy artist **Charlie Russell,** whose oil paintings and watercolors portrayed the austere beauty of the Missouri River's bluffs and coulees, badlands, breaks, and buttes. Isolated by the harsh climate, forbidding terrain, and sheer space of the Big Open, this million-acre range provides sanctuary for at least 200 species of birds, 45 different mammals, and a wide variety of reptiles and fish. Bighorn sheep have replaced the now extinct Audubon sheep that once grazed this prairie wilderness. Mule deer are the refuge's most abundant big game animals and elk its most surprising. Together with the UL Bend, a 20,800-acre peninsula of federally protected wilderness within the refuge, this is the only place in Montana where elk still occupy their native prairie year-round. Prairie dog towns make this a good spot for burrowing owls that nest in the rodents' holes, and plovers thrive on the shortgrass and sagebrush.

The prospect of seeing strutting grouse or eavesdropping on a spring convention of Canada geese make the refuge well worth visiting, but the undefiled footprint of history makes the C. M. Russell Refuge a national treasure. Dinosaur bones, buffalo kill sites, and tepee rings mark the nothingness of the prairie like random tombstones, while abandoned homesteaders' shacks and wagon-wheel ruts reveal more recent hardships. Paleontologists and archaeologists from museums and universities throughout the country visit the refuge and surrounding area each summer in search of clues to the past.

This isolated landscape is not easily reached, but a visit here is well worth the effort. Wildlife watchers should approach the refuge from US 191, north of Lewistown and south of Malta. A 20-mile, self-guided driving tour starts near the west end of the refuge (off US 191) and follows an all-weather road into the bottomland of the Missouri River as it makes its way east to Fort Peck Lake. Other roads are passable only in dry weather. Best seasons for visiting are spring and fall; best times of day to drive through are morning and early evening, the hours when animals are more likely to be out and about.

The U.S. Fish & Wildlife Service manages three outlying refuges southwest of the Russell Refuge as breeding sites and migratory rest stops for a variety of birds. Pelicans, cormorants, great blue herons, gulls, eagles, owls, and grouse are commonly seen at the **War Horse, Hailstone,** and **Lake Mason** refuges. The sage and shortgrass prairie surrounding these small lakes provides habitat for game animals, too. Located on backroads and lacking developed recreation facilities, these outposts see few visitors.

The Big Open is for nesting grebes and dancing grouse. It is for bobcats and bighorn sheep—animals seldom seen in the rugged prairie wilderness of the Missouri breaks. It is for grass that needs little moisture and people who need few conveniences. The Big Open is for beasts and birds whose very existence depends on open, unpeopled places. It is for a very few people whose spirit requires the same.

THE BUFFALO DRIVE

*O*n the north we passed a precipice about one hundred and twenty feet high, under which lay scattered the fragments of at least one hundred carcases of buffaloes, although the water which had washed away the lower part of the hill must have carried off many of the dead. These buffaloes had been chased down the precipice in a way very common on the Missouri, and by which vast herds are destroyed in a moment. The mode of hunting is to select one of the most active and fleet young men, who is disguised by a buffalo skin round his body; the skin of the head with the ears and horns fastened on his own head in such a way as to deceive the buffalo: thus dressed, he fixed himself at a convenient distance between a herd of buffalo and any of the river precipices, which sometimes extend for some miles. His companions in the meantime get in the rear and side of the herd, and at a given signal show themselves, and advance towards the buffalo: they instantly take the alarm, and finding the hunters beside them, they run towards the disguised Indian or decoy, who leads them on at full speed towards the river, when suddenly securing himself in some crevice of the cliff which he had previously fixed on, the herd is left on the brink of the precipice: it is then in vain for the foremost to retreat or even to stop; they are pressed on by the hindmost rank, who, seeing no danger but from the hunters, goad on those before them till the whole are precipitated and the shore is strewed with their dead bodies. Sometimes in this perilous seduction the Indian is himself either trodden underfoot by the rapid movements of the buffalo, or missing his footing in the cliff is urged down the precipice by the falling herd. The Indians then select as much meat as they wish, and the rest is abandoned to the wolves, and creates a most dreadful stench. The wolves who had been feasting on these carcases were very fat, and so gentle that one of them was killed with a spontoon.

—Meriwether Lewis, journal entry from Arrow Creek
along the upper Missouri River on May 30, 1805

SOUTHEAST TRIANGLE

SOUTHEAST
TRIANGLE

IF THE MISSOURI RIVER IS A WINDOW on Montana's past, then the Yellowstone embodies its future. The longest free-flowing river in the Lower 48, the Yellowstone is a river's river, valued for what it is, not what it could become with a little intervention from, say, the Army Corps of Engineers. From its headwaters in the mountains of Wyoming's northwest corner to its confluence with the Missouri 670 miles downriver, the **Yellowstone River** is unshackled by dams. As it makes its way along a gradual northeasterly course, the river forms the hypotenuse of Montana's southeast triangle.

Born in snowmelt at 12,000 feet, the Yellowstone cascades down mountains, catches its breath on the Yellowstone Plateau, then gouges out canyons, carves mountain valleys, races traffic along Interstate 94, and hurries past Montana's largest, most industrialized city before it settles down to the broad and braided, cottonwood-lined prairie river that dumps four trillion gallons of water into the Missouri each year. Along the way, it flowers the plains, irrigates croplands and hay pastures, supplies municipal water needs, powers industry, builds side channels, islands, and bottomlands for wildlife, sustains abundant fish populations, and provides unrivaled recreation for floaters, anglers, hunters, rockhounds, and all who find renewal in the presence of a Great Spirit.

Rising like tabletops out of the plains, the Chalk Buttes, near Ekalaka,
are part of the southeastern Montana mosaic.

■ WATER WARS

In the early 1970s, the Yellowstone was a river under siege. Proposals to dam the river had been debated off and on for 40 years, but the real threat came after the Arab oil embargo, when the federal government, together with the mining and utility industries, began eyeing the potential of eastern Montana coal fields for powering huge electrical plants. The power plants would require unprecedented diversions of water for cooling, and the logical source was the Yellowstone and its tributaries. When it was discovered that up to 80 percent of the river's total flow might be drained off in dry years, even the most ardent boosters of economic development began to question the wisdom of selling off their river as a solution to the energy problem.

After three years of intensive research and public debate, the Montana Board of Natural Resources and Conservation set aside 5.5 million acre-feet of water in the Yellowstone and its tributaries for fish, wildlife, recreation, and protection of water quality. Water for the sake of water. It was unheard of in the West, where once-great rivers like the Colorado and the Columbia have been dammed nearly to death. Even in Montana, with 10 dams on its main stem, the Missouri ain't what she used to be.

The board's action reversed more than Montana's traditional, consumptive approach to water use. It challenged a century of resource exploitation by outside interests and said, in effect, "This is our river and we will determine its fate." With millions of tons of coal still lying in shallow underground seams nearby, the Yellowstone's future is by no means secure, especially as state officials start eyeing those coal reserves as a solution to power shortages caused by deregulation of the utility industry in the late 1990s. But the precedent set by state policy makers in 1978, backed by public support, and bolstered by a solid framework of water protection laws assures that anyone who tries to tame the Yellowstone will have to put up quite a fight to do it.

■ THE LAND

Like the Big Open, southeastern Montana is dramatically Big Country. It is a land of canyons and badlands, fossils and agates, timbered hills, treeless plains, and rivers that sustain life in a near-desert climate. Southeastern Montana is good grass country, and therefore, cattle and cowboy country. It is Indian country, more specifically, Crow and Northern Cheyenne country. It is the site of one of our history's most violent native vs. non-native clashes, and of today's heated rancher vs.

coal developer resource debates. It includes Montana's largest city—Billings—along with a cowtown straight out of *Lonesome Dove,* a string of river settlements that owe their existence to the Yellowstone and the Northern Pacific Railroad, and a smattering of one-horse towns in the middle of nowhere.

Montana's southeast corner was developed in much the same way the rest of the plains regions were. Before the end of the 18th century, explorers and fur traders had discovered the Missouri's great southern tributary, which carried a French name—"la Roche Jaune," or Yellow Rock. Crow Indians knew it as the Elk River, but the French name stuck when Captain William Clark anglicized it. In July 1806, after Lewis and Clark had divided their forces to further explore Montana on their return trip to St. Louis, Clark reached the Yellowstone near present-day Livingston and drifted all the way downriver to the Missouri where he and Meriwether Lewis were reunited. The only physical evidence of Clark's Yellowstone River trip is the frontier graffiti he left on a rock outcropping about 30 miles east of Billings. He carved his signature in what he described as a "remarkable rock" and named it Pompy's Tower in honor of Sacagawea's son, whom he had nicknamed "Pomp." The federal Bureau of Land Management manages the landmark, now known as **Pompeys Pillar** *(map below, A-1),* as a national monument.

SOUTHEAST TRIANGLE

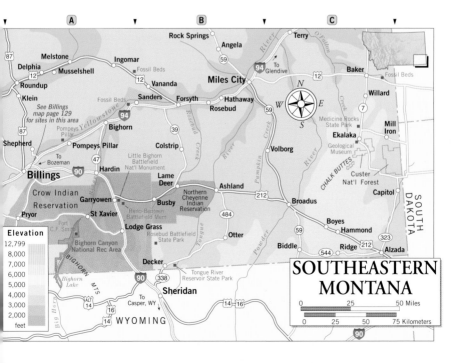

■ CATTLE COUNTRY

Later in the century, while prospectors were rushing to the gold camps of western Montana, Texas cowboys began trailing hundreds of thousands of longhorn cattle north to the rich grasslands that had once supported great buffalo herds. Growing demand for beef, not only in the Eastern cities but in Western mining camps, at military forts, and on railroad construction sites, provided the market. The northern territory's vast open range provided free grass and water. The sheep industry was not far behind, but the "woolies" never matched the numbers of Montana's open range cattle. Montana's top sheep-producing counties are Carter and Garfield, where the woolies outnumber people about 40 to one.

■ MILES CITY   *map page 123, B-1*

Trappings of the stockmen's trade are readily apparent in any eastern Montana town. But the heart and soul of the livestock industry, particularly the cattle industry, resides in Miles City, midway between Billings and Sidney, where the Tongue River joins the Yellowstone. Long recognized as the "cow capital" of Montana, Miles City pulls on its Justin "Ropers" and Tony Lamas every morning, tunes into KATL for rock or KIK for country-western, and caps the work day with beers and bourbon ditches at the Bison Bar, the Range Riders, and a half-dozen other main-street saloons.

Powder River roundup, framed by army post photographer
L. A. Huffman. (Montana Historical Society)

Cheyenne Indians being interviewed about the Battle of the Little Bighorn by journalist Olin D. Wheeler. (Montana Historical Society)

END OF THE FRONTIER, 1876

*K*ind fate had it I should be Post Photographer with the (1876) Army during the Indian campaigns close following the annihilation of Custer's command. This Yellowstone-Big Horn country was then unpenned of wire, and unspoiled by railway, dam or ditch. Eastman had not yet made the Kodak, but thanks be, there was the old wet plate, the collodion bottle and bath. I made photographs. With crude home-made cameras, from saddle and in log shack, I saved something.

Round about us the army of buffalo hunters—red men and white—were waging the final war of extermination upon the last great herds of American bison seen upon this continent. Then came the cattleman, the "trail boss" with his army of cowboys, and the great cattle roundups. Then the army of railroad builders. That—the railway—was the fatal coming. One looked about and said, "This is the last West." It was not so. There *was* no more West after that. It was a dream and a forgetting, a chapter forever closed.

—L. A. Huffman quoted in Mark H. Brown and W. R. Felton,
Before Barbed Wire, 1956

◆ MILES CITY BUCKING HORSE SALE

In May, the city celebrates its cowboy culture with a three-day rodeo that fills the town with thousands of spectators and participants ranging from local ranch hands to U.S. senators. The Miles City Bucking Horse Sale is the season opener, and it is no ordinary rodeo. Unlike other rodeos on the summer circuit, where cowboys and girls shine in skilled events including bareback riding, calf roping, steer wrestling, and barrel racing, the Bucking Horse Sale is exactly what it says it is: a showdown between the wildest, orneriest, most ill-behaved horses, and cowboys who are compulsive enough to climb aboard because "it's there." The guys who stay on top of the meanest horses longest get the prizes, and the horses that give the wildest rides sell for top dollar to rodeo stock contractors who come from throughout the United States and Canada. At the end of each day, participants and spectators mingle in downtown saloons, where videotapes of the day's buck-outs are shown on big-screen TV, and the latest fashions run to canvas dusters and teal chaps.

◆ DOWNTOWN MILES CITY SHOPPING

If you can't make the Bucking Horse Sale, there are plenty of places to soak up cowboy lore year-round in Miles City. Downtown, the scent of leather wafts from the door of the **Miles City Saddlery,** drawing you inside the way a sidewalk bakery does. Tourists delight in the racks of Western clothing, and the hats and boots stacked floor to ceiling on the main level, while working cowboys head downstairs for overalls, long underwear, bits and spurs, shoeing hammers, hoof knives and rasps, nippers, and ferrier aprons—the essential gear of their trade. A couple of blocks up the street is the exquisitely restored **Montana Bar,** built in 1902 "for those early cattlemen who stayed in Montana and parlayed a bull and a handful of heifers into herds that, when trailed, were about half the size of Connecticut."

◆ RANGE RIDERS MUSEUM

The cowboys and pioneers who settled these parts are memorialized at the Range Riders Museum, a sprawling complex on the western outskirts of town, that exhibits relics of the range and homestead eras, period clothing, Indian artifacts, a 400-piece gun collection, and replicas of early buildings and street scenes. The museum occupies the site of a military cantonment established in 1876 by the city's namesake, Col. Nelson A. Miles, who gets most of the credit for removing the Indian "menace" from the plains after Lt. Col. George Armstrong Custer's humiliating defeat at the Battle of the Little Bighorn. The cantonment was abandoned in 1877 when Fort Keogh was built two miles to the west. Once Montana's largest army post, Fort Keogh now serves all of eastern Montana as a USDA Livestock and Range Research Station, specializing in range improvement and the science of cattle breeding. *For museum information, call 406-232-6146 or 232-2890.*

☆　　☆　　☆

Lonesome Dove fans will remember Miles City as the place where their favorite cowboy, Gus McCrae, bit the dust after he and Captain Call trailed their herd of stolen cattle from the Mexico border to the grass bonanza of Montana Territory. Much has changed in Montana since those glory days, but much remains the same. Though the range is now fenced, ranches are still measured in miles, and many are still in the hands of the families that first staked them out.

While southeastern Montana is largely cattle country, the rich bottomlands along the Yellowstone River invited homesteaders to try their luck at farming. Completion of the Northern Pacific Railroad in 1883 brought another wave of settlers into the area. Russian Germans saw the climate and soil of the Yellowstone River Valley as prime sugar beet country; today, sugar beet farms stretch all the way from Laurel to Sidney, and Montana ranks among the nation's top sugar beet–producing states. In addition to sugar beets, other irrigated crops grown in this region include corn, alfalfa, oats, wheat, and barley.

■ BILLINGS   *map page 123, A-1 and page 129*

The farm and livestock industry is the first order of business for most of the cities and towns of southeastern Montana, but energy production also plays a prominent role in this part of the state. The 1951 discovery of the Williston Basin—a huge underground oil field beneath eastern Montana, western North Dakota, and southern Saskatchewan—brought prosperity to small communities including Glendive, Sidney, Baker, and Wibaux.

◆ INDUSTRIAL CENTER AND COWTOWN

The state's biggest winner was Billings, which emerged as headquarters for the state's promising new petroleum industry. The energy crisis of the early 1970s brought major-league mining and four new coal-fired generating plants to the coal

*Billings is a business town, and its Moss Mansion is a monument to one of
the city's early banker-developers, Preston B. Moss.*

fields of nearby Rosebud County. By the mid-1980s, world oil prices had col-
lapsed. As Montana's largest and most diversified city, Billings withstood the decline, but not without substantial losses of businesses, jobs, and people.

Located midway between Minneapolis and Seattle east to west and Denver and
Calgary north to south, Billings remains a major trade and distribution hub. It
serves as the nerve center for the region's farm and ranch economy; as the medical
center for all of eastern Montana and northern Wyoming; as a cultural oasis and
prime convention center for the area; and as a gateway to both Yellowstone Park
and the Little Bighorn Battlefield. With its handsome, new performing and fine
arts centers, two college campuses, sprawling shopping malls, high-rise hotels, and
buttoned-down, pin-striped business community, Billings puts on big-city airs.

But behind the neon lights and theater marquees, the symphony balls and
country club shindigs, Billings is a stockmen's town at heart. From the annual

stockgrowers' and woolgrowers' conventions to the Northern International Live-stock Exposition and Cowboy Christmas Reunion, Billings is where cowboys go when they get all slicked up for business or a night on the town. If ever there were doubt about the city's allegiance to the cattle industry, it vanished in the dust of 10,000 hooves in September 1989. Billings residents lined city streets to cheer the riders and wranglers of the "Great Montana Centennial Cattle Drive" on the last leg of their six-day, 60-mile celebration of the way things used to be—here on the range—before plows turned the grass upside down and fences got in the way.

A heroic-size bronze sculpture of a cattle drover commemorates the "Drive of '89" and welcomes travelers to the **Billings Visitor Center.** This is a worthwhile stop for first-time visitors to the greater Billings area, which numbers about 90,000 residents concentrated primarily between the prominent rimrock terrace of the city's north face and the Yellowstone River on the south. *South 27th Street, just off Interstate 90; 406-252-4016.*

SOUTHEAST TRIANGLE

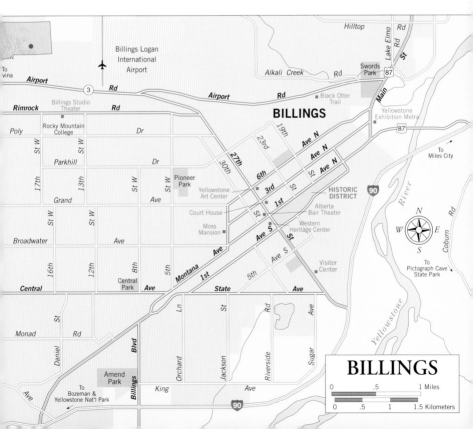

AUTHOR'S FAVORITE BILLINGS LODGINGS AND RESTAURANTS

Lodgings

Dude Rancher Lodge.
415 North 29th St.;
406-259-5561 or 800-221-3302
A downtown institution; western decor done just right. Great breakfasts.

Josephine B&B. 514 N. 29th St.;
800-552-5898 or 406-248-5898 $$$
Gracious hosts welcome guests to this historic home just four blocks from downtown Billings. Some private baths, inviting wraparound porch.

Radisson Northern Hotel.
N. 28th St.; 406-245-5121
This 160-room hotel in downtown is a Billings classic, with beautiful views and a lobby with a huge fireplace. Ranchers from nearby come here to dine at the **Golden Belle** when they want to get dressed up for a night on the town.

Sanderson Inn B&B.
2038 South 56th St. West;
406-656-3388
Renovated farmhouse on five acres just west of the city.

Restaurants

The Granary.
1500 Poly Dr.; 406-259-3488
Beef, seafood, chicken, and a great salad bar, offered in a restored flour mill. Outdoor patio seating in summer. Reservations advised.

Juliano's.
2912 Seventh Ave. North
406-248-6400
Fine continental cuisine served in an intimate atmosphere. Lunch and dinner, and tempting desserts. Reservations advised.

Montana Brewing Company.
113 North Broadway; 406-252-9200
Upscale pub menu with a beer for every taste, including its own specialty brews. Popular for lunch and dinner; be prepared for a short wait.

Pug Mahon's.
3011 First Ave. North; 406-259-4190
Good Irish stew, pasties, and other traditional Irish fare for lunch and dinner. Sunday brunch is popular: a dozen omelets and complimentary champagne.

The Rex.
2401 Montana Ave.; 406-245-7477
The best for beef, seafood, chicken, pasta; great desserts, too. Reservations advised.

Stella's.
110 North 29th St.; 406-248-3060
Where downtown Billings gathers for breakfast and lunch. Homemade breads and giant cinnamon rolls.

The Windmill.
3921 First Ave. South; 406-252-8100
A Billings institution specializing in chicken, steak, and shrimp.

◆ ARTS AND CULTURE CENTERS

In addition to its many shops, restaurants, motels and hotels, hospitals and clinics, Billings has several cultural and historic attractions. The curtain rises one night out of three at the **Alberta Bair Theater**, downtown Billings' beautiful performing arts center. *(Call 406-256-6052 for hours.)*

The newly expanded **Yellowstone Art Museum** boasts a permanent collection that ranges from historic works by Joseph Henry Sharp, Charles M. Russell, and Will James to an impressive collection of contemporary works by Russell Chatham, Deborah Butterfield, Theodore Waddell, Rudy Autio, Peter Voulkos, and many others. *See pages 72–73 for images and more information on the museum; to reach the museum, call 406-256-6804.*

Not to be outdone by the arts community, a dedicated bunch of Billings boosters opened **ZooMontana,** a 70-acre wildlife park and botanical garden, in 1993. The **Western Heritage Center** draws residents and visitors to its changing exhibits about the Yellowstone River Valley and the West. **The Moss Mansion** preserves the elegance of one of the city's early bankers, while **Pictograph Cave State Park** preserves the drawings of a prehistoric culture.

■ CROW AND CHEYENNE

Like the plains north of the Missouri River and the mountain valleys to the west, the "ground-of-many-gifts" south of the Yellowstone was Indian country long before it was exploited by fur traders and trampled by trail drives. Crow Indians once ranged across a gigantic sweep of mountains and plains from the upper Yellowstone River near what is now Yellowstone National Park, across southern Montana and into Wyoming's Wind River country and Bighorn Basin. A series of treaties with the U.S. government confined them to their current two-million-acre reservation, which encompasses most of Big Horn County between Hardin and the Wyoming state line. Their immediate neighbors to the east, on a much smaller reservation, are their historic enemies, the Northern Cheyenne. Unlike other tribes that now inhabit Montana, the Crow developed friendly relations with the federal government before and during the Indian war years. They saw the government as a potential ally in their attempt to protect their land from encroachment by Northern Cheyenne and Sioux, many of whom had left their reservation in the Black Hills of South Dakota when it was overrun by gold prospectors.

■ LITTLE BIGHORN BATTLEFIELD   *map page 123, A-2*

The **Little Bighorn Battlefield National Monument** and **Rosebud Battlefield State Park** memorialize an explosive moment in Western history. The U.S. campaign to rid the plains of Indians and to open the West to development began after the Civil War and was achieved by 1890. Within 25 years, one culture crushed another, and for the people whose borders had always been defined by mountains and rivers, and whose sustenance—the great buffalo herds—was rapidly disappearing, life could never be the same.

Scholars and Custer buffs from all over the world visit the Little Bighorn Battlefield each year in search of clues to explain the mystery of the Seventh Cavalry's misguided strategy. Casual visitors come by the thousands to walk the grounds of a battle so deeply entrenched in the lore of the American West. Some say the site is haunted by ghosts, spirits still troubled by the violence that detonated these plains more than a century ago. A mass grave atop "Last Stand Hill" makes it a likely spot for disembodied visitors. Ironically, until 1991, Little Bighorn Battlefield was a place where all of the monuments were to the losers. Reversing 120 years of history slanted toward Custer and his cavalry, Indian activists won placement of a monument at the battlefield to the Sioux and Cheyenne victors, as well as a change of name from Custer Battlefield to Little Bighorn Battlefield.

◆ CHIEF PLENTY COUPS STATE PARK   *map page 123, A-2*

Visitors to the Little Bighorn Battlefield are in good position to explore the culture and history of the neighboring Crow and Northern Cheyenne tribes. Chief Plenty Coups State Park, at Pryor, preserves the home and burial site of Plenty Coups, last chief of the Crows. The Indian leader, whose name means "Many Achievements," is remembered for trying to save the Crows' beloved homeland by getting along with the white man. A museum at the site houses a cultural center for Crow tribal history. *For information, call 406-252-1289.*

◆ NORTHERN CHEYENNE RESERVATION AND INDIAN MUSEUM
map page 123, B-2

At Ashland's Cheyenne Indian Museum, on the adjacent Northern Cheyenne Reservation, artifacts, clothing and beadwork, even models of a sweat lodge and tepee encampment illustrate the culture of the tribes that inhabited this area. To this day, a careful observer driving through a reservation can detect random plumes of smoke, indications that Indians are heating rocks in outdoor lodges for a therapeutic or ceremonial sweat bath.

THE BATTLE OF LITTLE BIGHORN

Few events seem so fixed in the American psyche as the 1876 "massacre" of Lt. Col. George Armstrong Custer and his men at Little Bighorn. The battle seems to reverberate through the years with echoes of that entire tumultuous era when whites and Indians fought over the West. Born to a middle-class Michigan family in 1839, George Custer began his military career as a rather undistinguished student at West Point. He graduated—last in his class—just as the Civil War was beginning, and proved himself an able and daring soldier, moving quickly up the ranks and becoming a major general of the Michigan volunteers. After the war, he gained attention for his exploits in the West, and his autobiographical *My Life on the Plains* attracted national attention. Despite a court-martial for ordering deserters to be shot, Custer's star was rising, and there was even talk of future presidential ambitions for the man whose flowing yellow hair became a trademark.

Sitting Bull, Sioux chief
(Montana Historical Society)

Lt. Col. George Armstrong Custer
(Montana Historical Society)

GOLD IN THE HILLS

The events leading up to the climactic confrontation at Little Bighorn were familiar ones, centering around the discovery of a glittering yellow rock, gold. It was the same substance that had earlier stimulated the heady rush of miners and profiteers of all stripes to California, Colorado, and western Montana. This time it was to the Black Hills of Dakota Territory.

The Black Hills had long been fought over by various Indian tribes, but the 1868 Fort Laramie Treaty promised the land to the Sioux, for "as long as the grass shall grow and the buffalo shall roam." According to the treaty, "no persons except those designated herein… shall ever be permitted to pass over, settle upon, or reside in the territory described in this article." As with previous treaties, however, this one proved difficult to enforce, particularly when reports kept surfacing of rogue miners emerging from the hills loaded down with gold dust. To check out these rumors, Lt. Col. Custer was sent to head a massive expedition of 1,000 men into the Black Hills in 1874. His geologists/miners did indeed find gold, an event quickly trumpeted by newspapers across the nation. Unfortunately, the 1868 treaty stood in the way of thousands of whites anxious to get rich on the latest mother lode.

Although the government officially disapproved of whites invading the Black Hills, little was done to halt their advance. Gen. William T. Sherman commented, "I understand that the President and the Interior Dept will wink at it." Even if they *had* wanted to do something, it is unlikely that the Army could have stopped the hordes of miners clamoring to get into the Black Hills. When the government attempted to buy the land for $6 million, the Sioux responded by demanding $600 million along with a guarantee of food and clothes for the next seven generations. The United States then took the next predictable step: they decided to simply take the Black Hills by force.

THE BUILDUP

By the fall of 1875, Sioux on the reservations faced starvation due to negligence by the U.S. government and the corruption of its Indian agents. Many of the Sioux headed west to Montana, joining the Cheyenne on hunting grounds along the Little Bighorn River. The government issued an order that all Indians who did not reach the reservations by January 31, 1876, would be considered hostiles and subject to whatever action the U.S. Army might take. The Sioux and Cheyenne either ignored the order or were too far away to be aware that it even existed. In either case, the Army was sent out to bring them in.

*Some say ghosts haunt the Little Bighorn Battlefield, spirits still troubled by the
violence that detonated these plains more than a century ago.*

The Army converged on the Sioux and Cheyenne from three directions under the overall command of Gen. Alfred H. Terry. General George Crook headed north from Fort Fetterman in Wyoming, while Gen. John Gibbon moved in from western Montana. The third column rode west from Fort Abraham Lincoln in Dakota Territory, headed by Gen. Terry, and including Lt. Col. Custer's Seventh Cavalry.

Gen. Crook's column, reinforced by Shoshone and Crow warriors and scouts, met a force of more than a thousand Indians in the Rosebud Valley (south of the present-day Northern Cheyenne Reservation) on June 17, 1876. The Battle of the Rosebud was more or less a draw, but Crook was forced to retreat back to the south. Meanwhile, Gen. Gibbon was moving toward the Bighorn from the west, joining up with Gen. Terry on June 21. Custer and his men were directed to follow an Indian trail from the south into the Little Bighorn Valley while the force of Terry and Gibbon pressed down from the north.

The Sioux and Cheyenne were well aware that an attack was imminent. Not only had scouts warned of the advancing columns, but so had visions. Chief Sitting Bull had taken part in a Sun Dance along Rosebud Creek in which 100 pieces of flesh were cut from his arms as a blood sacrifice. Afterwards, he dreamed of a great victory over the blue coats, a victory that was drawn out on the sand. Custer's scouts found the sand pictograph and understood its meaning. It was a warning that went unheeded by the blue coats.

THE BATTLE

On the morning of June 25, Custer's scouts had located the combined Sioux and Cheyenne village along the Little Bighorn River. His 600 men prepared to attack, unaware that at least 10,000 Indians and up to 4,000 warriors were waiting for him. To surround the village, Custer split his regiment into three battalions, putting one under the command of Maj. Marcus Reno and another under Capt. Frederick Benteen. Custer himself led the remaining 225 men.

When Reno attacked, his men were forced back by a fierce Indian counterattack, and were quickly joined by Benteen's force on the high riverside bluffs. Everyone knew that something must be terribly wrong with Custer and his men, for they heard gunfire and saw the smoke from a battle to the north. A messenger from Custer brought a note saying "Come on, big village, be quick, bring packs," but Reno and Benteen's men found themselves pinned down. Here they held out until the following evening, when the Indians who had encircled them finally withdrew.

(Although an official military inquiry cleared Reno and Benteen, many historians place the blame for Custer's destruction on their shoulders for not moving up to help.)

Meanwhile, Custer had met up with the full force of several thousand battle-hardened Sioux and Cheyenne warriors. None of his command survived the Battle of the Little Bighorn to explain what had happened. Sioux and Cheyenne accounts varied, but seemed to point to complete chaos among the cavalry, with many apparently going insane in the battle and committing suicide. It appeared a fate better than being tortured to death. Among the 225 who died were Custer himself, along with two brothers, his brother-in-law, and a nephew. Probably fewer than 50 Indians were killed.

THE AFTERMATH

After the battle, Indian women moved onto the site, stripping off the soldiers' clothes and joining in a macabre mutilation of the bodies. Lt. Col. Custer (whose hair was cut short at the time) was one of the few whose heads remained unscalped. His body was relatively untouched; some say because it was protected by two women who knew that Custer had taken a Cheyenne girl as a wife. It is also said that the two women punctured Custer's eardrums with a sewing awl so that he would be able to hear better in the next life. He had certainly not heard the warnings in this one. Two days later, the Army finally stumbled upon the gruesome carnage at Little Bighorn, the place that the Sioux called Greasy Grass.

A magnificent triumph for Sitting Bull, Crazy Horse, Gall, and other Indian leaders, victory was nonetheless short-lived for the Sioux and Cheyenne. Back East, word of the massacre came as tragic news to a spirited nation in the midst of its first centennial celebration, evoking an immediate national outcry for revenge. The War Department dispatched a third of the U.S. Army to Montana Territory to put an end to the Indian resistance. Many Sioux and Cheyenne fled to temporary safety in Canada, but with the buffalo gone and their ancestral lands seized by American interests, there could be no return to the old days. Custer's Last Stand was in many respects the last stand of the Plains Indians as well. Within a few years, the last of a proud people straggled into the reservations, desperate for food. The death knell came in 1890 when medicine man Sitting Bull was shot by Indian policemen in a botched arrest.

—Don Pitcher

◆ TONGUE RIVER RESERVOIR   *map page 123, B-2*

The reservation lies west of the rolling, pine-studded hills of Ashland Forest and north of Tongue River Breaks, an austere, wind-scrubbed landscape of red shale and juniper canyons near Montana's southern border. A gravel road parallels the river through Tongue River Canyon, providing fine views of the coulees and breaks. **Tongue River Reservoir State Park** offers good fishing for walleye, crappie, and bass. Four species of fish from the reservoir hold state records for size.

◆ HARDIN   *map page 123, A-1*

The city of **Hardin,** on the northern edge of the Crow reservation, has an excellent visitor center to orient travelers to the area's past and present. A complex of restored buildings and rotating exhibits, the **Big Horn County Historical Museum and Visitor Center** portrays local history from the settler's point of view. With its outdoor park, well-stocked bookstore, and gift shop, it makes a pleasant stop. Should you decide to spend the night in Hardin, the **Kendrick House B&B** on North Custer is a pleasant Victorian offering five guest rooms convenient to the Little Bighorn Battlefield and the Bighorn River. *Call 406-665-3035.*

■ BIGHORN CANYON   *map page 123, A-2*

Less than an hour's drive south is **Bighorn Canyon National Recreation Area,** a scenic gorge between the Pryor and Bighorn Mountains on Montana's southern border. Canyon walls tower above 71-mile-long Bighorn Lake, created by Yellowtail Dam near the park's northern entrance. Water sports and walleye fishing are the main attractions here, but the area also draws hikers, birders, and wildlife watchers. Threatened and endangered species such as bald eagles, peregrine falcons, and even an occasional whooping crane round out the Bighorn Canyon bird list to 260 species. Backcountry camping, scenic drives, canyon overlooks, historic homesteads and ranches, and one of Montana's least-visited mountain ranges await visitors to the west side of the canyon.

◆ PRYOR MOUNTAINS: ICE CAVES AND WILD HORSE RANGE
   map page 123, A-2 (extreme left south of Pryor)

The Pryor Mountains are a remote, highland junction of desert and ice on the west side of Bighorn Canyon. Low-lying limestone peaks and plateaus are rutted with deep canyons and dotted with ice caves so numerous that visitors can still find some that have never been explored. The best known is **Big Ice Cave,** which tunnels into a hillside blanketed with wildflowers during the summer.

(opposite) Bighorn Canyon National Recreation Area, from the Devil Canyon overlook.

But the Pryors' biggest attraction is its **wild horse range,** the nation's first. Established in 1968, this outback preserve is home to about 130 mustangs managed by the Bureau of Land Management. Descended from both Spanish stock and horses of local ranchers, they have reverted to truly wild animals in the sequestered meadows and box canyons of this 44,000-acre refuge. Visitors frequently see the horses from the Trans-Park Highway (Montana State Highway 37), on the west side of Bighorn Canyon.

◆ BIGHORN RIVER   *map page 123, A-1/2*

Bighorn River below Yellowtail Dam, on the east side of the canyon, is a nationally renowned trout stream; it supports as many as 10,000 trout per mile, most of them good-sized browns. These may sound like great odds, but statistics are not synonymous with success. Fishing for wild trout in mountain rivers and streams is not as easy as it may appear. Beginners' luck aside, landing trout is directly proportional to knowledge of the water. And here on the Bighorn, there are plenty of fishing guides who know every inch of the river. If you are new to this or any river in Montana, it's a good idea to hire a guide the first day out. Drill your guide for information, then head out on your own the next day. One day's guide service on a new river is a good investment in any fishing vacation.

■ FISHING AND FLOATING THE YELLOWSTONE RIVER

Native cutthroat and other trout give the upper Yellowstone River its national reputation among anglers. Somewhere between Columbus and Laurel, however, the Yellowstone and its tributaries give up their cold-water traits and take on a prairie personality. The climate becomes warmer and so does the water. The river supports 45 species in all, including sauger, walleye, bass, pike, burbot, sturgeon, and channel catfish.

The lower Yellowstone's most exotic fish is also its oldest and largest. More than 65 million years old, the bottom-dwelling **paddlefish** has a distinctive, spatula-like snout and a hulking frame of cartilage and meat covered with a tough, leathery skin. The Yellowstone and the Missouri Rivers support one of the world's few remaining reproducing populations of paddlefish. In May and June, the fish make spawning runs up the two rivers from Lake Sakakawea in North Dakota, signaling the start of one of Montana's most athletic sporting events. Anglers crowd the Yellowstone's banks at Intake Diversion Dam, between Glendive and Sidney. Because paddlefish are plankton eaters that filter microscopic organisms through their gills, they are never caught the conventional way, but by snagging. So, with a little blind luck, fishermen may snag one of these 25- to 50-pound beasts. The prize, besides a memorable catch and photo opportunity, is a freezer full of boneless, white, lobster-like steaks. Hoping to cash in on a resource that lies literally under its nose, the Glendive Chamber of Commerce has even begun marketing paddle-fish caviar, primarily to cruiselines.

■ AGATES

Other treasures from the lower Yellowstone include colorful moss agates, jasper, and petri-fied wood. Formed some 50 million years ago, agates are a form of quartz that contains dendritic, or branchlike, patterns in the shape of trees, flowers, and other "pictures." They range in color from yellow and or-ange to brown and black, making distinc-tive jewelry when cut and polished.

Agates can be found all the way from Custer, where the Bighorn joins the Yel-lowstone, to Sidney, near the North Dakota state line. The best times to look are in early spring, when ice breaks up and scours the riverbed, and after June, when spring runoff has exposed new stones. Raw agates are not easily spotted by amateur rock-hounds, but there are plenty of rock shops along the lower river, where tips and guidance are freely given.

Not much for looks, the ancient paddlefish provides
great sport for fishermen along the lower Yellowstone and
Missouri Rivers. (Travel Montana)

One of Montana's finest agate collections is displayed in Glendive's Best Western Holiday Lodge on North Merrill, where guided float trips can be arranged for agate hunters. *To reach the Glendive Best Western, call 406-377-5555.*

Whether searching for agates, fish, white-tailed deer, a family of Canada geese, or simply peace of mind, drifting down the Yellowstone is a lovely introduction to southeastern Montana. Unlike the upper river—where trout fishing and white water draw thousands of recreationists each year—the lower river is relatively unknown, a forgotten place where you can float for two or three days without seeing another person.

■ BORDERLAND BADLANDS

◆ MAKOSHIKA   *map page 110, C-2*

Land lovers will enjoy a similar, off-the-beaten-path experience most anywhere in southeastern Montana, but two of the more accessible sites are Makoshika and Medicine Rocks State Parks. Just outside of Glendive, Makoshika is a badlands park that has been shaped for 70 million years by wind and water. Derived from a Sioux Indian word meaning "bad" or "stinking earth," Makoshika preserves 8,800 acres of sculpted sandstone and shale dotted with pine, juniper, and a frenzy of wildflowers. Fossilized remains of primitive plants and dinosaurs open windows to the prehistory of this area, once a vast swamp covered by giant ferns and inhabited by reptiles. During the summer, visiting paleontologists conduct "dig-a-dinosaur" tours to teach amateurs how to identify fossils without disturbing them.

The **Frontier Gateway Museum** in Glendive has a fine collection of fossils from the area. The park's most popular current inhabitants are the turkey vultures that return each spring from the Southwest. Area residents mark the event, usually around mid-April, with "Buzzard Day," an excuse to get together at the park for games and activities. The park has a visitor center, campground, picnic tables, scenic drives, nature trails, and archery and shooting ranges.

◆ MEDICINE ROCKS   *map page 123, C-1*

Medicine Rocks is another badlands park, south of Makoshika in Montana's isolated southeast corner. As its name implies, this was a place of big medicine, where Indian tribes came to seek strength and guidance from the spirits that dwelled here. The Sioux name for medicine rock, *Inyan-oka-la-ka,* means "Rock with a hole in it." In fact, these rocks look more like Swiss cheese than sandstone. The steady wind that sweeps the plains appears to be the master craftsman at Medicine Rocks, sculpting the soft sandstone deposits over millions of years into sand castles, knobs, pillars, and buttes. An early visitor to this quiet corner of Montana, Theodore Roosevelt, was captivated by the sight of "as singular a bit of country as I have ever seen." He described the formations as "caves, columns, battlements, spires, and flying buttresses... mingled in the strangest confusion." Once the domain of giant herds of buffalo, this area still hosts mule deer, pronghorn, coyote, fox, and raptors of all kinds. Relatively undeveloped, Medicine Rocks State Park provides camping, picnic tables, toilets, drinking water, and a loop road with scenic turn-outs.

Makoshika is a badlands park near Glendive; its Sioux Indian name means "bad" or "stinking earth." (photo by Douglas O'Looney)

■ EKALAKA, CARTER COUNTY   *map page 123, C-1*

A trip to this out-of-the-way corner of the world would be incomplete without a visit to Ekalaka, in Carter County, said to be founded by a bartender who was out here hunting buffalo when his horses balked and his wagon bogged down. "Hell," he said, "any place in Montana is a good place to build a saloon." Whereupon he dropped his load and built the Old Stand Bar, which still serves as the social center of this small but spirited outpost. While the county was named after the bartender, Ekalaka, its county seat, derived its curious name from a Sioux Indian girl said to be the niece of Sitting Bull. A town of only 430, Ekalaka has one of the most significant local museums in Montana.

(above) A well-placed sign beats a highway map when you leave the pavement in eastern Montana.(opposite) The post office, general store, and gas station are the social center of tiny Volborg in southeastern Montana.

The **Carter County Museum** is nothing short of a prehistory bonanza. In addition to the 35-foot-long skeleton of a duck-billed dinosaur, assembled bone-by-bone from fossilized remains found nearby, the museum houses the half-ton skull of a *Triceratops,* the remains of a giant marine lizard, a bonehead dinosaur, and artifacts from a much more recent find—an 11,000-year-old archaeological site where ancient peoples killed and butchered buffalo. All of the museum's treasures were found in Carter County. *For more information, call 406-775-6886.*

South of Ekalaka are the Chalk Buttes, Ekalaka Hills, and Long Pines, three distinct scenic areas managed as units of the **Custer National Forest.** A number of enjoyable scenic gravel roads cut through this remote country, offering the chance to savor an austerely beautiful landscape. One of the nicest, Powderville Road, crosses the plains to tiny Powderville and then on to Chalk Buttes. Together with the Pryor Mountains, the Ashland Forest, Makoshika and Medicine Rocks, the diverse public lands of southeastern Montana have little in common except their isolation and the region's ubiquitous cattle crop. Canyons and mesas, badlands and breaks, limestone cliffs, terraces, pine forests, meadows, and grasslands are all part of the southeastern mosaic. Not long ago, many of these lands were regarded as sacred places where Indians gathered to seek visions and spiritual renewal. Largely overlooked by visitors who seek the grander scale of Glacier and Yellowstone, they remain an appealing destination for modern vision seekers.

SOUTHEAST
TRIANGLE

CENTRAL HEARTLAND

Map page 155
●Great Falls

IN GEOGRAPHIC AND GEOLOGIC TERMS, CENTRAL MONTANA may be no more than the transitional land between eastern and western Montana, but economically and socially, it has its own character; for if Montana has a heartland, this is it. From Roundup to the Rocky Mountain Front, it rises gradually from semi-arid plains and low-lying hills to fertile valleys, benches and buttes, forested mountains and isolated peaks. Along the way, grass and sage give way to cultivated fields of wheat and barley as the rainfall increases. Baseball caps outnumber cowboy hats and the people who wear them use tractors, not horses, to get the work done.

■ GOLDEN TRIANGLE

The tallest structures on the skyline are grain elevators, and one of the most pleasing sights in all of Montana is the inland ocean of plump, golden grain that ripples across the plains of central and northern Montana in late summer. Central Montana shares the grain-rich Golden Triangle with the Hi-Line. Find Great Falls, Havre, and Cut Bank on a map, and you will have traced the triangle's outline, but you will not see it labeled as such. It exists in the minds of Montanans, a perceptual region made real by the cash receipts of its annual output of grain. In a state that consistently ranks among the nation's top five wheat and barley producers, this area produces fully 40 percent of the statewide total. Indeed, it is one of the nation's most important breadbaskets. Headquarters for the region's agriculture

A field of spring wheat, east of Great Falls.

industry are Great Falls, which services the Golden Triangle, and Lewistown, a smaller city that pinpoints the state's geographic center. Dozens of small farming communities dot the heartland, survivors of Montana's homestead experiment.

■ GREAT FALLS   *map page 149*

Great Falls, a city of about 57,000, straddles the Missouri River where a series of waterfalls once roared, giving the state's second-largest city its name. It was at this point on the river that Lewis and Clark encountered one of the most formidable challenges of their entire expedition. Meriwether Lewis described the falls as a "sublimely grand specticle" when he first saw them in June 1805, but the enchantment wore off quickly. He and co-captain William Clark were stalled at this site for nearly a month while they portaged 18 miles around the falls before continuing upriver. Later harnessed by dams for their hydroelectric power potential, the falls also gave the city its most enduring nickname, the "Electric City." Scenic overlooks at some of the dams give visitors a chance to stretch their imaginations as they envision an earlier obstacle course of freeflowing falls and cascades.

◆ LEWIS AND CLARK NATIONAL HISTORIC TRAIL
   INTERPRETIVE CENTER

By Montana standards, Great Falls is a large city with a diversified economy. Yet, it is in the city's past that civic leaders see their city's future. Through their efforts, the entertaining and educational **Lewis and Clark National Historic Trail Interpretive Center** opened in 1998 on the east edge of town. Perched on—and built into—a scenic bluff overlooking the Missouri River and housed in an imposing, modern edifice, the center emphasizes every angle of the Corps of Discovery's pivotal journey. The 30-minute introductory film by Ken Burns is a good place to start your visit. The self-guided tour through the 5,500-square-foot complex retraces the expedition's route, includes a lifesize diorama of the grueling portage around the Great Falls, and several exhibits chronicling the Corp's various interactions with the Indian tribes of the Plains and the Pacific Northwest. Costumed interpreters, hands-on, interactive exhibits, and entertaining lectures make it a wonderful place for kids—young and old—to spend the day. *4201 Giant Springs Road; 406-727-8733.*

Karl Bodmer's painting The Steamer Yellow-Stone on 19th April 1833 *shows the crew unloading the boat so it could pass over a sandbar. (Library of Congress)*

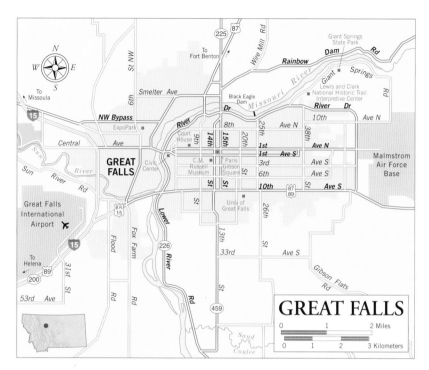

◆ C. M. RUSSELL MUSEUM

The C. M. Russell Museum in Great Falls has assembled one of the world's largest collections of Charles M. Russell original art and personal objects. Great Falls is the logical spot for this national treasure because this is where the cowboy artist spent his most productive years as a painter, sculptor, and master storyteller of the romantic West. The city celebrates Russell's life and legacy every year by throwing a colossal birthday party for him in March during the C. M. Russell Auction, when artists, art lovers, and collectors of Western art from throughout the world come to Great Falls to immerse themselves in four days of seminars, exhibits, and auctions during this event. Over 30 years old, the event has raised more than $3 million for the Russell Museum, which includes galleries, Russell's turn-of-the-19th-century home, and his original log cabin studio. Covering 76,000 square feet, the museum features the work of Russell and his contemporaries, and houses 11,000 works in its permanent collection. *400 13th Street North; 406-727-8787.*

(chapter continues on page 153)

C. M. RUSSELL, COWBOY ARTIST

Cowboy artist Charles Marion Russell was born in 1864 to a wealthy St. Louis family, but spent his childhood in rebellion against the strictures of society. In desperation, Charlie's father sent the lad to Montana at age 16 to give him a dose of reality. His family expected to see a chastened young man return to their doorstep, but instead, Charlie fell in love with the wide open spaces of the West. His first Montana job—as a sheepherder along the Judith River—proved a disaster when Charlie lost the entire flock of sheep. Shortly thereafter, mountain man Jake Hoover found the shivering kid hunkered beside a flickering fire. Under Jake's tutelage, Charlie learned

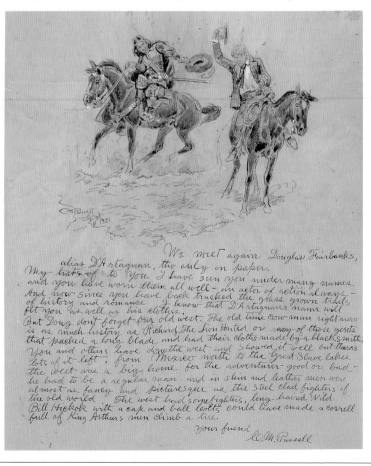

(above) Charlie and Nancy Russell visit actor Douglas Fairbanks (dressed for his role as D'Artagnan) on the set for The Three Musketeers. *Fairbanks, a great admirer and collector of Russell's work, later received a letter from Russell (opposite) with depictions of Russell as a cowboy and Fairbanks as D'Artagnan.*

to survive on the open range. An exact replication of the small, sod-covered cabin he shared with Jake stands along the South Fork of the Judith, an unmarked but unmistakable shrine to the romance and freedom he sought out West.

Eventually, Charlie landed a job as night wrangler for a cattle outfit. The job provided a perfect outlet for his pent-up creative energy; it meant his days were free to paint, draw, or make models from clay or wax. Russell continued to wrangle cattle for more than a decade, gaining first-hand knowledge of the cowboy life that became a central feature of his art work. Our most enduring reminder of the disastrous winter of 1886–87 is a small watercolor of a starving steer painted by Russell, who titled it "Waiting for a Chinook." Stalked by coyotes, the dying animal portrayed the end of an era.

Russell was a humorous, lighthearted man given to good times with good friends. Those who knew him were delighted by his marvelous, long-winded tales of the Old West. But Russell was saddened by the changes and injustices he saw during the rapid development of the West. A cowboy at heart, he had no affection for the homestead movement, which turned the plains "grass side down." Writing to a friend in 1913, he said, "The boosters say it's a better country than it ever was but it looks like hell to me. I liked it better when it belonged to God. It was shure his country when we knew it."

Russell spent a summer near the Blood Indians, a branch of the Blackfeet, and learned enough sign language to communicate with many of the Plains Indian tribes. He lamented the demise of their culture and the government's policy of displacing the West's native inhabitants. "Those Indians have been living in heaven for a thousand years," he once told a friend, "and we took it away from 'em for forty dollars a month." Russell was one of several prominent Montanans who lobbied for creation of the Rocky Boy's Reservation in 1916 for landless members of the Chippewa and Cree tribes.

Russell documented the West he loved in more than 4,500 oil paintings, watercolors, sculptures, and illustrated letters. In later years, he gained an international following for his self-taught artwork, commanding up to $20,000 for a single painting. Despite national acclaim, he continued to live in Great Falls, working in an artifact-filled log cabin studio next to his home. Russell died in 1926, but left behind his passionate legacy of paintings documenting the American West, many of which are on display in the outstanding C. M. Russell Museum in Great Falls.

Charles M. Russell. (C. M. Russell Museum)

■ FORT BENTON *map 155, B-1*

Once a military installation, Fort Benton is now a peaceful community loaded with history and small-town charm. Lewis and Clark camped here, less than an hour downriver from Great Falls, in June of 1805. Because of the trouble they and other early travelers encountered with waterfalls upriver, Fort Benton became the head of commercial navigation on the great river route of the West. Fort Benton came to be known as the "birthplace of Montana" after the first steamboat from St. Louis arrived in 1859. Within a year, it was also a terminus on the Mullan Road, which linked the Missouri to the Columbia River and the Pacific Northwest. Other wagon

Frontier still life Fort Benton's Museum of the Upper Missouri.

roads soon radiated from this river port like spokes from a hub, and by the mid-1860s, thousands of miners were passing through en route to the gold camps of southwestern Montana. It is said that two-and-a-half tons of gold dust were shipped downriver from Fort Benton in 1866, and that between 1872 and '82, 445,000 buffalo robes made the same trip. By the same token, tons of supplies and equipment destined for Montana's gold camps were freighted upriver and dumped on the landing at Fort Benton, then hauled overland by ox or mule teams.

Fort Benton today is a mature, law-abiding town of about 1,600, its ambience a far cry from the lynchings and gunfights that marked its renegade youth. Paved, tree-lined streets have replaced mud- and manure-caked wagon roads. Sleek canoes and motor boats glide where sternwheel steamers once chugged into port. Neat rows of wood-frame houses now stand where Indian trading houses, a brewery, an adobe fort, and at least a dozen saloons once sprawled along the river. Fort Benton's preservation-minded residents have rescued their past and now share it with visitors at their riverfront park, historic landmark district, Lewis and Clark Memorial, and museums focusing on agriculture and the historic Upper Missouri.

■ NUCLEAR HEARTLAND

If Russell condemned his nation's early incursions, he undoubtedly would have had some salty comments about today's military presence in Great Falls and the plains and grainfields of central Montana. Beneath this quiet, life-sustaining landscape lie 200 long-range nuclear missiles, each equipped with three warheads, each capable of producing a nuclear firestorm up to 100 times greater than the blast that incinerated Hiroshima in 1945. Originally installed as Minuteman II missiles during the height of the Cold War, they comprise a portion of the 500 to 600 Minuteman and MX missiles seeded in the plains of Montana, Wyoming, and North Dakota. When entire military bases were being closed during the military

OPEN HOUSE ON THE PRAIRIE

*T*he Air Force personnel who look after the missiles in Montana are stationed at Malmstrom Air Force Base, just outside of Great Falls. The public information officers there answer questions by mail about the Minuteman system with a vague line drawing of a missile in a silo. To callers who wish to chat about the missile installations, they reply in the most general terms. Then, in the summer, the base holds an open house for anybody who wants to come, and officers and enlisted men show their visitors around and tell them just about anything they want to know. This event, called Big Sky Days, is usually on a weekend in July. One year, along with about twenty-nine thousand other people, I went. At the gate, an Air Force guy in a short-sleeve blue uniform shirt was directing traffic. Nearby he had parked a Chevy Blazer with the doors open, so he could listen to the radio. "Standing in the Light," by Fleetwood Mac, was playing. Malmstrom is mostly runway. The thousands of cars parked together took up only a little piece of it. In the distance, heat shimmers rose where it seemed to disappear around the curve of the earth.

Big Sky Days was the kind of summer event where people in shorts walk around dazed and asquint. Long lines waited to go up into the camouflage-painted B-52. In a big hangar, Air Force wives and local groups ran booths selling "Rambo Hotdogs" and "Commie Busters" T-shirts. At one booth, kids could get their faces painted camouflage. By the end of the day, about half the kids had. An M-60 tank in the middle of the hangar drew kids by the hundreds. It was like the most popular rock at monkey island. Members of Air Force security in mesh flak jackets and black berets, with automatic rifles across their backs, helped kids climb on and off. By the hangar doors, pilots in flight suits walked up to each other and put their heads together. Then, after a moment, they threw back their heads and laughed big openmouth pilot laughs.

—Ian Frazier, *Great Plains,* 1989

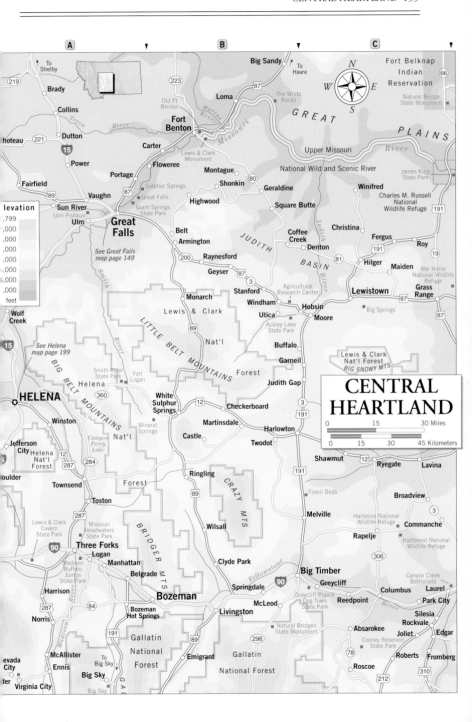

downsizing of the early 1990s, Great Falls business interests successfully defended Malmstrom Air Force Base as the logical site for a national stockpile of intercontinental ballistic missiles (ICBMs). Residents and visitors rarely know that they are traversing nuclear Ground Zero when driving through central Montana because the missiles are housed in underground silos—out of sight, out of mind. Covered by concrete slabs and surrounded by tall, chain-link fencing, they resemble small electrical power substations. Innocuous as they seem, they are controlled around the clock by personnel of the 341st Strategic Missile Wing based in Great Falls.

■ LEWISTOWN   *map page 155, C-2*

Lewistown got an earlier start as a trading post on the Carroll Trail between Helena and the mouth of the Musselshell. It has served as a regional trade center ever since. With a population of about 5,800, Lewistown has the heart of a small town and a head for exploiting its assets. Its central location, together with a busy main street, the preservation of historic buildings erected by Croatian stone masons-turned-homesteaders, and plenty of outdoor recreation opportunities all contribute to Lewistown's appeal. Set against a backdrop of three mountain ranges—the Snowies, the Judiths, and the Moccasins—it is one of Montana's most attractive small towns.

CENTRAL HEARTLAND

Karl Bodmer's etching of The White Castels on the Upper Missouri *was done in the 1830s during his explorations in eastern Montana.*

■ EXPLORING THE UPPER MISSOURI RIVER

Just as it did more than a century ago, Fort Benton still serves as an important starting point for river travel. Not only can you enjoy scenic boat tours right from town, but more adventurous explorers can raft, kayak, or canoe the **Upper Missouri National Wild and Scenic River,** which stretches 150 miles downriver from Fort Benton to Fort Peck Lake. The Bureau of Land Management maintains a visitor center in Fort Benton to orient floaters to the only major portion of the 2,300-mile-long Missouri that remains in its natural, freely flowing state.

As it courses through this landscape of badlands and breaks, past sagebrush and sandstone, this turbid stretch of the Missouri moves slowly and quietly, with a calm and measured pace that seems appropriate for a river so weighty in historic significance. The Missouri River offers neither white-knuckle rapids nor icy, refreshing water. But its serene beauty can be captivating, and the undeniably key role the river played in American history and culture can be fascinating.

♦ HISTORY ON THE MISSOURI

Once the domain of Blackfeet, Assiniboine, and Cree Indians, the Missouri served as a kind of moving stage where many major players in Montana history made their debuts. Lewis and Clark marveled at the "seens of visionary inchantment [sic]" they viewed in the scenic White Cliffs area. Prince Maximilian, Albert Bierstadt, Karl Bodmer, and other European explorers and artists, anxious for a look at the New World's exotic frontier and seeking a romantic view of the American West, depicted the river it in priceless paintings of the landscape, wildlife, and native cultures they encountered as they made their way upriver. Indians and fur traders swapped beaver pelts for beads and whiskey at riverside trading posts. Near the end of their ill-fated, three-month march to Canada, Chief Joseph and his band of Nez Perce crossed this stretch of river en route to a place they never reached. Steamboats puffed upriver, creating a steady market for fuel that was supplied by "woodhawks" along the river. Cattlemen turned their herds out to graze the river's rough edges, a formidable landscape that came in handy for cattle rustlers and outlaws. Homesteaders found this country too harsh to cultivate but not before they built the weathered shacks that remain as evidence of their optimism.

♦ BOATING ON THE MISSOURI

For all the action this river has seen, it is hauntingly quiet now, the perfect tonic for anyone wishing to escape the babel of humanity. But for an occasional chorus of Canada geese or the distant song of coyotes calling, the isolated breaks of the

Missouri are silent and refreshingly lonesome. Despite the disappearance of some of its earlier residents, like the grizzly bear, wolf, and buffalo, the Missouri still provides refuge for a diverse bunch of mammals, birds, amphibians, reptiles, and fish.

Rattlesnakes are among the strangers you might encounter here, so be prepared to rely on yourself, because you are miles—on river and bad roads—from medical help. Essential gear, besides food and camping equipment, includes hiking boots, rain jackets, plenty of fresh water, and all manner of sunscreens: lotion, long sleeves, wide brims, and sunglasses. A canoe trip on the Missouri can last from a day to a week, the longer the better. Popular launching spots, besides Fort Benton, are Coal Banks Landing and Judith Landing.

In January 2001, in his last Presidential gasp, Bill Clinton signed off on a fleet of environmental protection laws, and the stretch of river below Fort Benton was designated a national monument, **Lewis and Clark Cruises** provides boat tours down the Missouri from Fort Benton, and the BLM in Lewistown has a list of canoe rental outfitters along with a detailed information packet for floating the river on your own. *Call 406-538-7461.*

But while this part of the river has been preserved for its historic value, the stretch of the **Missouri above Great Falls** is prized as one of Montana's **great trout streams.** Fed by mountain headwaters and regulated by four dams, the upper river supports sizeable populations of catchable rainbows and browns. No slouch in the scenery department either, this stretch of river is also popular with rafters and canoeists, who often follow its course through canyons, past mountains, and onto open plains. Diverse habitats—ranging from bottomlands and backwater sloughs to dense forests and short-grass prairies—provide sanctuary for a variety of wildlife, including deer, elk, smaller mammals, and furbearers, as well as waterfowl, raptors, and upland game.

■ CENTRAL MONTANA RIVERS AND STREAMS

To the east are the plains, rivers, and isolated mountain ranges of central Montana. Not as famous as southwestern Montana's Madison and Gallatin, the streams that meander through central Montana are uncrowded and fun to fish. Not as postcard-perfect as the high-rise peaks to the northwest, the mountains are smaller, more manageable, and easily reached. Two of the most uncommonly beautiful river valleys in all of Montana carry the deceptively ordinary names of the Smith and the Judith. Both rivers rise in the mountains of central Montana and find their separate ways to the Missouri.

◆ SMITH RIVER   *map page 155, A-2/3*

Born in the Castle Mountains east of White Sulphur Springs, the Smith River winds beneath imposing limestone walls and through remote, largely private sheep and cattle ranching country between the Little Belt and Big Belt mountain ranges. Because of its isolation and limited public access, the Smith is a floater's river. Overcrowding has become a problem in recent years, necessitating the state fish and wildlife agency to regulate the number of people on the river.

◆ JUDITH RIVER   *map page 155, C-1/2*

In contrast, the Judith River, farther east, is surrounded by national forest lands and not so stand-offish. Accessible by improved gravel roads, this is a valley for leisurely driving, biking, hiking, or horseback riding. Not as big a river as the Smith, the Judith and its mountain-fed tributaries support smallish trout. What they lack in sporting appeal, however, is compensated by the surrounding beauty of lush meadows and limestone canyons.

■ GOLD, SILVER, AND GEM MINING TOWNS

◆ UTICA AND SAPPHIRES   *map page 155, B-3*

West of the Judith River and south of US 87, the tiny outpost of **Utica** carries a sizeable reputation as one of the liveliest towns of the open-cattle-range era, when cowboys from throughout the grass-rich Judith Basin came to town to spend their week's earnings on Saturday night. This area has also enjoyed on-again-off-again eminence as one of the world's few producers of gem-quality sapphires. Valued worldwide for their clarity and deep blue color, sapphires have been mined from Yogo Gulch, in the Little Belt Mountains southwest of Utica, since 1896. Over the years, this lode has produced $10 million worth of gemstones. Synthetic sapphires have crowded the market and devalued the real thing, but rich veins of sapphire-bearing clay still exist in the gulch, making it a popular spot for rockhounds.

◆ SILVER AND GOLD

Some of the serious money in central Montana's development came from gold and silver. While the gold rush of the 1860s and the silver strikes of the eighties were concentrated in the highly mineralized mountains of southwestern Montana, the boarded skeletons of saloons and assay offices in the Castle, Judith, and Little Belt Mountains confirm a fever of epidemic proportions. Fortunes were fabulous but fleeting in the mining camps of Castle, Maiden, Kendall, and Hughesville.

Delayed rail service and distant smelting facilities, combined with a panic on the silver market, caused the more isolated camps of central Montana to collapse nearly as quickly as they sprang to life.

A few homes and outbuildings are all that remain of the silver mining center of **Castle,** once a 14-saloon town in the Castle Mountains southeast of White Sulphur Springs. In the Judith Mountains, northeast of Lewistown, there is even less evidence of **Maiden,** where an estimated $18 million in gold was produced before a fire leveled the town in 1905. Another mining camp in the Judiths was overestimated in nearly every respect, including its name. Mining operations never amounted to much in **Gilt Edge,** but legend has it that Calamity Jane was a frequent guest of its jailhouse. Nearby **Kendall,** in the low-lying Moccasin Mountains north of Lewistown, was a more serious venture. At the turn of the century, it boasted a two-story hotel, opera house, two churches, a mercantile, four stagecoach lines, and several saloons. Kendall became a ghost in 1912, when a branch line of the Milwaukee Road (a partly electrified railroad that spanned central Montana) sidestepped it to establish the town of Hilger nearby. Many of Kendall's buildings collapsed and others were moved to area ranches. In the Little Belts, several small camps rose briefly to prominence, including Hughesville, Barker, Lehigh, Monarch, and Neihart. Once the trade center of this mining district, **Neihart** remains a small but active jumping-off place for year-round recreation in the surrounding mountains.

■ MOUNTAINS

◆ BIG SNOWY MOUNTAINS   *map page 155, C-3*

An icicle-lined cave with a frozen waterfall is one of the attractions that draws explorers on hot summer days to the Big Snowy Mountains, less than an hour's drive from Lewistown. Lake fishing, hiking trails, more caves and waterfalls, fossils, camping, picnic grounds, and stunning, 360-degree views lure visitors. **Big Spring Creek,** which offers some of Montana's finest trout fishing and best drinking water, originates in these mountains. About seven miles south of Lewistown, where the creek emerges from one of the largest freshwater springs in the United States, visitors to the Big Springs Trout Hatchery can see where many of Montana's famed trout get their start. Unlike the wild, self-propagating trout that dwell in

Castle is one of dozens of ghost towns that haunt the mountains and hillsides of central and western Montana.

THE FOREST OF THE SUN

I stopped writing and thought about Bill Bailey, who runs the Excelsior Grain elevator and knows a great deal about wheat. He can tell whether it has smut or rust or garlic in it, or why the top of the sheaf is empty or what is the best seed to plant. Bill Bailey likes to talk, and he says, "If you know a man's wheat over a few years you've got a pretty good line-up on the man himself…"

I went on writing: "I love the wheat and I hate it. I love the green blades of winter wheat in the spring. They show through the snow on the ground and make the only bright color in that winter world of grays and blacks and whites. I love the spring wheat that always seems trying to catch up with the winter wheat. It is like a person without much education or background trying to measure up with a person who's had years of both. The beardless wheat always seems to me like a young boy, and the shaggy bearded wheat like an old man.

"When the wheat is an even ripeness, the color of the crust of the fresh-baked bread it will go to make, and the wind sings across it, I love it so I could sing too, just to look at it. My mother says the wind in the wheat makes her think of the wind in the forests of northern Russia, only this is a sharper, thinner sound. When I was a little girl, I used to lie on my back in the field of wheat where my mother and father were working and play I was in a forest. The trees of wheat reached high above me and the wind sang in their tops; only my forest was golden instead of black like Mother's forest. Perhaps mine was the forest of the sun and hers was the forest of the night."

—Mildred Walker, *Winter Wheat,* 1944

A golden wheatfield in the foothills of the Little Belt Mountains.

Montana's rivers, these hatchery trout will be planted in freshwater lakes and reservoirs. Annual output of up to three million trout and kokanee salmon accounts for a sizeable proportion of the state's total production.

◆ CRAZY MOUNTAINS   *map page 155, B-4*

To the south are the Crazy Mountains, supposedly named after a westering woman who became deranged and wandered the area alone after everyone else in her family was killed during a Blackfeet Indian raid. Today these mountains are known simply as the Crazies. This small but magnificent range is a favorite of hikers, riders, and hunters. Soaring peaks, alpine lakes, cascading streams, and sweeping views make the Crazies one of Montana's most spectacular alpine areas. To the Crow Indians these were sacred peaks, a place to summon spirits. Later travelers sought landmarks to measure their progress, and few were more dramatic than the Crazy Mountains, rising 7,000 feet above the plains, 11,000 above sea level.

■ ROCKY MOUNTAIN FRONT

Along the western edge of the heartland, travelers find another clearly defined transition point. Here, the plains pour out of the mountains, rolling east of US 89/287 as far as the eye can see. The vertical wall of the Rocky Mountains rises abruptly to the west. This is the Rocky Mountain Front, a visual feast cooked up about a hundred million years ago in a superheated, over-pressurized underground kitchen. Today's apparent calm belies the intense forces still at work beneath this transition zone. Earthquakes rumble frequently through western Montana, indicating that these mountains are still on the move.

Rocked by human conflict, the visible landscape is equally dynamic. What appears to be a land of quiet beauty has become a battle zone, where developers and conservationists, ranchers and wildlife advocates square off almost daily over the issues of oil and gas exploration, logging, wilderness protection, and grizzly bear habitat. Oil and gas deposits are believed to lie beneath the overthrust belt that was created when huge slabs of rock formations slid over one another. While conservationists, including Blackfeet Indian traditionalists, have fought to preserve these pristine lands, the oil industry has defended its right to explore their potential for commercial drilling. In 1997, the Forest Service surprised both sides with a decision to ban oil and gas development along the Rocky Mountain Front for 20 years. Four years later, in 2001, the agency implemented a similar 20-year ban on hardrock mineral exploration.

CENTRAL
HEARTLAND

Arrowleaf-balsamroot grows in the foothills of the Rocky Mountain Front.

One of the Front's most controversial residents, the grizzly bear, has stirred debate over another complex issue that raises a fundamental question: Whose land is this, anyway: the wildlife populations that were here first, or the human community that came later? The grizzly's leading defender, the late A. B. Guthrie, Jr., was a celebrated resident of the Front until his death in 1991. Pulitzer Prize–winning author of *The Way West, The Big Sky,* and several other novels about the early development of the West, Guthrie described the grizzly as "a living, snorting incarnation of the wilderness and grandeur of America." His allegiance to the bear was a sore point with his rancher-neighbors, most of whom run their cattle and sheep on the fringe of prime grizzly habitat.

Recognizing the importance of the Rocky Mountain Front to this and other wildlife and plants, The Nature Conservancy has preserved 18,000 acres of prairies, wetlands, foothills, and forests along the east slope of the Rockies, a lowland extension of the adjacent Bob Marshall Wilderness. The Conservancy's **Pine Butte Swamp** is the grizzly's last prairie stronghold, a place where the threatened beast and other wildlife can migrate freely between mountains and plains. Here, the bears come each spring to feed and raise their young in a lush lowland while snow still covers the high country. This merger of diverse habitats is home to some of Montana's rarest native plants and animals, plus a rich prehistory that includes the nesting sites of dinosaurs, a buffalo jump, and a portion of the Great North Trail, used by Asiatic peoples migrating across the land bridge to North America more than 10,000 years ago. Visitors to Pine Butte Swamp, less than 30 miles west of Choteau, can explore the preserve on their own or participate in week-long natural history tours and workshops that feature the area's plants, animals, geology, and paleontology.

From cattle and sheep to wheat and barley, plains to alpine peaks, the Central Heartland embodies the physical diversity of Montana. An agricultural giant, it is but a pinpoint on America's demographic map. The heartland was built on the backs of farmers and small-town folks who still celebrate the rural lifestyle at county fairs, church suppers, and community dance halls. But their way of life is threatened, their future as uncertain as the grizzly's. As more and more Americans desert the farm, central Montana supports fewer and fewer residents. Yet, it remains the kind of place most people would love to call home.

CENTRAL
HEARTLAND

Aspens are especially prevalent along the Rocky Mountain Front.

(following pages) Horses gallop near the Crazy Mountains.

SOUTH CENTRAL
YELLOWSTONE COUNTRY

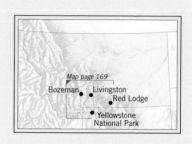

IF YELLOWSTONE PARK WERE SIMPLY a piece of real estate defined by the legal boundaries that established it as the world's first national park in 1872, Montana would hardly be justified in claiming it as a major attraction. Barely overlapping Montana's southern border, the park's 2.2-million-acre expanse lies almost entirely in Wyoming's northwest corner. But Yellowstone is more than the largish square it occupies on both states' highway maps. It is the centerpiece of one of the nation's most intact ecosystems, the so-called **Greater Yellowstone Ecosystem,** which shapes the landscape and penetrates the mindset of three states—Wyoming, as well as Montana and Idaho. An immense wilderness plateau, it straddles the Continental Divide radiating an aura of elemental power.

Rising in the mountains of Yellowstone's backcountry, icy creeks gather size and strength as they surge north, providing Montana with some of the world's finest trout streams. Elk, grizzly bears, buffalo, geese, swans, and other Yellowstone residents migrate freely in and out of the park, making Montana a second home. It is conceivable that even the park's thermal waterworks gurgle north through underground plumbing to create the random hot springs that dot southwestern Montana. Indeed, the forests and wilderness areas, pristine waters, wildlife refuges, and roadless areas that surround the park, together with the park itself, constitute some 14 million acres of wild country within the Northern Rockies. Montana's claim on

Yellowstone Country extends north from the park roughly to Bozeman, Livingston, and Big Timber on Interstate 90. To the west, it stretches to the Madison River and beyond to the Gravelly Range and the Tobacco Root Mountains; to the east, it reaches to the mountain town of Red Lodge, at the base of the 12,000-foot-high Beartooth Plateau.

Given the nature of the landscape, Yellowstone Country is as close to heaven as most outdoor lovers will get in this life. Sacred sites range from the Grand Canyon of the Yellowstone to 12,799-foot-high Granite Peak (Montana's apex), from the trout-rich Madison River to feather-friendly Red Rock Lakes, a wildlife sanctuary for the trumpeter swan. Most residents devote their leisure time to fishing and hunting, hiking, biking, climbing, camping, horseback riding, and in winter, skiing and snowmobiling. Even driving is a pleasure when the road follows a sparkling river and promises glimpses of golden eagles, elk, and bighorn sheep along the way.

Four scenic highways—the Beartooth, along with the Paradise, Gallatin, and Madison Valley routes—provide access from south-central Montana into Wyoming's Yellowstone National Park. All four are destinations in their own right. Three flank great rivers, and one, the Beartooth Highway, has been stealing hearts and testing flatlanders' acrophobia since its completion in 1936.

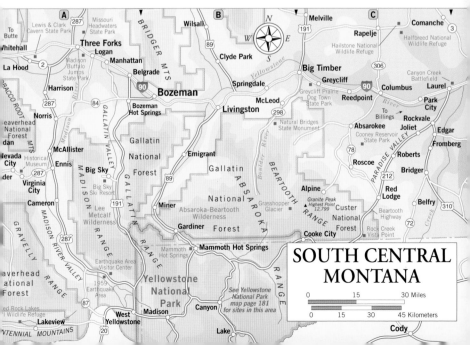

SOUTH CENTRAL MONTANA

■ BEARTOOTH HIGHWAY   *map page 169, B/C-3*

The Beartooth Highway (US 212) is an engineering triumph. Ascending the glacier-carved walls of Rock Creek Canyon south of Red Lodge, it teeters up switchbacks and hairpin curves with names like "Mae West" and "Frozen Man," delivering travelers from one heart-in-the-throat view to the next until it levels off at about 11,000 feet on the Beartooth Plateau. Snow-white peaks and plateaus, alpine lakes, elk, moose, lupine, buttercups, and daisies are all part of the view from the top of the world. First-time visitors are literally breathless by the time they reach the rarefied air on top. After catching their breath and stabilizing their knees, most put the Beartooth Highway near the top of their Most Loved Trips list. The late Charles Kuralt once called it "the most beautiful roadway in America."

The highway is generally open from late May to mid-October, but snow can fall at any time in this high country. While marmots celebrate summer by sunning themselves on newly exposed rockslides, visitors play in snowfields by the side of the road, and Olympic-class skiers descend snow-encrusted headwalls as part of their training at the Red Lodge International Ski Race Camp. Give yourself at least three hours to drive the 68-mile-long Beartooth Highway between Red Lodge and Yellowstone's northeast entrance. This is a drive to be relished, not rushed.

A creek near Red Lodge in the Beartooth Mountains.

■ RED LODGE   *map page 169, C-2*

Born as a coal-mining camp, Red Lodge grew on the backs and brawn of European immigrants. Today, this spirited mountain village relies on agriculture, recreation, and tourism for its economic well-being, but it has never lost sight of its proletarian roots. Ethnic distinctions have been diluted here as elsewhere in Montana, but neighborhoods still wear names like Finn Town, Little Italy, and "Hi Bug"—a schoolyard tag invented by kids to describe where the English-speaking upper class lived. Every August, the international stew that simmered here is served up at Red Lodge's nine-day-long **Festival of Nations.**

Sitting at the base of the skyscraper Beartooth Range, Red Lodge can count on a good six to seven months of snow, making it one of the state's top ski and winter sports areas. A dumping of six feet of snow in April is not uncommon. While the rest of Montana is rejoicing in green grass and crocus, hardcore skiers are stretching the season at **Red Lodge Mountain,** one of the Northern Rockies' premier spring skiing areas. *(See page 67.)* When the snow finally retreats, Red Lodge embraces summer and plays with a vengeance: kayaks, fly rods, and mountain bikes are the toys of choice. *To stay in Red Lodge, summer or winter try calling **Red Lodging,** a central reservations service: 406-446-1272 or 800-673-3564.*

■ ABSAROKA-BEARTOOTH WILDERNESS   *map page 169, B-2*

The Absaroka-Beartooth Wilderness is to hikers what Yellowstone National Park is to motorists. Just as adjacent Yellowstone Park was envisioned more than a century ago as a national pleasuring ground for the masses, the Absaroka-Beartooth Wilderness is the legacy of visionary conservationists who recognized the value of keeping this heavenly plateau forever wild. Remote and rugged, this alpine wilderness encompasses the Lower 48's largest single expanse of land above 10,000 feet. Indeed, 28 peaks, all within the Beartooth Range, rise to 12,000 feet or higher. At their base, mammoth boulders and icy lakes are strewn across the landscape like giant fistfuls of confetti. The less rugged, more rounded mountains of the Absaroka Range form the western half of a backcountry playground that covers nearly a million acres within two national forests in south-central Montana.

Snow can come at any time to this high country, making it one of Montana's least hospitable destinations. Yet backpackers arrive like pilgrims at this high ground, making it one of the most heavily used wilderness areas in America.

Rough Lake is one of almost 1,000 lakes dotting the alpine plateaus of the Absaroka-Beartooth Wilderness in south central Montana.

(opposite) Wildflowers embroider the plains and the mountains with color. Pictured here (clockwise from top left) are false lupine, fairy slipper, lupine, and shooting stars.

About 700 miles of trails take visitors seemingly to the top of the world. Many of the lakes are stocked with trout, mostly cutthroat and brookies, but also prized golden trout and arctic grayling. Rocky cliffs and remote river drainages shelter some of the Northern Rockies' most distinguished residents, including bighorn sheep, mountain goats, elk, bear, and moose. Prolific wildflowers defy one of Montana's harshest climates with audacious blossoms of phlox, orchids, and lilies during a spring season that lasts right through summer.

July and August are the most reliable months for dry weather, but a trip into the Absaroka-Beartooth Wilderness is never to be taken upon lightly. The Bear-tooths stir up their own weather, and violent storms frequently pound the plateau as if Zeus himself were hurling thunderbolts from Granite Peak. This is not to say that wilderness visitors invariably encounter snow, sleet, hail, rain, wind, or hypothermia in the wilderness. But they had better be prepared for all of the above, as well as the blinding purity of sunlight at more than two miles above sea level.

■ PARADISE VALLEY   *map page 169, C-2*

For some travelers, particularly those from the East and Midwest, the Beartooth Highway is too much, too soon. A devious service station owner in Billings used to delight in directing Yellowstone Park-bound tourists up the Beartooth, insisting it was the only way to get to the park from Billings. Most went on their way and were never heard from again, but a few made a point of returning to blister their informant for sending them on a journey that unnerved them from the very first switchback. Especially when they realize there is another route a 100 miles west.

For those who prefer to see their mountains from a distance, US 89 through the Paradise Valley delivers stunning alpine scenery along a well-mannered riverside route. To the east lies the imposing face of the Absarokas; to the west, the foothills of the Gallatins. Gouging out the broad valley between these two ranges is the **Yellowstone River,** one of Montana's finest fishing and floating rivers.

Encircled by mountains, the Paradise Valley has a way of lifting your eyes upward, which seems a good enough explanation for the origin of its name. Horace Albright, once superintendent of Yellowstone Park and later the head of the National Park Service, said of the valley, "If that area were in any other state, it would have been a national park." Area ranchers would never put up with such a foolish notion, but even the most vocal opponents of land-use planning now wish the valley had been protected from free market economics in 1981, when the late publisher Malcolm Forbes sold his 12,000-acre ranch along the north edge of

Yellowstone Park to the Church Universal and Triumphant (CUT). A highly controversial cult-like church that claimed a worldwide membership of 30,000 to 150,000, CUT transferred its headquarters from Southern California to Park County, Montana, when it bought the ranch and went about transforming the landscape: housing developments, mobile home parks, farm operations, even a massive, underground fallout shelter occupying 30,000 church-owned acres. Then in 1998, with CUT's spiritual leader, Elizabeth Clare Prophet, in declining health and all but ousted from power, CUT struck a complex deal with the federal government and the Missoula-based Rocky Mountain Elk Foundation that, when finalized in 1999, transfered close to 8,000 acres—including critical wildlife migratory corridors—to the custodianship of the public lands agencies. Further downsizing in 2001 led to the proposed sale of another 9,300 acres in the north end of the Paradise Valley.

Whether due to its scenic appeal, its isolation, or its fly-fishing, the valley has attracted another unusual crowd in recent years, this one from the celebrated world of arts, letters, and film. Over the years, fame's exiles, including writers Tom McGuane, William Hjortsberg, and Tim Cahill, artist Russell Chatham, movie director Sam Peckinpaugh, and actors Peter Fonda, Margot Kidder, and Jeff Bridges all sought refuge in the Paradise Valley. They come and go, but some, like Chatham and Cahill, have stayed, and others, like McGuane, have abandoned the Paradise Valley for even more remote properties.

■ LIVINGSTON: *map page 169, B-1*
RAILROADS AND FLY FISHING

About an hour north of Yellowstone Park, this small city was once a principal operations center for the Northern Pacific Railroad. With hundreds of workers employed by the NP's extensive machine shops, Livingston's dependence on the railroad made it vulnerable to every national recession that came along. In the early 1980s, the railroad, then under the ownership of Burlington Northern, consolidated its operations and laid off well over half the workers at the Livingston shops. But the real blow came in 1986, when BN abandoned the shops altogether. A new business, Montana Rail Link, bought BN's southern Montana line. Another new company, Livingston Rebuild Center, refurbished the BN facilities and now employs up to 150 mechanics, machinists, and painters to rebuild locomotives, railcars, and other heavy equipment from throughout the United States and Canada. Once boss of the Livingston economy, the rail industry now shares the reins with recreation and tourism, with fly-fishing being a premier attraction.

SOUTH CENTRAL
YELLOWSTONE COUNTRY

Livingston Depot Center

The ornate Livingston passenger depot, built around 1900, proclaimed the Northern Pacific's prominence as the "Yellowstone Park Line" and Livingston as the "Original Entrance to Yellowstone Park." Now a museum and exhibition hall, the Depot Center anchors Livingston's downtown historic district, characterized by the elaborate brickwork and cornices on turn-of-the-19th- century commercial and residential buildings that once housed the town's founders, its blue-collar workers, and a busy red-light district.

Dan Bailey Fly Shop

Across from the depot is another Livingston landmark, the Dan Bailey Fly Shop. A must-see for anglers, the shop was opened in 1938 by one of the sport's founding fathers, Dan Bailey. Bailey's sells everything from $400 graphite fly rods to 75-cent scraps of dyed rabbit fur. Bailey's employs about two dozen fly tiers on a piecework basis to produce more than half a million trout flies a year. Thousands of pro and amateur tiers visit the shop to watch as these professionals turn out royal wulffs, blue-winged olives, and other intricate patterns with remarkable speed and precision.

Federation of Fly-Fishers

Livingston's scenic location and its prominence as a fly-fishing destination have inspired an abundance of fine landscape, wildlife, and Western art. This community of 6,700 supports a half-dozen art galleries plus small, specialized collections within fly-fishing shops. Here too are the headquarters of the Federation of Fly-Fishers, which offers classes and houses the Fly-Fishing Museum. *Call 406-222-9369 for information on fly-fishing classes.*

■ GALLATIN CANYON   *map page 169, A-2/3*

The Yellowstone River is but one of dozens of renowned rivers in south-central and southwestern Montana that draw anglers from around the world. Another is the Gallatin, which stood in for the Big Blackfoot for many of the fly-fishing scenes in *A River Runs Through It*. Born in the northwest corner of Yellowstone Park, the Gallatin dodges boulders and scours tree-lined banks as it rushes down mountains and through canyons to meet the Missouri at Three Forks. Along the way, it furnishes habitat for fish and wildlife, rapids for rafters, riffles and pools for anglers, and refuge for campers, picnickers, and foot danglers.

From Bozeman to Yellowstone Park, it shares the Gallatin Canyon with US 191, a narrow, twisting highway that ushers motorists to the splendid Spanish Peaks area of the Lee Metcalf Wilderness, Cottonwood Canyon, Hyalite Canyon, and the Palisades Falls National Recreation Trail. Dozens of campgrounds and picnic areas and hundreds of miles of trails cater to outdoor enthusiasts. Accommodations along the route include Montana's most complete, all-season, destination resort at **Big Sky**, plus cabins, guest ranches, fishing and hunting lodges, and even an elegantly restored railroad hotel. In winter, there are enough slopes, lifts, trails, lodges, and restaurants along this route to keep downhill and cross-country skiers and snowmobilers happy for a week, if not the entire season.

■ BOZEMAN   *map page 169, B-1*

Gallatin Canyon is peopled at each end by two contrasting communities, both wholly devoted to outdoor recreation. At the north end, Bozeman has enough other interests to stand on its own as a regional trade center and the home of **Montana State University.** But underlying this academic and cultural façade is a sports-crazy town that lives for the ski season and longs for opening day on nearby trout streams. A 1998 issue of *Sports Afield* even ranked MSU as the "No. 1 fly-fishing college" in the nation. A city of 27,500 Bozeman is jammed with mountain bikes, kayaks, ski racks, and car-top carriers, and has more than its share of sporting goods shops, guides and outfitters, outdoor writers and photographers. With its proximity to Yellowstone National Park, Bridger Bowl and Big Sky ski areas, hiking, climbing, and fishing, as well as a favorable quality-of-life/cost-of-living ratio, it is easy to see why Bozeman is one of Montana's fastest-growing cities.

Inspired, perhaps, by their city's beautiful setting, Bozeman cares about its appearance and puts its best face forward. Bookstores, art galleries, a cozy coffee house, and half a dozen memorable restaurants are reason enough to spend a day in downtown Bozeman, which has withstood the threat of outlying shopping malls better than most Montana cities. And visitors return every year for festive events like the **Taste of Bozeman,** when Main Street is closed to traffic so that all those good restaurants can serve up their specialties to hundreds of guests outdoors, banquet-style.

◆ MUSEUM OF THE ROCKIES

Famous in paleontological circles for the residency of dinosaur guru Jack Horner, Bozeman's top attraction greets visitors with life-like, robotic replicas of a *Triceratops* family roaring and rooting in a fern garden. Although Horner's presence casts an aura of paleontological primacy over the institution, the museum is more than a testing ground for new thinking on a growing collection of timeworn bones. With the ambitious goal of explaining the Northern Rocky

AUTHOR'S FAVORITE BOZEMAN LODGINGS AND RESTAURANTS

Lodgings

Bergfeld B&B.
8515 Sypes Canyon Rd.;
406-586-7778
Great location for skiers and anglers;
hearty breakfasts. Hot tub with a view.

Bridger Inn B&B.
3691 Bridger Canyon Rd.;
406-586-6666
North of town in Bridger foothills; four
elegant rooms with private baths and full
breakfast.

Fox Hollow B&B.
545 Mary Rd.;
406-582-8440 or 800-431-5010
Five rooms with private baths; cozy wrap-
around porch; hot tub.

Lehrkind Mansion B&B.
719 North Wallace Ave.;
800-992-6932
This 1897 Queen Anne–style mansion

is impeccably restored and tastefully furnished with period antiques. Plush
rooms, wonderful hosts, and hearty delightful breakfasts are hard to beat.

Silver Forest Inn B&B.
15325 Bridger Canyon Rd.;
406-586-1882
Bed-and-breakfast located in a lovely
rural spot near Bridger Bowl Ski Area.

Torch & Toes B&B.
309 South Third St.;
406-586-7285 or 800-446-2138
Historic bed-and-breakfast home.

Voss Inn B&B.
319 South Wilson Ave.;
406-587-0982
Set in a beautiful Victorian home centrally
located near downtown, this B&B is dec-
orated with Edwardian antiques. Gourmet breakfasts and afternoon tea.

Restaurants

Bistro.
242 East Main St.;
406-587-4100
The Bistro has an eclectic menu and specializes in seafood, but also features Mexican dishes, pasta, stir fry, two-story
omelets, and an award-winning wine list.

Boodles.
215 Main St.; 406-587-2901
Innovative menu incorporates staples
from Central America, India, and Native
American cultures into creative dishes like
quinoa-crusted salmon with guava bas-
mati. Creative cocktails, too.

O'Brien's.
312 East Main St.; 406-587-3973
Fine cuisine, excellent wine list.

Mountain region over the past 80 million years, the museum gives nearly equal time and space to prehistoric peoples, the birth of the Rockies, the impact of man on the region, and Plains Indian history and culture. In addition, Taylor Planetarium—the only digital planetarium in the Northern Rockies—is open to the public. *Kagy Boulevard and Greek Way; 406-994-2251.*

■ WEST YELLOWSTONE   *map page 169, A-3*

Ninety miles south of Bozeman, **West Yellowstone** is a city of visitors. Well over one million people enter the park each year through this small town of 900 year-round residents, making it the busiest of the park's five gateways. In July and August, at the height of the season, "West" looks like a tourist trap, but give it a chance and it will grow on you, especially if you came to fish. Listen to the conversation as you stroll down Madison or Firehole or Gibbon Avenue, and you will know why the streets are named after some of the world's best-known trout streams, all located within 30 minutes of town. West Yellowstone is to serious anglers what Carnegie Hall and the Metropolitan Opera are to music lovers. It has top billing on every angler's dream list of places to go and things to do.

Not far from town, dead trees poke surreally through the surface of **Quake Lake,** an eerie reminder of the mega-jolt that toppled half a mountain into the Madison River canyon on the night of August 17, 1959. The landslide dammed a river, created a lake, and buried 28 campers in an unmarked grave. About 250 vacationers were trapped overnight in the canyon when whole sections of US 287 cracked like eggshells and dropped into existing Hebgen Lake. Registering 7.1 on the Richter scale, the earthquake was one of the strongest in U.S. history and shook an eight-state region. People across Montana were startled from their sleep, but the heaviest damage was at this site, where the U.S. Forest Service maintains a memorial visitor center and vista point.

The vast majority of tourists visit the West Yellowstone area during the summer, but fall and winter have become increasingly popular. Up until recently, West Yellowstone proudly promoted itself as the "the snowmobile capital of the world," but may have to reinvent itself in light of Yellowsone Park's new winter use ruling which may ban snowmobile activities in the park. Nevertheless, West Yellowstone remains a base camp for hundreds of miles of snowmobile trails on national forest lands outside the park. It is also popular for cross-country skiers, who can access the park by snowcoach, which may become the only accepted form of motorized travel inside the park. An excellent public trail system, right in town, provides early winter training for the U.S. Nordic and Biathlon teams.

SOUTH CENTRAL
YELLOWSTONE COUNTRY

YELLOWSTONE NATIONAL PARK

Wyoming's Yellowstone National Park is the magnet that pulls most visitors into south-central Montana, where three of the park's five entrances are located. America's largest national park outside of Alaska, Yellowstone has been drawing curiosity seekers from throughout the world ever since mountain man John Colter reported tales of hissing geysers, burbling mud pots, and pools of boiling paint to an unbelieving public in 1810. For many years, this mysterious place was known simply as "Colter's Hell." In his journal of American travel notes, Rudyard Kipling described it as "a howling wilderness of three thousand square miles, full of all imaginable freaks of a fiery nature."

Several short, self-guiding trails introduce visitors to headline attractions, like the Grand Canyon of the Yellowstone and Upper Geyser Basin, which encompasses the world's greatest cluster of geysers, including Old Faithful. A longer but lovely introductory trail is the three-mile climb to the top of Mount Washburn, between Tower and Canyon. From the summit, visitors enjoy panoramic views of Yellowstone Canyon, Hayden Valley, Yellowstone Lake, and on clear days, the Tetons, Absarokas, and Gallatins. Hikers can also view the mosaic burn pattern created by the historic fires of 1988. More than a third of the park's 2.2-million-acre landscape was altered by the fires, with more than 790,000 acres of forest blackened to one degree or another. But meadows and forest understory have bounded back, creating prodigious wildflower displays and increased forage and habitat for wildlife.

For those who want to know more about fire ecology, bears, geysers, or the many other features that make Yellowstone one of America's greatest outdoor classrooms, the **Yellowstone Institute** offers more than 125 field courses each year *(see page 54)*. The Institute is housed at the historic Buffalo Ranch in the Lamar Valley, near the park's northeast gate.

AVOIDING THE CROWDS

Close to three million people now visit the park each year. During the peak months of summer, traffic crawls along the park's Grand Loop Road and grinds to a standstill every time a bison or bull elk is sighted within camera range. There are a couple of ways to beat the crowds, however. One is to visit the park during the off-season. In September, hormone-crazed bull elk entertain visitors with their macho antics at the outset of breeding season. In spring, at the other end of the cycle, a drive through Yellowstone is like visiting a wildlife nursery. Satisfied bison and elk moms suckle their wobbly calves in roadside meadows, while Canada geese drill downy, yellow goslings on paddle-and-splash missions in a watery wilderness.

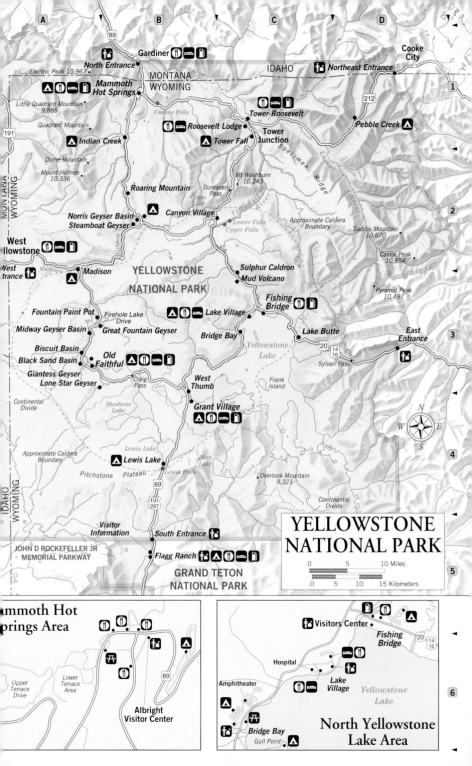

YELLOWSTONE NATIONAL PARK

Gardiner
North Entrance
MONTANA
WYOMING
IDAHO
Cooke City
Northeast Entrance
Electric Peak 10,967
Mammoth Hot Springs
Little Quadrant Mountain 9,885
Quadrant Mountain
Indian Creek
Undine Falls
Tower-Roosevelt
Roosevelt Lodge
Tower Fall
Tower Junction
Pebble Creek
212
Dome Mountain
Mount Holmes 10,336
Roaring Mountain
Dunraven Pass
Mt Washburn 10,243
Specimen Ridge
Saddle Mountain 10,670
191
Norris Geyser Basin
Steamboat Geyser
Canyon Village
Gibbon
Grebe Lake
Yellowstone River
Lower Falls
Upper Falls
Approximate Caldera Boundary
Castor Peak 10,854
West Yellowstone
West Entrance
Madison
Madison
YELLOWSTONE NATIONAL PARK
Sulphur Caldron
Mud Volcano
Pyramid Peak 10,497
MONTANA
WYOMING
Fountain Paint Pot
Firehole Lake Drive
Great Fountain Geyser
Midway Geyser Basin
Biscuit Basin
Black Sand Basin
Giantess Geyser
Lone Star Geyser
Old Faithful
Lake Village
Bridge Bay
Fishing Bridge
Yellowstone Lake
Lake Butte
20
14
16
Sylvan Pass
East Entrance
Craig Pass
West Thumb
Frank Island
Continental Divide
Shoshone Lake
Grant Village
N
W   E
S
IDAHO
WYOMING
Approximate Caldera Boundary
Lewis Lake
Pitchstone Plateau
Lewis Lake
Lewis Falls
Hart Lake
Overlook Mountain 9,321
Continental Divide
89
191
287
Visitor Information
South Entrance
JOHN D ROCKEFELLER JR MEMORIAL PARKWAY
Flagg Ranch
GRAND TETON NATIONAL PARK

0   5   10 Miles
0   5   10   15 Kilometers

Mammoth Hot Springs Area

Upper Terrace Drive
Lower Terrace Area
89
Albright Visitor Center

North Yellowstone Lake Area

Visitors Center
Fishing Bridge
20
14
16
Hospital
Amphitheater
Lake Village
Bridge Bay
Gull Point
Yellowstone Lake

*Preaching at Pulpit Terrace in the Mammoth Hot Springs area of Yellowstone Park.
(Montana Historical Society)*

A welcome hush settles over Yellowstone as it fills up with snow in winter. If the park's spouting geysers and fumaroles seem eerie in summer, they are unearthly in winter. Frosty bison move in and out of view as clouds of mist and steam roll through, transforming the powerful beasts into shaggy ghosts. Snow whites out the roads and confines travel to places accessible via skis, snowshoes, snowmobile, or guided snowcoach tour.

With the approval in 2001 of a controversial, new winter use ruling, one of those modes of transportation—the snowmobile—may be phased out of Yellowstone over a three-year period. The decision followed many years of study, which concluded the machines' adverse impacts on the park, its wildlife and its other visitors seriously outweighed its benifts to snowmobilers. The ruling, however, was still in question at the time of publication of this book.

INTO THE BACKCOUNTRY

The best way to avoid peak-season congestion is to abandon your car for day hikes or extended hiking and horseback trips through Yellowstone's spacious backcountry. The park has more than a thousand miles of backcountry trails to acquaint visitors with its many moods and curiosities. The privileged few who use them are gifted with sights never seen from a Winnebago: the secret eruptions of the remote Shoshone Geyser Basin, the terraced waterfalls and wilderness jacuzzis of the "Cascade Corner," the chance view of a golden-tipped grizzly sow steering her cubs across Hayden Valley, the unexpected burps and splats of unnamed mud pots.

Yellowstone's backcountry is bear country. There are an estimated 700 bears in and around the park, including about 200 grizzlies. While few people actually see *Ursus horribilis,* the great bear ranges throughout the park. Hikers should generally avoid traveling alone, and should always check trail conditions and bear sightings before heading out. Given the National Park Service's aggressive efforts to reduce bear-human conflicts, it is difficult to avoid these precautions. Brochures, leaflets, and fliers litter the park.

The Gallatin Gateway Inn, south of Bozeman, was built in 1927 as a hotel and railway depot for visitors en route to Yellowstone Park.

Lodging Near Yellowstone

Emigrant

Paradise Gateway B&B.
US 89; 800-541-4113
Exceptional B&B on the Yellowstone River between Livingston and Yellowstone National Park. Four rooms with private bath; two cabins; good breakfast.

Yellowstone Country B&B.
5 mi. south; 406-333-4917
Two modern log cabins situated right on the Yellowstone River. Gracious hosts serve an excellent breakfast.

Gallatin Gateway

Gallatin Gateway Inn.
76405 Gallatin Rd.; 406-763-4672
Restored, Spanish Colonial–style inn built by the Chicago, Milwaukee & St. Paul Railway in 1927 as a hotel-depot for tourists en route to Yellowstone. Comfortable guest rooms, some with shared baths. Swimming pool, hot tub, and tennis courts on premises. Restaurant offers seasonal menus and fresh ingredients.

Gardiner

Maiden Basin Inn.
5 miles north on US 89; 800-624-3364
Clean and quiet inn on the Yellowstone River with a variety of rooms including family suites with full kitchens.

Pray

Chico Hot Springs Lodge.
Off Hwy. 89, 406-333-4933
Rustic lodging and year-round mineral hot springs near the Yellowstone River and Yellowstone Park, as well as one of Montana's favorite dining rooms.

Red Lodge

Pitcher Guest Houses. 2 South Platt St.; 406-446-2859
Two distinctive homes and two one-bedroom log cabins.

The Pollard.
2 North Broadway; 406-446-0001
Elegantly turn-of-the-19th-century inn; sophisticated dining in **Greenlee's**.

Rock Creek Resort.
US 212, south of town; 406-446-1111
Deluxe lodging, meeting rooms, condos. Tennis, swimming, horseback riding, fishing. **Old Piney Dell restaurant** offers good dinner, great Sunday brunch.

Willows Inn.
224 South Platt St.; 406-446-3913
Victorian B&B near Rock Creek, Beartooth Highway, and Red Lodge Ski Area.

Firehole Ranch.
11500 Hebgen Lake Rd.;
406-646-7294 or 406-646-9093
This Orvis-endorsed fly-fishing lodge north the park is elegant in a cowboy kind of way. Cozy common room, hearty food.

Yellowstone

TW Recreational Services.
Yellowstone Park, WY; 307-344-7901
Advance reservations required at the park's lodges and cabins.

Zortman

Buckhorn Cabins.
406-673-3162
Seven cabins, five with kitchens, and RV park in the Little Rockies of north-central Montana. Hunting spoken here.

A LOVE STORY

I was at the Top Hat having a drink with Little Troy Burnham, talking about the deer season, when a woman who had been sitting at the front of the bar got up and came over to us. I had seen this woman other times in other bars in town. She would be there in the afternoons around three, and then sometimes late at night when I would be cruising back. She danced with some men from the air base, and sat drinking and talking late. I suppose she left with someone finally. She wasn't a bad looking woman at all. Blond, with wide, dark eyes set out, wide hips, and dark eyebrows. She could've been thirty-four years old, although she could've been forty-four or twenty-four, because she was drinking steady, and steady drink can do both to you, especially to women. But I had thought the first time I saw her: Here's one on the way down. A miner's wife drifted up from Butte, or a rancher's daughter just run off suddenly, which can happen. Or worse. And I hadn't been tempted. Trouble comes cheap and leaves expensive is a way of thinking about that.

"Do you suppose you could give me a light," the woman said to us. She was standing at our table. Nola was her name. Nola Foster. I had heard that around. She wasn't drunk. It was four o'clock in the afternoon, and no one was there but Troy Burnham and me.

"If you'll tell me a love story, I'll do anything in the world for you," Troy said. It was what he always said to women. He'd do anything in the world for something. Troy sits in a wheelchair due to a smoke jumper's injury, and can't do very much. We had been friends since high school and before. He was always short, and I was tall. But Troy had been an excellent wrestler and won awards in Montana, and I had done little of that, some boxing once was all. We had been living in the same apartments on Ryman Street, though Troy lived there permanently and drove a Checker cab to earn a living, and I was hoping to pass on to something better. "I *would* like a little love story," Troy said, and called for whatever Nola Foster was drinking.

"Nola, Troy. Troy, Nola," I said, and lit her cigarette.

"Have we met?" Nola said, taking a seat and glancing at me.

"At the East Gate. Some time ago," I said.

"That's a very nice bar," she said in a cool way. "But I hear it's changed hands."

"I'm glad to make your acquaintance," Troy said, grinning and adjusting his glasses. "Now let's hear that love story." He pulled up close to the table so that his head and his big shoulders were above the tabletop. Troy's injury had caused him not to have any hips left. There is something there, but not hips. He needs bars and a special seat in his cab. He is both frail and strong at once, though in most ways he gets on like everybody else.

"I *was* in love," Nola said quietly as the bartender set her drink down and she took a sip. "And now I'm not."

"That's a short love story," I said.

—Richard Ford, *Rock Springs*, 1987

■ MADISON RIVER VALLEY   *map page 169, A-1/2/3*

Flanked on the east by the soaring peaks of the Madison Range, this drive along US 287 offers skyward views of Montana's second-highest mountain range and the broad, alluvial plains that fan out from its base to create one of the state's most handsome valleys. Heavy timbers frame entrances to ranches that lie at the end of long, gravel roads. The names etched into these gates—Bar Seven, Longhorn, Jumping Horse—are clues to one of the major occupations that drive the economy of the valley.

But the real evidence is a landscape dotted with cattle and sheep as far as the eye can see. Year after year, Madison County ranks among Montana's top cattle- and sheep-producing counties. And year after year, the **Madison River** draws more nonresident anglers to its banks than any other trout stream in Montana. Originating in Yellowstone Park, the river follows US 287 for about 60 miles from West Yellowstone to Ennis, then leaves the highway before joining the Gallatin and Jefferson Rivers at Three Forks to form the Missouri.

■ ENNIS   *map page 169, A-2*

Ranching and fishing converge in the small community of Ennis, where well-heeled anglers meet high-heeled cowboys over beers in watering holes like the Longbranch and Silver Dollar. Over the years, fly shops and art galleries have replaced farm and ranch supply stores, but the atmosphere in Ennis remains distinctly Western. At no time is the valley's love affair with livestock more apparent than during rodeo weekend, when the population of Ennis swells to accommodate contestants and spectators at one of Montana's most popular Fourth of July rodeos. An attractive purse, a sure crowd, and a wild horse race make Ennis one of the top rodeos for professional cowboys and cowgirls working the summer circuit, as well as for local ranch hands. When the dust has settled and the professionals have moved on to the next arena, spectators turn their attention to the many nearby attractions that make Ennis such a popular base camp for summer visitors.

■ HISTORICAL GHOST TOWNS AND STATE PARKS

Three state parks north of Ennis reach back still further in history. Just outside the aptly named community of Three Forks, three great Montana rivers—the Jefferson, the Madison, and the Gallatin—join to form the Missouri River. The site was an important crossroads for several Indian tribes, and the Lewis and Clark expedition camped here in July 1805, 2,500 miles above their starting point in St. Louis.

◆ GHOST TOWNS

Two of Montana's liveliest ghost towns, **Virginia City** and **Nevada City**, lie just 15 miles west of Ennis, on Montana State Highway 287. An 1863 gold strike brought thousands of prospectors to the area and secured Virginia City's place in history as Montana's second territorial capital. *(See pages 215–218 for more about this area.)*

◆ MISSOURI HEADWATERS STATE PARK   *map page 169, A-1*

When Lewis and Clark camped here, where the Missouri feeds into the Mississippi, Meriwether Lewis recorded in his journal that he and his co-captain, William Clark, had agreed to name the forks after President Thomas Jefferson, "the author of our enterprize," Secretary of the Treasury Albert Gallatin, and Secretary of State James Madison. They proceeded westward along the Jefferson, certain, as were most early explorers, that the Missouri headwaters would take them to the Pacific Ocean. The history of the area is preserved in a beautiful setting at Missouri Headwaters State Park, popular for camping, picnicking, hiking, fishing, and floating.

*Most Montana communities support a historic home or museum like the
Missouri River Headwaters Heritage Museum in Three Forks.*

◆ LEWIS AND CLARK CAVERNS   *map page 169, A-1*

Montana's first and best-known state park preserves one of the largest limestone
caverns in the Northwest, less than 20 miles west of Three Forks on MT 2. Lewis
and Clark Caverns began forming more than 300 million years ago. Sediments at
the bottom of a shallow inland sea hardened into limestone and were eventually
exposed to air as the sea drained away and the nearby Tobacco Root Mountains
were uplifted. As groundwater penetrated and dissolved fractured limestone, a network of channels began forming. Today, these channels and caves are punctuated
by stalactites, stalagmites, columns, and crystals. Visitors can explore the caves on
guided tours during the summer. The park also has a visitor center, café and gift
shop, campground, picnic area, and nature trail.

◆ MADISON BUFFALO JUMP STATE PARK   *map page 169, A-1*

For 2,000 years before the arrival of guns and horses, Indians killed the buffalo they needed for food, clothing, shelter, and tools by stampeding them en masse over cliffs. Not far from the Missouri Headwaters, Madison Buffalo Jump State Park preserves one of these early killing grounds. Layers of bones and remnants of primitive tools mark these slaughtering sites, where Indian parties often spent several days gutting carcasses, removing hides, and drying meat.

■ ROADS LESS TRAVELED

For those who seek a more intimate, less developed view of this landscape, several rugged roads wind tentatively through the wild country that borders Yellowstone Park. Starting as ordinary, two-lane highways, they taper off first to gravel, then dirt. Some wind up at trailheads that designate foot and horse traffic only. These memorable trips make few demands in proportion to the pleasures they yield. A flexible itinerary and a tolerance for bumpy, dusty roads are a small price to pay for a chance view of a golden eagle feeding by the side of the road or mountain goats perched on rocky outcrops overhead. For extended visits, most travelers are self-sustained. There are some private cabins and guest ranches, however, in addition to a number of public campgrounds.

◆ CENTENNIAL VALLEY   *map page 169, A-3*

The remote Centennial Valley, just west of the park, is an essential trip for photographers, birders, and wildlife watchers. The valley is bordered on the south by a wall of mountains that approach the 10,000-foot level. The rugged Centennials catch heavy snow that serves to replenish the lakes and marshes of 42,000-acre **Red Rock Lakes National Wildlife Refuge**, which provides sanctuary for the trumpeter swan. This vast wetland sustains a multitude of other birds and animals. Because of its location halfway between West Yellowstone and Monida on a dirt and gravel road, passage is slow and subject to weather conditions. The best time to visit is between May and September when the road is generally dry. Recently designated a national scenic backroad by the BLM, the Centennial Valley Road has its own built-in speed bumps to ensure that motorists take it slow.

◆ COLUMBUS   *map page 169, C-1*

North of the park, Columbus is the starting point for a cluster of secondary routes into the Beartooth Range along the Stillwater and Rosebud drainages. Though

Flowers grow along a "jack fence" in the Centennial Valley.

long dependent on farming and ranching, this Yellowstone River community is enjoying an economic revival tied to mining and manufacturing. The Stillwater Mining Company, located at the edge of the Absaroka-Beartooth Wilderness near Nye, is the nation's only producer of platinum-palladium metals, used widely in industry and technology. Columbus is also the home of Montana Silversmiths, the world's largest manufacturer of Western-style silver products, including belt buckles, jewelry, and saddle and bridle trim.

◆ ABSAROKEE   *map page 169, C-2*

The last outpost of any size before heading into the mountains is Absarokee, 15 miles south of Columbus on Montana State Highway 78. The small town bears an Indian name that originally was used to identify the Crow tribe. Once part of the Crows' vast homeland, Absarokee was on the Crow Reservation until the reservation was reduced to its current size and location near Hardin. The historic Bozeman Trail also crossed through this southern portion of Stillwater County. In 1862, founder John Bozeman envisioned the route as a shortcut from eastern Wyoming, through Indian territory, and on to the gold fields of Virginia City. Despite its ease of travel and abundance of water, grass, and game, the trail was abandoned in 1868 due to persistent attacks by the Sioux. Today, travelers can experience pioneer travel on short wagon-train vacations. *(See page 91).* Visitors can enjoy another Western tradition, still very much alive in Montana, at either of two lively rodeos held in Absarokee each summer. In early June, the Northern Rodeo Association kicks off its season here, and in July, seasoned contestants from throughout the area entertain a spirited crowd at the Old Timers' Rodeo.

Absarokee is the jumping-off point for deeper exploration of Beartooth country on different routes, each constituting a variation on the theme of grandeur. Follow East Rosebud Creek 14 miles to the tiny settlement of Roscoe, then another 12 miles on gravel to East Rosebud Lake, which marks the beginning of one of the Beartooth's most spectacular canyons. A short hike up East Rosebud Creek reveals a Yosemite landscape with an El Capitan–like upthrust at nearly every bend in the trail. An extended hike or horseback ride on the same trail takes conditioned explorers over the top of the boulder-strewn, lake-studded Beartooth Plateau before dropping down to Cooke City, at the northeast corner of Yellowstone Park.

A 20-mile road follows West Rosebud Creek from Fishtail to a hydroelectric plant below Mystic Lake. Early in the century, the Montana Power Company chose the site to build its 300-foot-long concrete dam and power plant in these

Beartooth country is a wilderness of granite peaks, boulder-strewn fields, and alpine lakes.

highest of all Montana mountains because of its vertical drop and massive snow-fall. Considered an engineering feat at the time of its construction, such a proposal today would generate far more controversy than electricity. Hikers and horsemen en route to the Absaroka-Beartooth Wilderness begin their journey with a three-mile ramble up to Mystic Lake, itself a popular fishing spot.

A 40-mile trip along the Stillwater River packs plenty of scenic views, camping, and stream fishing in the heart of Beartooth country. The route also leads to the the nation's richest deposits of platinum, palladium, and related metals, and the Stillwater Mining Company's highly automated mining operation near Nye.

■ BOULDER RIVER

The 1964 Wilderness Act, passed to preserve the pristine qualities of certain natural areas forever, defines wilderness as "an area where the earth and its community of life are untrammeled by man, where man himself is a visitor who does not remain." The act prohibits motorized travel within wilderness boundaries, but people who shun hiking and horseback riding can still surround themselves with wilderness on the **Boulder River Road.**

Reaching some 50 miles south of Big Timber to the abandoned mining town of Independence, this partially paved, partially rugged road fingers its way into the Absaroka-Beartooth Wilderness along a non-wilderness corridor. As a result, travelers are enveloped by wilderness for about a third of the distance. For the entire distance, they are encircled by sublime views of rivers and peaks, canyons and gorges, and meadows and hay fields where sheep mingle with elk and deer. Eagles and hawks soar overhead, while rainbow trout flash in rivers and streams below. The road is strung with a handful of attractive Forest Service campgrounds.

"They don't make land like that anymore," commented newsman Tom Brokaw after purchasing a ranch on the nearby West Fork of the Boulder. "Montana is special in the world. I come over a rise there and I feel like I'm in Tibet." Other celebrities attracted to the exotic front of the Boulder Valley are Brooke Shields, Michael Keaton, Tom McGuane, and Robert Haas, chairman of Levi Strauss. They come for the unspoiled beauty and the unhurried lifestyle. Here, they come and go without a fuss, even in nearby **Big Timber,** a small Western town of about 1,650.

The cosmopolitan views of visiting anglers and hikers, combined with those of the valley's new luminaries, are tempered by the rock-hard, conservative politics of Sweet Grass County and the mores of ranchers whose families have been raising sheep and running cows here for a century. The sociology of Big Timber is nearly as engaging as the landscape that surrounds it.

Boulder River, south of Big Timber.

SOUTHWEST MONTANA

FEWER THAN 60 YEARS AFTER LEWIS AND CLARK entered the unmapped wilderness of what is now Montana, miners and merchants were beating a path across the mountains and deserts of California, Colorado, and Idaho to reach its southwestern gold fields. News of gold strikes on Grasshopper Creek in 1862 and Alder Gulch the following year traveled fast. By the mid-1860s, Montana had nearly 30,000 permanent, non-Indian settlers, where five years earlier there had been none. Another strike in 1864, this one on Last Chance Gulch, established Helena as the "Queen City of the Rockies" and southwest Montana as the progenitor of the state's most enduring nickname, the Treasure State.

In the 1860s at the height of the gold rush in Montana, the strikes were so rich it was said that a prospector could shake a dollar's worth of dust from an uprooted sagebrush. In five years, the digs at Alder Gulch (now Virginia City) produced $30–40 million worth of gold; Last Chance Gulch produced an estimated $19 million in just four years. By 1866, Montana was second only to California as a gold producer. But the gold played out, and so did silver. Then in 1882, the fortuitous discovery of a thick vein of copper beneath the undistinguished gold camp of Butte ushered in the greatest era of all in Montana mining history and immortalized Butte as "the richest hill on earth."

Right behind the miners came the stockmen, who supplied the fresh meat for Montana's mining camps. The valleys were as rich in grass as the mountains were in precious metals. While the plains of eastern Montana fattened hundreds of thousands of cattle for the export market during the state's great open range cattle era of the 1870s and '80s, Montana's early mining camps provided a ready market for pioneer stockmen. Those who mastered the basics of building a herd and selling in the Deer Lodge and Beaverhead valleys emerged as leaders of Montana's developing livestock industry.

Computerized livestock breeding programs and technology-driven mining operations are still the bones and sinew of this corner of the state. But its spirit resides in the weathered ghost towns, Victorian mansions, and carriage houses that bespeak the bonanza years of Montana's colorful mining frontier. Much of Montana's political and economic history was written in this part of the state, and it is easily revisited in galleries, museums, mansions, and miners' union halls. Where prospectors once mined these hills and panned these streams for the sparkling "color" that meant instant prosperity, visitors today mine the area not just for its history but also for its natural beauty and recreational opportunities—its trout streams and forested mountains. Georgetown Lake, the Anaconda-Pintler Wilderness, the Big Hole River, and Gates of the Mountains are just some of the getaways that make this part of the state so attractive to sightseers and sportsmen.

Most of the region's small cities grew from primitive mining camps after the discovery of gold placers and silver lodes, as well as rich deposits of copper, lead, and zinc. The two largest are Helena and Butte.

■ HELENA   *map page 199*

Helena's early fortunes were made of gold. The city's main street is still called **Last Chance Gulch,** a souvenir to the four discouraged prospectors who declared this unlikely spot to be their "last chance" after following strike after played-out strike all over the West. It turned out to be their best chance when, in 1864, they discovered the first of several gold deposits that catapulted Helena into second place, right behind Alder Gulch, as Montana's leading gold producer. Within 10 years, tents and crude log cabins had given way to mansions, mercantiles, and hundreds of small businesses. By 1888, an estimated 50 millionaires lived here, making Helena the richest city per capita in the United States. Strategically located on early travel routes and at the center of Montana's mining district, Helena could be confident of its survival. In 1875, it became Montana's third territorial capital (after Bannack and Virginia City, the sites of Montana's first two major gold strikes). Then, in 1894, it became the permanent state capital in a runoff election against Anaconda, after a $3 million campaign financed by rival copper barons Marcus Daly and William A. Clark.

Helena, the state capital of Montana, can boast a spectacular natural setting as well as lavish, often intriguingly eclectic architecture.

Much of Helena's early history has been preserved in its architecture, both downtown and in adjacent residential neighborhoods. The extravagant jumble of Baroque, Gothic, Italianate, and Romanesque designs reflects the exuberance of Helena's Victorian period. Arched windows, ornate pillars, masonry, wrought iron, and detailed carvings are all visible on the massive stone buildings anchoring Helena's historic Last Chance Gulch. While fires, earthquakes, demolition, and decay have leveled many of Helena's historic buildings, close to a hundred stand as reminders of the city's golden era. The growth of Helena can be traced from the gulch eastward as downtown fixtures such as the original Governor's Mansion and the original State Capitol (now the Lewis and Clark County Courthouse) were abandoned for more modern buildings on the east side of town.

◆ WESTSIDE: GOVERNOR'S AND SANDERS MANSIONS

Within the century-old mansions of Helena's venerable westside neighborhoods can be found an opulent mix of styles and designs that combine parquet floors, Tiffany windows, tile fireplaces, handcrafted oak and cherry woodwork, high-ceilings, spacious front porches, gazebos, and carriage houses. The original **Governor's Mansion**, at 304 North Ewing, was built as a home in 1888 by entrepreneur William Chessman; it is open to the public for tours.

At 328 North Ewing stands the **Sanders Mansion,** built by politician and vigilante Wilbur Fisk Sanders. The high-ceilinged Queen Anne–style home, still with its original furnishings, is now a gracious inn with seven guest rooms; 406-442-3309.

◆ CATHEDRAL OF ST. HELENA

Towering above all these secular monuments to the earthly treasures of an earlier period is the magnificent Cathedral of St. Helena. Modeled on the Votive Cathedral of the Sacred Heart in Vienna, it boasts stained-glass windows from Bavaria, a white marble altar from Italy, and twin spires crowned with gilded crosses that face east and west to catch the first and last light of day. Rising 230 feet above the tree-lined streets of Helena—as if to compete with the surrounding peaks of the Rocky Mountains—the cathedral lends European dignity to the city's skyline.

◆ ART AND CULTURAL CENTERS

History and the arts are a source of pride to Helena residents. Many are involved in efforts to restore downtown buildings and mansions to house halls and galleries.

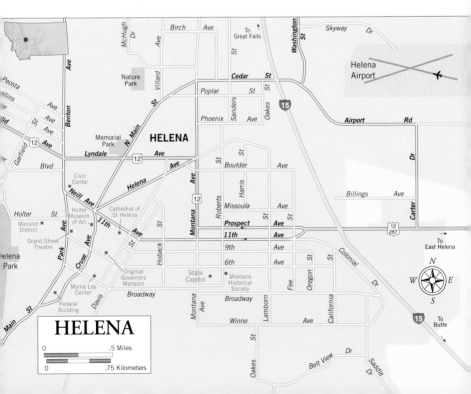

HELENA

0	.5 Miles
0	.75 Kilometers

An ambitious arts group transformed an abandoned, century-old jail into the **Myrna Loy Center,** a performing arts and film center. **Grandstreet Theatre** is a lively school and stage for lively arts. **The Archie Bray Foundation** is internationally recognized for its ceramic arts.

The Montana Historical Society, at 225 North Roberts, houses two smaller museums, the **Montana Homeland Historical Museum** and the smaller **F. Jay Haynes Museum** for frontier photography. Also here are works by C. M. Russell, along with a fine archives and historical library.

◆ STATE CAPITOL

While the city's early growth was financed by gold dust and nuggets, Helena now owes its existence to the less tangible but self-perpetuating occupation of politics. Much of the business of state government is conducted beneath the dome of the **State Capitol,** which was returned to its original elegance during a major restoration and remodeling project completed in 2000. Walls adorned with ornate fabric coverings, floors tiled in a ceramic mosaic and a stained glass canopy known as a barrel vault, are highlights of the $26 million dollar restoration project. Crowned in copper, the capitol serves as a reminder that while gold shines brighter, the reddish-brown ore coming out of Butte, beginning in the 1880s, was the dominant star in Montana's mining and political history.

SOUTHWEST
MONTANA

(above) The State Capitol in Helena. (opposite) The Cathedral of St. Helena is modeled after Vienna's Cathedral of the Sacred Heart.

COPPER MONEY

*W*hen the late Senator Robert LaFollette listed [William A.] Clark as one of one hundred men who owned America, and cited fourteen great corporations in his hands to prove it, he neglected to recite a more revealing fact. Differing from the other ninety-nine "owners of America," Clark stood alone, unique, in the fact that of all the great enterprises with which he was connected, not one share of stock nor bond issue by any one of them was either listed or quoted or could be bought on any stock exchange in the United States.

William A. Clark, "copper king."
(Montana Historical Society)

WILLIAM ANDREWS CLARK
PIONEER PROSPECTOR AND MINER
MERCHANT BANKER RAILROAD BUILDER
BENEFACTOR OF CHILDREN AND PHILANTHROPIST
THIS MEMORIAL IS ERECTED BY
THE SOCIETY OF MONTANA AND OTHER FRIENDS
AS A TRIBUTE TO HIS GREAT ACHIEVEMENTS
AND TO PERPETUATE HIS MEMORY

Inscription from bas-relief in capitol rotunda in Helena

—C. B. Glasscock, *The War of the Copper Kings:*
Builders of Butte and Wolves of Wall Street, 1935

■ BUTTE   *map page 204, D-4*

The discovery of rich copper ores in Butte coincided with the introduction of the electric light bulb and telephone on the world market, and the rest, as they say, is history. Large mining interests turned to Butte, and between 1882 and 1890 copper production increased from nine million to 130 million pounds, and the city's population tripled. The population peaked right around World War I with an estimated 20,000 miners and 100,000 residents, making it one of the West's largest inland cities. Once Montana's largest city, Butte now ranks fourth, with about 34,000 residents.

This mile-high mining town is known affectionately as "Butte, America," because the valley in which it lies was lost in a frontier twilight zone between the Louisiana Purchase and Oregon Territory, and never legally procured as part of either chunk of real estate. A true melting pot, it drew thousands of foreign-born immigrants in search of a living wage. They clustered together in ethnic neighborhoods that still bear names such as Corktown, Dublin Gulch, Finntown, Chinatown, and Little Italy. Some of these enclaves were literally devoured by the huge open-pit mine that began replacing underground mining operations in 1955, but Butte, more than any other city or town in Montana, has retained its ethnic character. While the Irish dominate Butte in body and spirit, there still remain distinct pockets of Finns, Slavs, Italians, and small populations of many other nationalities.

The Wah Chong Tai Co. thrived in Butte's melting pot, circa 1900. (Montana Historical Society)

SOUTHWEST
MONTANA

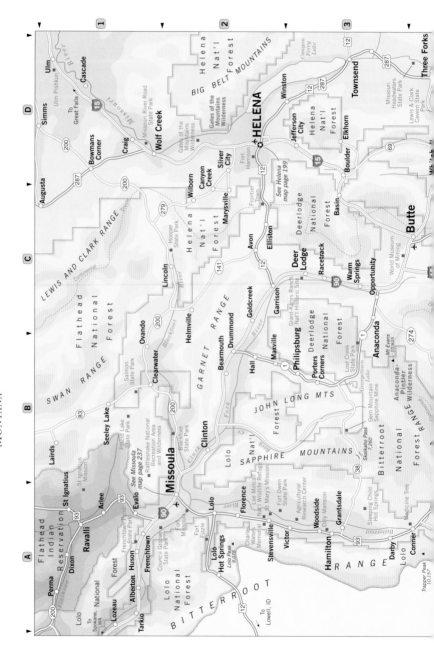

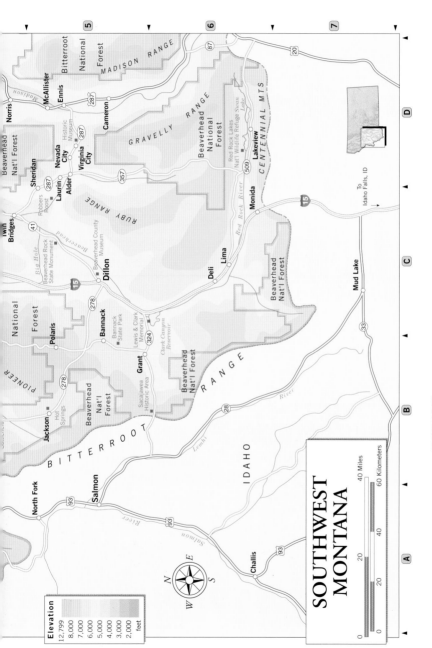

SOUTHWEST MONTANA

Whether due to its ethnic roots, its labor heritage, or both, Butte is a rough town with a tender heart. Surrounded by gallow frames, mine spoils, ore dumps, and mine shafts, and perched on the edge of the defunct, mile-wide Berkeley Pit, Butte stands uncontested as Montana's most unattractive city. It has been described in the national press as "the ugliest city in America." Behind its bleak, pock-marked face, however, shine the smiling eyes and indomitable spirit of its residents. People are the power behind Butte and they have been ever since they muscled the ore and fought the labor wars that made Butte the most militant union town in the nation.

Butte was all business when it went to work, but when the shift changed, Butte knew how to have fun. Hundreds of saloons and gambling parlors stayed open around the clock to serve three shifts of miners. This was a town that never shut down and never gave up. Market fluctuations, changes in mining technology, overseas production, and depletion of high-grade ores all inflicted near-fatal blows to the economy of Butte over the years. What everyone but Butte interpreted as the final blow came in 1983, when the Atlantic Richfield Company (ARCO) announced the suspension of all mining operations in Butte. Mining in Butte will never be what it was during the nation's industrial era, but small-scale copper mining

These gold bricks (above), not as pure as they look, will be further processed outside the state.

(opposite) Molten gold.

has made a comeback, and Butte has diversified its economy with a sound mix of businesses built on mining, energy and environmental research, along with public utilities, education, and medical services.

◆ BUTTE MINING TODAY

For most of its existence, Butte was a company town, held captive by global markets and corporate policies beyond its control. Forced to take control of its destiny when it was abandoned by arco, Butte today stands as a role model for other Montana towns singing the American heartland blues. While Butte had the vision to contemplate life after copper, it never lost sight of its rich ethnic-labor heritage and mining history. The entire city is a living museum, with real-life exhibits in the card room of the M&M bar and café, the tightly packed miners' shanties that cling to steep hillsides, uptown mansions that memorialize the copper kings, Irish wakes that celebrate the lives of the departed, Christmas Eve at the Serbian Church, St. Urho's Day at the Helsinki Bar, and St. Patrick's Day in every bar and on every sidewalk.

◆ MINING HISTORY FOOD, LODGING, AND SIGHTS

Visitors can familiarize themselves with Butte's mining heritage on walking tours of uptown Butte, driving tours of underground mines, guided trolley tours of the city, and at the **World Museum of Mining; the Mineral Museum;** and the visitors center at the **Berkeley Pit,** for many years the nation's largest truck-operated open-pit copper mine, and now one of the nation's largest Superfund sites.

Visitors can also get a glimpse into the lives of mine-industry Buttians rich and poor by living—at least temporarily—like a prince or a pauper. **The Copper King Mansion B&B** is a three-story Elizabethan-style residence once owned by William A. Clark that's today an eight-room B&B. Guests can stay in the rooms that are part of the guided tour during the day. *219 West Granite Street; 406-782-7580.*

The Scott B&B was once a boarding house for miners, now renovated for guests, now it's on the National Register of Historic Places. There are seven rooms with private baths. *15 West Copper Street; 406-723-7030.*

For lunch, try **Nancy's Pasty Shop** *(2810 Pine Street)*, which sells the meat pies that Welsh and Cornish miners asked their wives to bake for them. When a miner found a pasty in his lunch bucket, he referred to it affectionately as "a letter from 'ome." Pasties have endured as a Butte's ethnic tradition. **The Pekin Noodle Parlor** *(117 South Main)* dates back to Butte's mining heyday. The no-frills walk-up is as popular for its atmosphere as it is for its pork noodles and boiled wonton.

◆ HIGH ALTITUDE SIGHTS

Two attractions stand as monuments to "Buttians'" characteristic determination to beat the odds. One, a 90-foot, 51-ton lighted statue of *Our Lady of the Rockies* overlooks Butte from atop the Continental Divide.

The other, the multi-million-dollar **U.S. High Altitude Sports Center,** grew out of Butte's speedskating tradition and serves as a training facility and competition skating rink for Olympic-class athletes. The new Butte Chamber of Commerce *(1000 George)* has information on all these options, plus a fly-fishing display featuring the work of master fly-tier and conservationist George Grant.

At first glance, Butte appears to offer little more than a tarnished landscape and the sort of bland services you might find at an interstate highway junction. But venture past the gas stations and fast-food joints clustered at the exit ramps and poke around uptown Butte. Drop into any cafe for a hot cup of joe, or any tavern for a cold beer. A warm reception is guaranteed, and it won't be long before "yous guys" see the heart of gold that beats behind the homely façade of the city built on copper.

■ ANACONDA   *map page 204, C-3*

About 25 miles west of Butte is another small city that owes its existence to copper. Indeed, Anaconda would be known today as "Copperopolis" if its founder, Marcus Daly, had had his way. Hand-picked by Daly as the site of a giant reduction works to process the ores coming from his Anaconda mine in Butte, Anaconda became a classic company town whose fortunes were tied directly to those of Daly's mining operations. When the mines were producing, life was good in Anaconda, and Marcus Daly was its patron saint. Besides providing good jobs for hundreds of smelter workers, he endowed his beloved Anaconda with a trolley line, an amusement park, a magnificent hotel, and a racetrack. At one time, the 585-foot-high smelter stack was the tallest in North America; the plant had the world's largest smelting capacity.

By the end of World War II, the Anaconda Copper Mining Company (ACM), which had absorbed the interests of Daly and the other early copper barons of Butte, had also acquired copper mines in Chile and Mexico, becoming the world's largest producer of copper. Beyond copper, ACM controlled lumber, railroad, and even newspaper operations.

Anaconda Mining Company lost its monolithic stature in the worldwide copper industry in 1970, when a Marxist government rose to power in Chile and nationalized all of that nation's copper mines. Trouble in Latin America coincided with the domestic challenge of meeting new air pollution standards, and the company began divesting itself of its Montana properties, one by one. In 1977, ACM merged with the Atlantic Richfield Company, and in 1980, the company suspended its smelting operations in Anaconda and Great Falls indefinitely. For the first time in its existence, the company town of Anaconda was without a company.

Unsure of its future, Anaconda has taken a firm grip on the significance of its role in Montana history. It is said that seven truckloads of printed material from the Anaconda Reduction Works are preserved by the local historical society, as are maps, photographs, and memorabilia from Anaconda's early ethnic cultures, immigrant groups, and social organizations. For those who prefer their history condensed, try a historic walking tour (see the chamber of commerce), or head to the museum and art gallery.

Washoe Theater and Hearst Free Library
Washoe Theater is an art deco classic, and its Hearst Free Library (donated to the city by newspaper eminence Phoebe Hearst, whose husband helped finance Daly's mining ventures), is yet another reminder of the outside money that aided the development of southwestern Montana. *406-563-6161.*

Montana's natural resources made many a millionaire. Evidence of their lavish tastes can be seen today at Anaconda's elaborate Washoe Theatre (opposite), an art deco classic, and at Deer Lodge's Towe Ford Museum, where Henry Ford's camper is on display (above).

Lost Creek State Park

Nearby Lost Creek, one of the best-kept secrets in the state parks system, boasts spectacular limestone cliffs, granite formations, and waterfalls. The mountain goats and bighorn sheep you'll see wandering around make this a worthwhile sidetrip for anyone visiting Anaconda.

Washoe Park

Given to the city by Marcus Daly, Washoe Park is still Anaconda's favorite playground with its ball fields, flower gardens, picnic areas, swimming pool, and state fish hatchery. vorite playground, with its ball fields, flower gardens, picnic areas, swimming pool, and state fish hatchery.

■ STOCKGROWERS' TOWNS

Southwestern Montana has two other mid-sized communities, both firmly rooted in the livestock industry. **Deer Lodge,** 25 miles north of Anaconda, and **Dillon,** about 80 miles south, lie along major rivers flowing through broad mountain valleys. Just as the mountains around Butte and Helena yielded rich gold and copper deposits, these valleys provided the resources for Montana's cattle industry.

◆ DEER LODGE AND THE GRANT-KOHRS RANCH   *map page 204, C-3*

Canadian trapper and mountain man Johnny Grant was the first to make a go of ranching in the Deer Lodge Valley, and many consider him the founder of the industry in Montana. In 1853, he acquired a few sickly cows, and by 1863 he was running 4,000 head and nearly as many horses on his Deer Lodge property and supplying most of the beef for the mining camps of Bannack and Virginia City. Grant sold his spread in 1866 to a German immigrant, Conrad Kohrs, who built it into one of the most prosperous cattle ranches in the West. As headquarters for an empire that covered more than a million acres of grazing land in the western United States and Canada, Kohrs' operation was one of few that survived the brutal winter of 1886–87.

Today, the Grant-Kohrs Ranch is preserved on the outskirts of Deer Lodge as a national historic site. Visitors can poke around in the early barns and outbuildings, or tour the original ranch house, once regarded the finest in the Territory. Cattle still graze here and draft horses are still used to work the land, making this the next best thing to a working ranch for visitors curious to know more about

Hay bales dot the landscape in Montana's southwest region.

ranching without getting their cowboy boots dirty. Plan to stay awhile in Deer Lodge, especially if you enjoy history, because the **Old Montana Prison,** the **Montana Law Enforcement Museum,** the **Towe Ford Museum,** and the **Powell County Museum** are all located in the same block downtown.

◆ BIG HOLE BASIN   *map page 204-205, B-4*

For a larger view of the livestock industry, you can't do better than a drive through the scenic Big Hole Basin in the heart of the region. Watered by the meandering Big Hole River, the hay grows wild in this high mountain valley, contributing heavily to Beaverhead County's standing as the top cattle and hay producer in the state. Mountain valleys were "holes" to the early trappers and mountain men, and this was one of the biggest in the area, so the name stuck. Known today as the "valley of 10,000 haystacks," the Big Hole looks like an agrarian landscape from the past, with haystacks piled high as houses throughout the valley's 50-mile length and 15-mile width. Cutting a cleaner profile than the haystacks are the 30-foot-high beaverslides that are used to stack the hay. The derrick-like, wooden structures were devised by two Big Hole ranchers in 1907.

◆ DILLON   *map page 205, C-5*

The trade center for Big Hole and Beaverhead Valley ranchers is **Dillon,** which got its start as a railroad town on the route to mineral-rich Butte. The stately homes of early merchants and stockmen still preside over Dillon's older, tree-lined neighborhoods. Once Montana's largest wool shipping point, Dillon is better known today as the home of **Western Montana College,** which specializes in improving rural education and serves as a branch campus of the University of Montana.

Dillon is also a base camp for recreation in the surrounding Beaverhead National Forest, the nearby Beaverhead and Big Hole Rivers, Clark Canyon Reservoir, and the Wise River-Polaris scenic byway. Dillon's **Labor Day Rodeo,** locally billed as "Montana's Biggest Weekend," ranks among the state's best rodeos with its dances, rodeo performances, a wild horse race, parade, and barbecue. *See pages*

■ GHOST TOWNS

For every gold camp that survived, there are dozens that went bust when the diggin's played out. The century-old drama of prospectors, road agents, vigilantes, harlots, and abandoned wives and children is etched in the weathered frames of cabins, saloons, hotels, and assay offices that once lined the folds and gulches of these mountain valleys. A few ghost towns, especially Bannack and Virginia City, have been preserved, their stories intact. Most, however, are blown-down, rusted-out relics whose stories can only be conjured up in the imaginations of the visitors who seek them out.

◆ BANNACK   *map page 205, B-5*

For beginning students of ghost town lore, Bannack is an illustrated primer on Montana's gold mining history. The site of Montana's first major gold rush, Bannack erupted when hundreds of prospectors flocked to a strike on nearby Grasshopper Creek in 1862. Within a year, the population had swollen to 3,000, and in 1864 Bannack became Montana's first Territorial capital. Eventually the gold played out and so did Bannack, but not before a sizable community had been established. Gunfights and hangings once shattered the silence of this remote valley, while more peaceable citizens crowded the saloons, dance halls, miner's court, church, and school. Today, Bannack is a quiet park, managed by the state for its historic value. A walking tour and visitor center familiarize visitors with the social and structural fabric of this 1860s' gold rush town. In late July, Bannack celebrates its history with a weekend of frontier crafts and food, music, buggy rides, gold panning, a black powder rifle shoot, and frontier church service. **Bannack Days** is the biggest weekend of the year in this otherwise lonely outpost. The park is located west of Dillon, off Montana State Highway 278.

◆ VIRGINIA CITY AND NEVADA CITY   *map page 205, D-5*

Visitors can still stroll the boardwalks of one of the West's richest and most colorful mining districts, about 60 miles east of Dillon, on Montana State Highway 287. Virginia City and Nevada City lie within a mile of one another along Alder Gulch. News of an 1863 gold strike here spread like knapweed, and within a year several thousand prospectors had crowded into makeshift camps along the gulch. The most enduring of these overnight mining camps was Virginia City, which mushroomed into a commercial hub of 10,000 and served as Montana's second territorial capital from 1865 to 1875. In one year, $10 million in gold nuggets was panned from the streams that feed into the gulch, and since the initial strike, an estimated $70 million has been taken from the area. Thanks to the painstaking restoration efforts of a Montana ranch family headed by the late Charles and Sue Bovey, and a new partnership between the private sector and the state of Montana, visitors can drop coins into a nickelodeon, photograph a two-story outhouse, and browse through shops, buildings, merchandise, and memorabilia that are true to

This weathered façade is one of several restored buildings from Montana's gold rush days at Virginia City.

MINERS AND MAYHEM

Of the settlements in Alder Gulch, Virginia City was the principal, though Nevada, two miles below, at one time was of nearly equal size and population. A stranger from the Eastern States entering the gulch for the first time, two or three months after its discovery, would be inspired by the scene and its associations with reflections of the most strange and novel character. This human hive, numbering at least ten thousand people, was the product of ninety days. Into it were crowded all the elements of a rough and active civilization. Thousands of cabins and tents and brush wakiups, thrown together in the roughest form, and scattered at random along the banks, and in the nooks of the hills, were seen on every hand. Every foot of the gulch, under the active manipulations of the miners, was undergoing displacement, and it was already disfigured by huge heaps of gravel, which had been passed through the sluices, and rifled of their glittering contents. In the gulch itself all was activity. Some were removing the superincumbent earth to reach the pay-dirt, others who had accomplished that were gathering up the clay and gravel upon the surface of the bed-rock, while by others still it was thrown into the sluice boxes. This exhibition of mining industry was twelve miles long. Gold was abundant, and every possible devise was employed by the gamblers, the treaders, the vile men and women that had come with the miners to the locality, to obtain it. Nearly every third cabin in the towns was a saloon where vile whiskey was peddled out for fifty cents a drink in gold dust. Many of these places were filled with gambling tables and gamblers, and the miner who was bold enough to enter one of them with his day's earnings in his pocket seldom left until thoroughly fleeced. Hurdy-gurdy dance-houses were numerous, and there were plenty of camp beauties to patronize them. There too, the successful miner, lured by siren smiles, after an evening spent in dancing and carousing at his expense, steeped with liquor, would empty his purse into the lap of his charmer for an hour of license in her arms. Not a day or night passed which did not yield its full fruition of fights, quarrels, wounds, or murders. The crack of the revolver was often heard above the merry notes of the violin. Street fights were frequent, and as no one knew when or where they would occur, every one was on his guard against a random shot. Sunday was always a gala day. The miners then left their work and gathered about the public places in the towns. The stores were all open, the auctioneers specially eloquent on every corner in praise of their wares. Thousands of people crowded the thoroughfares, ready to rush in any direction of promised excitement. Horse-racing was among the most favored amusements. Prize rings were formed, and brawny men engaged at fisticuffs until their sight was lost and their bodies pommelled to a jelly, while hundreds of on-lookers cheered the victor. Hacks rattled to and fro between the several towns, freighted with drunken and rowdy humanity of both sexes. Citizens of acknowledged respectability often walked, more often perhaps rode side by side on horseback, with noted courtesans in open day through the crowded streets, and seemingly suffered no harm in reputation. Pistols flashed, bowie-knives flourished, and braggart oaths filled the air, as often as men's passions triumphed over their reason. This was indeed the reign of unbridled license, and men who at first regarded it with disgust and terror, by constant exposure soon learned to become part of it, and forget that they had ever been aught else. All classes of society were represented at this general exhibition. Judges, lawyers, doctors, even clergymen could not claim exemption. Culture and religion afforded feeble protection, where allurement and indulgence ruled the hour.

— Nathaniel Pitt Langford, *Vigilante Days and Ways,* 1890

Road agent's grave at Boot Hill cemetery in Virginia City.

The town of Garnet (above) was a silver boomtown in the 1870s;

the era. One of Montana's foremost summer theater troupes, the **Virginia City Players,** performs a 19th-century melodrama on summer evenings at the Virginia City Opera House. *For information, call 406-843-5314 or 800-648-7588.*

Less developed but equally diverting are the 1870s gold camp of **Garnet,** north of Drummond; the 1880s silver boomtown of **Granite,** near Philipsburg; the 1870s mining camp of **Elkhorn,** near Boulder, which produced both gold and silver; and **Marysville,** north of Helena, home of the fabulous Drumlummon mine, which yielded $16 million in gold and silver. Dozens of other ghost towns haunt the mountains of southwestern Montana.

The **Ghost Town Hall of Fame,** at Fairmont Hot Springs east of Anaconda, displays photos and narrative descriptions of many of them. You can buy comprehensive guides to Montana's ghost towns at many bookstores around the state.

■ OUTDOOR RECREATION

The abiding treasures of this region are not the gold placers, silver lodes, and copper veins whose value is determined by a fickle metals market. In an increasingly crowded and polluted world, this mining district's trump card may well be its rivers and lakes, its vast, untrammeled wilderness and roadless areas, its unpeopled space, and natural beauty. Small cities and towns that once drew prospectors and immigrant laborers now attract retirees, sportsmen, and refugees from urban America seeking a simpler way of life.

◆ FISHING RIVERS: BEAVERHEAD AND BIG HOLE   *map page 205, C-4/5*

The centerpiece of the region's natural attractions is a superlative trout fishery nurtured by the headwaters of the Missouri River. Ever since August 22, 1805, when Meriwether Lewis noted in his journal that his party had landed "528 good fish, most of them large trout," the **Beaverhead River** has become famous for its "pork-chops," chunky browns and rainbows that tip the scales at four-plus pounds each. Indeed, the upper Beaverhead produces more trophy-size trout per mile than any other stream in the state.

More accessible and easier to fish, the **Big Hole** draws more anglers each year than the Beaverhead. Many come in June to fish the Big Hole's famed salmonfly hatch, which triggers Montana's most celebrated trout feeding binge. Rising as a trickle in the Beaverhead Mountains, the Big Hole flows through wild hay meadows, skirts the north end of the Pioneer Mountains in a grand, graceful arc, and plunges through a canyon before merging with the Beaverhead at Twin Bridges to become the Jefferson River.

◆ MAN-MADE LAKES AND RESERVOIRS

Beyond the veinous network of rivers and streams that surge through its valleys, the region is studded with lakes and reservoirs. One of the most scenic is **Georgetown Lake** *(map page 204, B-3)*, actually a reservoir built in 1901 by the Anaconda Company to ensure a lasting water supply for its smelting operation in nearby Anaconda. Shimmering beneath the 10,000-foot-high peaks of the Anaconda Range, Georgetown Lake is one of Montana's most popular boating and fishing spots, with reliable yields of rainbow trout and kokanee salmon.

To the south, near Dillon, **Clark Canyon Reservoir** *(map page 205, C-6)* is an excellent rainbow trout fishery with plenty of camping and boat-launching facilities. To the north, near Helena, three dams on the Missouri have created a chain of recreation opportunities on Canyon Ferry, Hauser, and Holter Lakes. Stretching 25 miles from the valley east of Helena to Townsend, Canyon Ferry Lake draws people from throughout the state to fish its waters, sail and surf its wind-chopped surface, and play on its sandy beaches.

♦ GATES OF THE MOUNTAINS WILDERNESS   *map page 204, D-2*

Lewis and Clark left their imprint just a few miles downriver where the Missouri flows through a narrow passage flanked by what Lewis described as "the most remarkable clifts that we have yet seen." Because these cliffs first appeared as if they would block the expedition's passage, then seemed to open as the explorers got closer, Lewis named this scenic gorge the Gates of the Rocky Mountains. Visitors today can see the same illusion on commercial boat tours departing from the Gates of the Mountains boat landing on Holter Lake.

Nearby Gates of the Mountains Wilderness is one of Montana's smallest and least visited wilderness areas. Most people are content to view a fraction of the wilderness from the tour boats that glide past it for specifics). For those willing to don hiking boots and a backpack, the "Gates" offer a truly primitive experience within the same distinctive limestone formations and cliffs that can be seen from the river. Canyons, coulees, and gorges invite deeper exploration. A popular hunting area, they provide a home to sizable populations of elk, bighorn sheep, mountain goats, and mule deer. *For more information, visit www.wildmontana.org.*

Storm clouds hover over Big Hole Basin.

Gates of the Mountains Wilderness is one of Montana's least visited parks.

The adjacent **Beartooth Game Management Area** furnishes winter range for the area's large elk herd. Another small, easily accessible recreation area is the **Humbug Spires Primitive Area,** south of Butte. Erratic limestone rock formations, located just off Interstate 15, draw hikers, rock climbers, and geology buffs.

◆ ANACONDA-PINTLER WILDERNESS   *map page 204, B/C-4*

Southwestern Montana's foremost wilderness area is the lofty Anaconda-Pintler, straddling the Continental Divide southwest of Butte and Anaconda. Much larger than the Gates of the Mountains or the Humbug Spires, the Anaconda-Pintler Wilderness receives surprisingly moderate use. This is high country characterized by alpine meadows, lakes, windswept ridges, and several peaks above 10,000 feet. Nearly all of the land is above 7,000 feet, meaning that snow can come at any time and remains on the ground for more than half the year. There are nearly 300 miles of trails in this wilderness, including 45 miles of the Continental Divide National Scenic Trail. The Anaconda-Pintler encompasses several lakes and streams, including headwaters of nationally renowned **Rock Creek,** an exceptional trout stream that flows north approximately 70 miles to its confluence with the Clark Fork, en route to the Pacific Ocean. Many of the lakes and streams in the wilderness area hold cutthroat and rainbow trout, while mountain goats, elk, moose, deer, bear, and mountain lion occupy the higher ground.

■ SCENIC BYWAYS

People need not climb these mountains nor fish these rivers to catch their spirit. Just being in their presence, surrounded by their majesty and grace, is enough for most visitors to the Northern Rockies. Two scenic roads penetrate the region, providing lavish views as well as access to hiking trails and trout streams, campgrounds, ghost towns, and other historic sites. Montana State Highway 1, known as the **Pintler Scenic Route,** is an inviting alternative to Interstate 90 between Missoula and Butte. For 60 miles, it parallels sparkling streams, climbs mountain passes, skirts the shores of Georgetown Lake, and visits the towns of Anaconda and Philipsburg, all beneath the towering backdrop of the Anaconda Range. When combined with Interstate 90, it forms a loop that takes in the community of Deer Lodge.

For a closer look at this Northern Rockies landscape, the **Wise River-Polaris National Forest Scenic Byway** (closed during the winter) bisects a half-million acres of peaks, lakes, and headwaters in the Pioneer Mountains. For half its 30-mile length, this partially paved road follows the Wise River, then crosses a divide and emerges from the Beaverhead National Forest near Dillon. Along the way, it delivers motorists to a variety of scenic, historic, and cultural gems, including the ghost town of **Coolidge,** which served as a base camp in the 1920s for miners working the nearby Elkhorn silver mine; 1930s-era campgrounds constructed by the Civilian Conservation Corps; prehistoric Indian sites; and a New Ager's mecca called **Crystal Park,** where small quartz crystals and amethysts are commonly found. Campgrounds, hiking trails, trout streams, and abundant wildlife can stretch what appears on the map to be a short jaunt into an extended tour.

Upon reaching Highway 278 at the south end of the Wise River-Polaris Road, Bannack State Park and Clark Canyon Reservoir are but a few miles to the south. To the northwest lies the town of **Wisdom** and the **Kirkpatrick Custom Hat Company,** whose congenial proprietors use frontier-era tools to craft cowboy hats for those in the trade (and for a few who aren't). Stop by for a chat and coffee.

A mule ranch along the Pintler Scenic Route, with the Anaconda Range in the background.

Big Hole Battlefield National Monument, (*map page 205, B-4*) site of an 1877 battle between the U.S. Army and Chief Joseph's Nez Perce Indians, lies 12 miles west of Wisdom on Highway 43. This was one of four major battles along the Nez Perce's flight to Canada. While the Nez Perce escaped the army here and technically won the Battle of the Big Hole, their numbers and morale were seriously diminished. A visitor center at the Big Hole Battlefield explains the significance of the Nez Perce Indian War. Trails take visitors to the camp site where soldiers surprised the sleeping Nez Perce, a wooded area where Col. John Gibbon and members of the Seventh Infantry were besieged by warriors for 36 hours, and the ridge where Indians captured the army's howitzer and a pack mule carrying 2,000 rounds of rifle ammunition.

■ PROSPECTING FOR SAPPHIRES

While the early visitors to this part of the state were fortune seekers lured by talk of fabulous gold strikes, many of today's visitors are rockhounds, drawn to one of the few places where modern prospectors can dig for sapphires. These brilliant gemstones are found in a rainbow of colors. The most common is green-blue, while blue is the best known and ruby one of the most highly prized. At commercial sapphire mines, visitors can screen "paydirt" from buckets or purchase bags of gravel to sift at home. Some of the mines also have custom gem-cutting shops on site. Most sapphire hunters spend a day or two at the mines for the fun of it, gathering gemstones that range from one-half to 10 carats. But it's easy to get hooked on these treasure hunts, knowing that sapphires as large as 150 carats have been found, then sold for thousands of dollars. Two of these mines line the Missouri River northeast of Helena—the **Spokane Bar** and **El Dorado**. Another large deposit lies along Rock Creek, southwest of Philipsburg. Once mined commercially by the St. Louis–based American Gem Mining Syndicate, today's **Gem Mountain Sapphire Mine** (*map page 204, B-3)* is open to rockhounds and recreational prospectors.

Big Hole Battlefield National Monument commemorates one of the four major battles fought by the Nez Perce along their flight to Canada.

MISSOULA AND
BITTERROOT COUNTRY

Map page 237
•Missoula

THE BITTERROOT VALLEY TAKES ITS NAME from the river that flows its entire length, the mountain range that forms its dominant western wall, and the diminutive flower that grows wild among its forests of ponderosa pine. This distinctive valley, which resembles a snout on the face of western Montana, appears isolated from the rest of the state but is central to its history.

■ HISTORIC BITTERROOT VALLEY   *map page 204, A-2/3/4*

Flathead Indians are said to have lived here as early as 1500, when they drifted east with other Salish-speaking tribes from the Columbia River country of the Pacific Northwest. They moved freely across the Continental Divide to hunt buffalo until around 1700, when the arrival of Shoshone and Blackfeet Indians east of the divide forced them back to the western valleys. By the time Lewis and Clark came upon them in 1805, they had established the Bitterroot Valley as their homeland.

◆ ST. MARY'S MISSION AND THE FLATHEAD INDIANS

In the 1830s, curious about reports of "Black Robes" who could speak to the Great Spirit, the Flatheads sent delegates east to St. Louis to request that a Catholic mission be established in their valley. In September 1841, the Jesuits founded **St. Mary's Mission,** the first church in the Northwest, in what is now the community of **Stevensville.** By Christmas of that year, more than 700 Indians had been baptized. But the original church did not last beyond its first decade. It faced

Jesuits established St. Mary's Mission in 1841; the church which stands today was built in 1866.

Early logging was done with horses. (Montana Historical Society)

a number of problems, including scarce funds, continual threats from hostile Blackfeet Indians, and growing disenchantment among the Flatheads. In 1850, the mission closed and the property was sold to Major John Owen, who transformed it into a lively trading post he named Fort Owen.

◆ FORT OWEN   *map page 204, A-2*

Never a military base, Fort Owen flourished as the commercial hub of Bitterroot Valley. John Owen himself had resigned his position as a licensed trader with the U.S. Army and began trading independently. At Fort Owen, he built on the grain and livestock operations established by the Jesuits of St. Mary's and soon became a major supplier to nearby gold camps. Fort Owen was also a popular gathering spot for adventurers, trappers, new settlers, and several Indian tribes. Here, travelers were welcome, parties and feasts were frequent, and Indians and whites were friends. Married to a Shoshone, Owen was sympathetic to the growing problems of the natives and became the agent of the Flathead Nation, a position he later resigned out of disgust with the federal Indian Bureau's indifference and neglect. Fort Owen served as Flathead Agency Headquarters until 1860, when the headquarters was moved to its existing location in the Jocko River Valley, north of Missoula. A remnant of this once humming "bastion of civilization" in the remote wilderness of the Northwest has been preserved in Stevensville as **Fort Owen State**

Park. Set on the banks of the Bitterroot River, surrounded by the lush pasturelands that supported Fort Owen's livestock, the dimly lighted East Barracks is about all that remains of the enterprise.

Less than a half-mile away is **St. Mary's Mission** *(map page 204, A-2)*, reconstructed in 1866 by an Italian Jesuit, Father Anthony Ravalli. St. Mary's remained an Indian mission until 1891, when the last band of Flatheads in the Bitterroot were forced to move north. A prominent Stevensville landmark, it memorializes not only the long-standing friendship between the Flathead Indians and the Catholic church, but also the importance of this valley to the peopling of Montana. In terms of permanent settlement, the Bitterroot Valley is where it all began.

■ THE VALLEY TODAY

To reach both St. Mary's and Fort Owen, travelers must leave US 93 and cross the Bitterroot River to reach the East Side Highway (State Highway 203/269). This secondary route stretches about 30 miles through the valley's interior, between Florence and Hamilton, and provides a leisurely alternative to its major north-south artery. With views of the low-lying Sapphire Mountains to the east and the canyons and peaks of the Bitterroot Range to the west, visitors will understand the

The logging and sawmill industry today is highly mechanized. (Montana Historical Society)

magnetic pull this valley has had on visitors ever since the Flathead Indians were first attracted by its mild climate. Stretching nearly 100 miles south of Missoula to the Idaho border, the valley lies in the protective rain shadow of the Bitterroot Mountains, whose 8,000- to 10,000-foot summits wring eastbound moisture from the Pacific out of the air before it reaches the valley. Logging and livestock are the traditional pillars of the Bitterroot economy, with a growing number of cottage and service industries that reflect the valley's appeal as a retirement community and refuge for urban emigrés. From gardening and beekeeping to horse breeding and log home construction, anything goes in this valley of scattered housing and small ranches.

■ HAMILTON   *map page 204, A-3*

The rapidly growing community of Hamilton is a crossroads of the Bitterroot Valley's loggers and ranchers, scientific and technical workers, and U.S. Forest Service personnel. As county seat of Ravalli County, it is also the government and commercial center for the valley's 36,000 residents. It has a substantial retirement population consisting largely of former visitors who were permanently attracted by the area's climate, rural lifestyle, and outdoor recreation. Prized assets are the Bitterroot River, which flows right through town, and Blodgett Canyon, a magnificent gorge through the Bitterroot Range just 20 minutes away.

◆ DALY MANSION

"Outsiders" have been discovering the Bitterroot ever since mining industrialist Marcus Daly traveled through the valley in 1864 searching for a mining friend, George Hearst, who was feared lost in Canada. Later in his career he remembered the valley's natural beauty and climate, not to mention its thick stands of timber, which he needed for his mine tunnels and smelter works in Butte and Anaconda. In 1888–89, he and his agents began acquiring land for timber as well as for Daly's personal use. He built a 28,000-acre estate on the outskirts of Hamilton that became his summer residence and stock farm. He called it "Riverside," and added a covered and heated horse track for his beloved race horses. After the copper king's death, the **Daly Mansion** was remodeled extensively by his wife, and is now open to the public during the summer. A beautiful, tree-lined driveway leads to the three-story, 42-room Georgian Revival residence with its 24 bedrooms and 15 bathrooms. *For more information, call 406-363-6004.*

◆ HAMILTON TODAY

The legacy of Daly's logging and milling operations may well be the log home manufacturing industry that now dominates the valley's economy. Nearly two dozen log home companies are headquartered here. The assembly yards where logs are peeled and notched, then shipped as kit log homes to buyers throughout the world, can be seen just off US 93 throughout the valley.

In the summer of 2000, Hamilton residents got a first-hand view of drought-induced fires that scorched nearly one million acres of Montana forest and range-lands and put 12,000 firefighters (from Puerto Rico, New Zealand, Australia, Canada, and 26 different states) to Montana. Blodgett Canyon was the site of one of the countless fires, which swept into residential areas as well: more than 70 homes were destroyed in the Bitterroot Valley alone.

DR. HOWARD T. RICKETTS AND ROCKY MOUNTAIN LABORATORIES

In addition to logging, the medical research and pharmaceutical industry has been a major employer in the Bitteroot Valley for almost a century. Around the turn of the 19th century, valley residents found themselves stricken with a deadly illness then called Rocky Mountain spotted fever, a disease whose mysterious origins soon drew researchers from around the country. One of many fine scientists to arrive in Hamilton was Dr. Howard T. Ricketts, who in 1906 discovered the link between the disease and a parasite borne by wood ticks prevalent in the foothills of the Bitterroots and other Western mountain ranges.

A successful spotted fever vaccine was developed in later years by scientists at **Hamilton's Rocky Mountain Laboratories,** built in 1928 by the U.S. Public Health Service and now an arm of the National Institutes of Health. During World War II, most of the vaccines for typhus and yellow fever were manufactured at the laboratory, where basic and applied research in immunologic, allergic, and infectious diseases continues today.

Ricketts himself died in 1910 of epidemic typhus—a disease related to spotted fever—which he had contracted in Mexico while studying the illness (and creating a potential vaccine) during an outbreak there. He is remembered by the species name rickettsia, the genus Rickettia, and the family Rickettsiaceae, some of whose members cause serious illness (including spotted fever and several other forms of typhus) in humans and animals.

(following pages) Trapper Peak, south of Missoula, is a distinctive landmark in the Bitterroots.

■ WILDERNESS AREAS

◆ SELWAY BITTEROOT-WILDERNESS   *map page 204, A-2/3/4*

The enduring appeal of the Bitterroot lies in a dramatic skyline etched by Trapper Peak, El Capitan, and other summits and spires that run the entire length of the Bitterroot Range. The crest of this glacially sculpted range forms the jagged border separating Montana from Idaho. The two states share not only one of the most rugged massifs in the Northern Rockies but also one of the largest federally protected wilderness areas in the Lower 48. The 1.3-million-acre **Selway-Bitterroot Wilderness** straddles the border, providing refuge for abundant elk and other wildlife. At first the sheer granite faces of these mountains appear cold and forbidding, but it won't be long before you feel the pull of their valleys and saddles, canyons and crests. Distinctive, U-shaped chasms cut east-west across the range, opening cool, pine-covered avenues of exhploration along trout streams fed by icy lakes in the wilderness interior. Several secondary roads lead from US 93 to trailheads at the mouths of these canyons.

◆ LEE METCALF NATIONAL WILDLIFE REFUGE   *map page 204, A-2*

Named after the late U.S. Senator Lee Metcalf, a native son and conservation giant, the refuge is an island of serenity in the midst of the rambling development of the Bitterroot Valley. It protects 2,800 acres of marshes, meadows, river bottoms, and uplands that sustain more than 200 different kinds of birds, notably blue herons, osprey, and a multitude of ducks, swans, and geese.

With the Bitterroots stealing the show, the valley's eastern rim, formed by the gentler ridges and folds of the Sapphire Mountains, is often overlooked. Easy to reach and well worth the effort, the Sapphires' high meadows and basins shelter elk, moose, bears, mountain lion, bighorn sheep, and mountain goats, as well as a number of smaller mammals and birds. A good trail system awaits hikers, but most visitors prefer driving the Skalkaho Pass Road, which climbs the east face of the range on Montana State Highway 38, west of Hamilton, crosses Skalkaho Pass at 7,260 feet, then drops into Rock Creek Valley and Georgetown Lake near Anaconda. This popular back road for summer loiterers is closed in winter.

Ponderosa pine in Blodgett Canyon, Bitterroot Mountains.

■ LOLO TRAIL   *map page 204, A-2*

At the north end of the Bitterroot Valley, US 12 takes motorists over the historic Lolo Trail into Idaho. This was a busy route, used by the Flathead and Nez Perce, and later by non-Indian explorers beginning with Lewis and Clark in 1805. After following the Bitterroot River in September of that year, their expedition camped at a place they named Travellers Rest, near the junction of US Routes 93 and 12 at Lolo. Shortly, they reached Lolo Pass on what is now the Montana-Idaho border, and began the most difficult leg of their westward journey. Hampered by deep snow, bad weather, and a scarcity of wild game, their progress was slow but they managed to reach the Pacific by November. The following July, on their return trip east, they camped again at Travellers Rest, and it was here that they split the outfit into two groups for further exploration of the Yellowstone, Marias, and Missouri Rivers. Well over a quarter of the expedition's entire 8,000-mile journey was spent here in Montana. The U.S. Forest Service maintains a visitor center at Lolo Pass that explains the significance of the Lolo Trail in the opening of the West. The history of the area was also illustrated by early Montana painter Edgar S. Paxson in several of the murals that adorn the walls of the Missoula County Courthouse in the valley's gateway city.

■ MISSOULA   *map page 204, A-2 and opposite*

Presiding over the north end of the valley is Montana's cultural superstar and second largest city. Best known as home to the **University of Montana**, Missoula is a yeasty brew of students and independent small businesspeople, professors, truckers, foresters, artists, and writers. The common denominator of this often factious community is a lifestyle revered by all. "One of the most sophisticated small cities in America"… "One of the top 10 universities for education and recreation"… "One of the top 10 bicycling cities in the United States": these are some of the badges of distinction Missoula wears, awarded over the years by national magazines and rating guides. At the head of five scenic valleys and the junction of three great rivers, Missoula has no shortage of recreational opportunities. Here is a city of 57,000 residents with nearly 140 restaurants, all within minutes of a wilderness trailhead. Here is western Montana's commercial, industrial, educational, and transportation hub, with a trout stream flowing through the center of town.

Loggers, foresters, railroaders, and merchants may have put this town on the map, but it is Missoula's writers, artists, and dramatists who keep it there. Past literary lights include critic Leslie Fiedler, the late poet Richard Hugo, and Western novelist Dorothy Johnson. Still shining brightly are novelists James Welch, James Crumley, Ian Frazier, and David James Duncan, essayist and novelist William Kittredge, writer and filmmaker Annick Smith, nonfiction writer Bryan Di Salvatore, and poet Patricia Goedicke. Many are the products of the university's fine creative writing program, which awards mfa degrees to a select group of graduate students from throughout the nation.

◆ THE UNIVERSITY INFLUENCE

With an enrollment of nearly 12,000, the university is Montana's leading liberal arts school. In addition to its College of Arts and Sciences, it maintains seven professional schools of business, education, fine arts, forestry, journalism, law, and pharmacy and allied health sciences. The university also conducts significant research at the UM Biological Station on Flathead Lake, the Lubrecht Experimental Forest, and the Bureau of Business and Economic Research.

Aside from the cultural, sports, and entertainment benefits supplied by the university, UM delivers a built-in clientele to the city's constellation of bookstores,

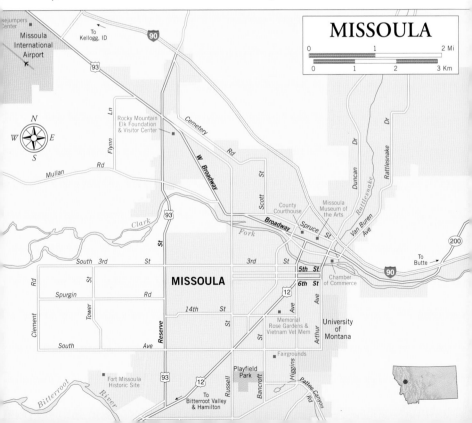

The annual Bobcat-Grizzly football game between Montana State University and the University of Montana dates back to 1897.

music stores, art galleries, restaurants, and food markets. Downtown Missoula has risen to the challenge of shopping malls, franchises, and fast-food restaurants by creating an appealing commercial district, complete with its inviting riverfront park and a farmers market that confirms its standing as Montana's "Garden City." Downtown Missoula is a place where people still practice the leisurely art of browsing as they drift from coffeeshop to bookstore to bakery, gathering up fresh herbs and spices, croissants, and imported cheeses along the way. Except for a few days in winter, when warm air aloft creates a temperature inversion and traps smog and wood smoke in the valley, Missoula's urban environment is as inviting as its natural setting.

◆ MISSOULA ART AND CULTURE

Readings and writing seminars are regular fare in and around Missoula. So are the live performances and exhibits of dozens of performing artists, musicians, dancers, painters, sculptors, potters, and crafters. Missoula is a town—perhaps the only one in Montana—where day in and day out, the mike is on and the curtain is up.

The campus of the University of Montana in Missoula.

MISSOULA AND
BITTERROOT COUNTRY

JEANNETTE RANKIN: ACTIVIST FOR PEACE

As the home of Montana's leading liberal arts university, Missoula attracts and nurtures political activists. But the city's most famous pacifist pre-dates the university, and even statehood. Born in 1880 on a ranch outside of Missoula, Jeannette Rankin became the first woman elected to the U.S. House of Representatives and the only member of Congress to vote against U.S. entry into both world wars. A progressive Republican, Rankin came to the peace movement through her involvement in the campaign for woman suffrage. As she worked on a variety of issues to benefit women and children, she became convinced that the quest for peace also belonged in the suffrage movement.

Rankin launched her political career in 1911, when she urged the Montana Legislature to grant women the right to vote. In 1916, she won her first campaign for Congress on a platform calling for woman suffrage, protective legislation for children, prohibition, and peace. After casting her first antiwar vote in April, 1917— five days after being introduced in Congress as its first female member— she said, "I have always felt that there was more significance in the fact that the first woman who was ever asked what she thought about war said NO and I believe that the first

Jeannette Rankin speaking in Washington, D.C., before proceeding to the Capitol to be installed as the first woman member of Congress, 1917. (Montana Historical Society)

vote I had was the most significant vote and a most significant act on the part of women, because women are going to have to stop war."

On that vote, she had the support of 56 other members of Congress. Twenty-four years later, after her re-election to Congress, Rankin stood alone in her opposition to war. On December 8, 1941, the day after Pearl Harbor, she cast the lone vote against U.S. entry into World War II. Asked to justify her unpopular position, she replied, "A just nation never votes unanimously for war." It was her political undoing. Defeated in her 1942 re-election bid, Rankin carried on her crusade through public appearances and antiwar statements. In 1968, the Vietnam War coalesced a group of women who marched on Washington under the banner of the Jeannette Rankin Brigade. In 1972, a year before her death, Ralph Nader noted, "If aging is the erosion of one's ideals, then Jeannette Rankin is young forever."

Statues of Montana's most outspoken feminist and pacifist stand today in both the U.S. Capitol and the State Capitol in Helena. Her ideals still inspire activists at Missoula's Jeannette Rankin Peace Resource Center.

Performing Arts

Missoula is the home of the **Montana Repertory Theatre**—a first-rate regional touring company. The **Missoula Children's Theatre** is the largest touring children's theater in America; they perform and host kids acting workshops for much of the year. *Visit www.mctinc.org, or call 406-728-1911.*

Also recommended are the String Orchestra **of the Rockies;** the **Garden City Ballet Company;** and other university and community music and drama groups.

On Wednesdays in summer, a few thousand Missoulians gather downtown at Caras Park for the city's **"Out to Lunch"** series of music and theater performances.

Museums

The Historical Museum at Fort Missoula provides a glimpse of the area's history.

Western and wildlife art, the staple of most Montana galleries, is underplayed in Missoula, where contemporary art is refreshingly "in." A former resident novelist accurately described Missoula as "a forgiving, liberal town in a conservative state." Over a half-dozen art galleries and the **Missoula Museum of the Arts** exhibit works of local and regional artists.

International Wildlife Film Festival

Every April, the world's top wildlife films are screened and judged at the week-long **International Wildlife Film Festival,** whose mission it is to increase public awareness of wildlife and habitat through outstanding films and visual media. Winners of the film competition are showcased at open screenings; panel discussions, film-making intensive, and various contests are also open to the public. Kids can participate in a parade or check out interactive wildlife displays. *For information, call 406-728-9380 or visit www.wildlifefilms.org.*

AUTHOR'S FAVORITE MISSOULA LODGING AND RESTAURANTS

Lodging

Goldsmith's Inn B&B.
809 East Front St.; 406-721-6732
Lovely rooms on the Clark Fork River, near town and university. Next door is a fabulous ice cream parlor/restaurant.

Greenough B&B.
631 Stevens Ave.; 406-728-3626
Handsome home on the National Registry of Historic Places with three guestrooms all with private baths.

Restaurants

Bernice's Bakery.
190 South Third St.; 406-728-1358
Missoulians gather here to eat baked delights, guzzle coffee, read the paper, and socialize while lounging on the outdoor patio. Great lunches, too.

Black Dog Cafe.
138 West Broadway; 406-542-1138
Tasty health food; great salad dressings. Very organic; very affordable.

Chinook.
420 South Orange St.; 406-728-6250
French bistro-inspired cuisine with a contemporary Northwest flair served in a cool, elegant-yet-casual atmosphere.

Hob Nob Cafe.
808 East Main St. (beyond the bar at the Union Hall); 406-542-3188 **$**
Try Marianne's great cooking and original menu. Funky atmosphere, great location, and heavenly breakfasts.

Mustard Seed.
419 West Front St.; 406-728-7825
"Fireworks Chicken" and "Tsing-Tsing Tofu" are just two selections on this original Asian menu. Fresh ingredients, light sauces, and reliably good. Great take-out.

Perugia.
1106 West Broadway; 406-543-3757
Old World cuisine prepared by a Syrian who was born to cook. This dining experience is not to be hurried.

The Shack.
222 West Main St.; 406-549-9903
One of Missoula's favorite breakfast places, beloved for its omelets, hotcakes, and "browns." Lunch and dinner are served, too.

Worden's Deli.
451 North Higgins Ave.;
406-549-1293
When you're on the fly, stop at Worden's for an array of amazingly delicious sandwiches, including tasty veggie selections; 700 wine labels and a different beer for every day of the year.

Zimorino Bros. Red Pies over Montana.
424 North Higgins Ave.;
406-549-7434
Thick-crust pizza, spaghetti, ravioli, lasagna, and Italian sausage, all homemade. Great service and good wines.

◆ Missoula Outdoors

There may be plenty happening on the cultural front—but a new stage production or concert probably wouldn't a fall hunting trip, or sell out as quickly as a Lady Griz basketball game or the annual Bobcat-Grizzly football game (one of the nation's oldest intercollegiate rivalries, reenacted alternately on the UM campus in Missoula and the msu campus in Bozeman). Even though many eastern Montanans discount it as "that liberal college town" on the state's western fringe, Missoula is still in Montana. And Montana priorities are firmly in place here.

Missoula is constantly abuzz with fit and active people, and as you drive around town you'll notice vehicles topped with all manner of gear essential to the Missoulian outdoor lifestyle: bikes, skis, kayaks, and rafts. Surrounded by national forests, mountains, and rivers, locals either inherit or quickly acquire a love of woods and water. Those who lack the time or ability to hike, hunt, bike, fish, or float can enjoy Missoula's addictive environment at one of Montana's most attractive urban parks, which stretches along the Clark Fork River as it passes through downtown Missoula on its way to the Pacific Ocean. Or they can hike the "M" trail that winds up Mount Sentinel behind the university, offering as incentive a panoramic view of the town below. Almost as convenient as the park and the "M" trail is the **Rattlesnake National Recreation Area and Wilderness,** a 61,000-acre preserve of hiking and mountain biking trails, rocky peaks, and lake-filled basins that lies literally in Missoula's backyard, with trailheads just a mile north of town.

Also based in town are the **Rocky Mountain Elk Foundation**, one of the nation's fastest-growing wildlife conservation organizations; **Adventure Cycling**, America's bike-touring headquarters; and a handful of well-stocked fishing, camping, climbing, rafting, and all-around outdoor stores.

As Northern Region headquarters for the U.S. Forest Service, Missoula has always been tied to the wood-products industry and the forestry profession. One of the university's strongest programs is its forestry school, which supplies the agency with many of its pros. Missoula is also the home of the **Smokejumper Visitor Center and Aerial Fire Depot,** the oldest and largest of its kind in the nation. Stationed west of town near the airport, this is one of the U.S. Forest Service's nerve centers during the summer firefighting season, generally July through mid-September. Visitors can tour the center during the summer and view the action as retardant-filled planes squat for refueling and smokejumpers fuss with their parachutes and wait for the call that will signal their next mission. Photos, murals, and videos further illustrate the highly technical business of fighting fires from the sky, and the unusual history of firefighting. *US 93 just north of town; 406-329-4934.*

NORTHWEST MONTANA
AND THE FLATHEAD

Map pages 248-249
Glacier Nat'l Park
Kalispell

IF MONTANA HAS A DESTINATION RESORT AREA, this is it. Bordered by wilderness, encircled by mountains, watered generously by lakes and rivers, and soothed by a Pacific Northwest climate, the Flathead Valley attracts a lot of guests. Art galleries, championship golf courses, ski resorts, whitewater sailing, skiing, and whitewater rafting are the industry of the Flathead. The raw materials are Flathead Lake and a stockpile of nationally protected recreational resources: Glacier National Park; the adjacent Bob Marshall Wilderness; the National Bison Range; Jewel Basin Hiking Area; Mission Mountains Wilderness; and Flathead National Wild and Scenic River. Add the Big Mountain ski resort and a chain of lakes called the Seeley Swan, and you have a year-round playground of immense proportions.

Summer is the high season here. Visitors cluster on beaches and mingle at resorts, marinas, and yacht clubs. They clog the parking lots and gift shops at Glacier Park. Local businesses cater to a growing nonresident market with fine wines and the cuisine of schooled chefs. But come September, after the crowds have subsided, residents take back their beloved Flathead and preoccupy themselves with the same concerns of other Montanans: squeezing in as many fishing trips as possible before hunting season begins and making ends meet in an area that supports few large employers. Outside of the service and forest industries and a highly successful technology manufacturer based in Kalispell, residents find work on family farms and ranches or in their own creative genius.

The rural lifestyle and natural beauty of the Flathead Valley have drawn a disproportionately large number of painters, sculptors, ceramicists, and artisans to the area. Their work can be seen at studios, galleries, and art fair exhibits throughout the valley, particularly in the Bigfork and Kalispell areas.

What little land is not textured by mountains and managed by the federal government as national forest is cultivated in crops peculiar to the climate and soil of the Flathead Valley, like peppermint, Christmas trees, cherries, and champagne grapes. West of the Continental Divide, copious precipitation enables that area's profitable yields of barley, wheat, oats, hay, and seed potatoes.

■ FLATHEAD LAKE   *map page 248, C-3*

The heart of Flathead Valley is a shimmering expanse of water stretching nearly 30 miles from Bigfork and Somers on the north to Polson on the south. The West's largest natural, freshwater lake, Flathead Lake not only governs the climate of this northern valley, but also facilitates a mini-economy unique in Montana and by extension dictates in part the disposition of all who choose dwell here.

Until recently, Flathead Lake was perhaps most famous for its cherry orchards. The moderating influence of the lake creates a micro-climate conducive to the commercial production of some of the nation's plumpest, sweetest cherries. Mile upon mile of orchards formed a fragrant boulevard of blossoms along the lake's east shore each spring, followed by summer's festive harvest.

But in 1989, orchardists around the lake were reminded that they, like the rest of Montana's farmers and ranchers, should know that the weather is not to be trusted. On February 1, a brutal, record-breaking cold snap sent temperatures plummeting 53 degrees in 24 hours, flash-freezing trees and destroying the valley's cherry industry. Since that year, some growers have replanted their orchards, but it will be several years before production reaches pre-1989 levels. Other growers are experimenting with apples, pears, peaches, and apricots. But the fruit that's getting the most attention grows in a vineyard on the lake's west shore, near Dayton.

◆ MISSION MOUNTAIN WINERY

A recent addition to the producers whose exotic crops distinguish the Flathead Valley from the grain and livestock mainstays of central and eastern Montana, Mission Mountain Winery grows pinot noir grapes that are bottled as a pale, ruby champagne. The pinots thrive on the Flathead's long, hot days and cool nights, but to survive in Montana, their vines must be buried in soil over the winter. Mission Mountain also bottles a white riesling, chardonnay, muscat canelli, and Johannisberg riesling, using grapes that are grown in the Yakima Valley of Washington. The tasting room is open daily from early May to late October. *In Dayton off US 93 on the lakeshore; call 406-849-5524.*

◆ SAILING AND FISHING FLATHEAD LAKE

Flathead Lake supports Montana's largest sailing community, as well as sizeable fleets of motor craft and charter fishing boats. The lake is a favorite among fishermen who enjoy the needle-in-the-haystack approach to fishing—that is, searching out large trout in deep lakes. Flathead is unrivaled in Montana as a prime fishery for trophy mackinaw, or lake trout. Because of the lake's size and depth, fishing on Flathead takes on the appearance of an ocean expedition. Serious anglers arm themselves with steel line and saltwater rods, and probe this inland sea at depths of 130 feet from large boats fitted for downriggers. For visitors who would like to try their luck at catching a 20-pound Mac, there are several guides on the lake, plus boat rentals, tackle shops, and marinas in lakeshore communities. Visitors who don't need to fish to enjoy a beautiful lake can choose from several boat tours.

Far West. Daily excursions on Flathead Lake in a 64-foot ship, departing from Somers on the north shore of the lake. 406-857-3203

Port Polson Princess. Daily cruises on the south end of Flathead Lake aboard a 41-foot tour boat departing from Polson. 406-883-2448 *(operated by Best Western Motel)*

Questa. Daily sailing excursions on Flathead Lake in a 51-foot racing sloop departing from Flathead Lake Lodge, Bigfork; 406-837-5569

In addition to several private campgrounds and resorts, there are six state parks with camping facilities and boat launches around the lake. A seventh state park, **Wildhorse Island,** sprawls across the southwest arm of Flathead Lake. Accessible only by boat, the island shelters about a hundred bighorn sheep, along with a variety

The heart of Flathead Valley lies in the shimmering expanse of Flathead Lake, largest natural freshwater lake in the West. Crimson sunsets like this were common during the summer of 2000, when wild fires burned nearly one million acres accross the state.

NORTHWEST MONTANA
AND THE FLATHEAD

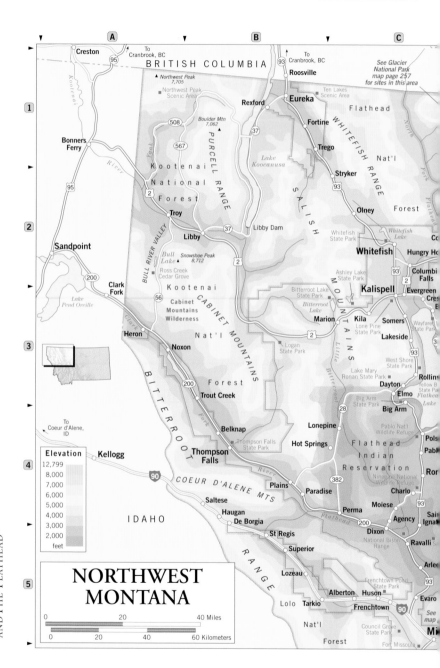

A   **B**   **C**

Creston
To Cranbrook, BC
95

BRITISH COLUMBIA

To Cranbrook, BC
93
Roosville

See Glacier National Park map page 257 for sites in this area

Northwest Peak 7,705
Northwest Peak Scenic Area

Rexford

Eureka

Ten Lakes Scenic Area

Flathead

1

Boulder Mtn 7,062
508

567

Fortine

Trego

Bonners Ferry

Kootenai

PURCELL RANGE

Lake Koocanusa

37

WHITEFISH RANGE

Nat'l

95

River

National

2

Stryker

93

Forest

Troy

Forest

Olney

Whitefish Lake

Flathead

2

BULL RIVER VALLEY

Libby

37

Libby Dam

SALISH

Whitefish State Park

Whitefish

Co

Sandpoint

200

Bull Lake

Snowshoe Peak 8,712

2

Libby Dam

Hungry Ho

Clark Fork

Ross Creek Cedar Grove

Kootenai

56

Ashley Lake State Park

Columbi Falls

Kalispell

Evergreen

Lake Pend Oreille

Cabinet Mountains Wilderness

CABINET MOUNTAINS

Bitterroot Lake State Park
Bitterroot Lake

MOUNTAINS

Cres

3

Heron

Nat'l

Marion

Kila

Somers

Lone Pine State Park

Lakeside

Noxon

Logan State Park

West Shore State Park

Rollins

Forest

Lake Mary Ronan State Park

Dayton

Elmo

Yellow B State Pa
Flathea Lake

200

Trout Creek

Big Arm State Park

28

Big Arm

To Coeur d'Alene, ID

BITTERROOT

Belknap

Thompson Falls State Park

Lonepine

Pablo Nat'l Wildlife Refuge

Pols

Elevation
12,799
8,000
7,000
6,000
5,000
4,000
3,000
2,000
feet

Kellogg

Thompson Falls

Hot Springs

Flathead

Indian

Pabl

4

90

COEUR D'ALENE MTS

Fork

River

Plains

Reservation

382

Ninepipe Nat'l Wildlife Refuge

Ror

Saltese

Paradise

Perma

Charlo

Moiese

93

IDAHO

Haugan

De Borgia

St Regis

Flathead

200

Dixon

Agency

Sai Igna

NORTHWEST MONTANA

Superior

National Bison Range

Ravalli

Lozeau

Frenchtown Pond State Park

Arle

5

Lolo

Tarkio

Alberton

Huson

Frenchtown

93

Evaro

RANGE

90

See map

Mi

Nat'l

Council Grove State Park

0   20   40 Miles

0   20   40   60 Kilometers

Forest

Fort Missoula

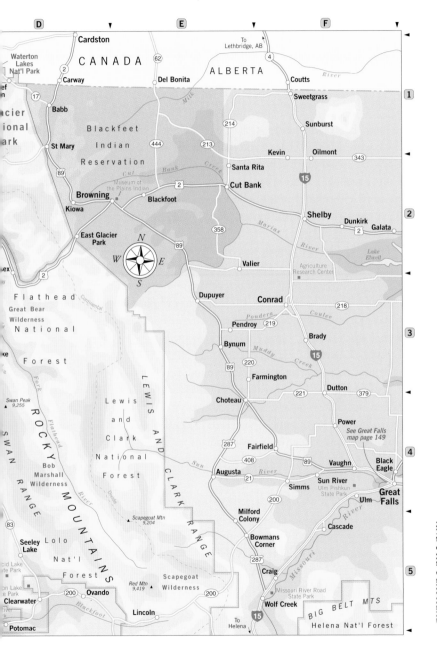

of other mammals and birds. Positioned within the boundaries of the Flathead Indian Reservation, the island was once used by Salish and Kootenai Indians as a hiding place for their horses when they were threatened by Blackfeet horse-raiding parties. Horses that were never retrieved gave the island its name.

■ KALISPELL   *map page 248, C-3*

With more than 14,000 residents, the city of Kalispell is as urban as it gets in this valley. Founded in 1891 along the main line of the Great Northern Railway, Kalispell has served northwestern Montana as a transport and trade center ever since. Its patriarch, Charles Conrad, was a pioneer entrepreneur who arrived in Montana on a Missouri River steamboat after losing his Virginia plantation during the Civil War. He rebuilt his fortune in the freighting business at Fort Benton, then moved to the Flathead Valley. In forming the Kalispell Townsite Company, he reserved 72 acres for himself and built a three-story, 23-room, Norman-style mansion, said to be the best example of luxurious, turn-of-the-century architecture in the Pacific Northwest. The **Conrad Mansion** remained in the Conrad family until they gave it to the city in 1975, and is open daily for guided tours from mid-May to mid-October. *Woodland between Third and Fourth; 406-755-2166.*

Several other historic homes grace the tree-lined residential neighborhoods of "old" Kalispell. Beyond these dignified roots, Kalispell has branched and sprawled into a typical small city that serves the surrounding valley with a revitalized downtown commercial district, convention facilities, a community college, airport, and numerous restaurants, motels, and art galleries. While Kalispell serves the functional needs of the valley, some of the Flathead's smaller communities better reflect the distinctive lifestyle enjoyed by area residents.

■ WHITEFISH   *map page 248, C-3*

This sports-loving town—nestled between the shores of Whitefish Lake and the base of Montana's largest ski resort, and just a short drive from Glacier Park, blue-ribbon trout streams, and miles upon miles of hiking and mountain biking trails —can convincingly back up its claim to be Montana's recreation capital. In summer, its 5,800 residents celebrate their place on Earth with canoe races, regattas, mountain bike and microbrew festivals, and Olympic-style summer games. In winter, snow-sport enthusiasts come to schuss the sloops of The Big Mountain resort, or pilot XC skis and snowmobiles across the frozen landscape. In January, they throw one of Montana's most festive parties: the Whitefish Winter Carnival.

■ COLUMBIA FALLS AND POLEBRIDGE   *map page 257, A-5 and A-3*

The timber products industry and the Columbia Falls Aluminum Plant are the major employers in Columbia Falls. Nearly as important as the paychecks they provide are the recreational benefits of living within minutes of Glacier Park, the North Fork of the Flathead River, 34-mile-long Hungry Horse Reservoir, and the Great Bear and Bob Marshall Wilderness Areas.

One of the most distinctive communities in this region is Polebridge, halfway up the gravel road that lines the western edge of Glacier Park. Consisting of a historic general store known as the Polebridge Merc, along with a hostel, café, saloon, and ranger station, Polebridge is the social center of the scattered North Fork community. Deep in logging country, the independent thinkers of Polebridge are among Montana's most outspoken proponents of wilderness protection. Typical of the Polebridge spirit is the sign outside the Northern Lights Café announcing "this business is supported by people from all walks of life." If you need to make a phone call while exploring the remote reaches of the North Fork of the Flathead, this is the place to do it. The Merc has the only public telephone in these parts, and it's a busy one.

■ BIGFORK   *map page 248, C-3*

Lying less than 60 miles south but feeling lightyears away is the picture-perfect village of Bigfork, overlooking Flathead Lake from a sheltered bay at the mouth of the Swan River. Influenced by the climate of the Pacific Northwest, winters are long and gray here and elsewhere in the Flathead Valley. But when the sun comes out of hibernation, Bigfork blossoms like the potted geraniums and petunias that line its main street and the sweet peas that grow wild in the draws and gullies at its outskirts.

With a year-round population of roughly 1,400, Bigfork swells in summer to accommodate the many visitors who come to enjoy its art galleries, live theater, sidewalk cafés, restaurants, resorts, golf courses, and genteel ambiance. Well known as one of Montana's leading fine arts communities, Bigfork also nurtures the performing arts at its new, million-dollar **Bigfork Summer Playhouse**. It is no wonder that urban refugees from San Francisco, Los Angeles, and elsewhere have settled in the so-called "village by the bay." Bright red barns stand out against the towering blue mountains of the Swan Range; cows graze on steep hillsides; neat rows of junior Scotch pine stretch for miles at Christmas-tree farms throughout the valley. Bigfork is the good life, Montana-style.

■ POLSON   *map page 248, C-4*

At the opposite end of Flathead Lake, Polson is a community of about 4,300 that reaches back to 1840, making it the first settlement on the lake. It is fitting that the community was named after pioneer rancher David Polson, who was also a fine fiddler. Every summer, in late July, Polson hosts the state's biggest fiddling contest when members of the Montana Oldtime Fiddlers Association come to town. All of Polson is a stage, as contestants—ranging in age from six to 90—tune up at various campsites around town. Formal competition takes place inside the middle-school gymnasium. Other attractions, besides the lake and the water-based lifestyle it supports, are the nearby Flathead River and one of the valley's oldest and loveliest lakeshore golf courses.

■ FLATHEAD INDIAN RESERVATION   *map page 248, C-4*

Polson is the largest city on the 1.2-million-acre Flathead Indian Reservation, which takes in the southern half of Flathead Lake and stretches south nearly to Missoula. This is the only Indian reservation in Montana west of the Continental Divide. Unlike the Plains Indians living on Montana's six other reservations, the Salish and Kootenai tribes of the Flathead Reservation are the descendants of a coastal culture. Together, the tribes are known as the Flathead Indians—a name whose origins are unclear. Some say that Lewis and Clark gave the Flatheads their name, but there is no evidence that these Indians ever adopted the practice of flattening their children's heads as some of the coastal tribes farther west are believed to have done. Before the arrival of non-native explorers, the Flathead moved freely throughout the Bitterroot and Flathead Valleys, with frequent forays east of the Rockies to hunt buffalo. Whatever its beginnings, the name Flathead carried over to many of the land forms in this area.

Intrigued by stories of Catholic missionaries—tales that had drifted West probably via some Iroquois Indians who'd visited in the 1830s—the Flatheads sent east for "Black Robes," thus bringing Roman Catholicism to Montana. One of the most historic monuments to the church's early development is the mission at St. Ignatius. Set against the magnificent backdrop of the Mission Range, the **St. Ignatius Mission** was established in 1854 by the Jesuits after they abandoned their original mission in the Bitterroot Valley. The new mission began as a simple wooden chapel, cabin, blacksmith, and carpentry shop. The imposing brick church that stands today was built a century ago and includes a number of spectacular murals depicting biblical history, painted by Brother Joseph Carignano. It is the oldest continuously operating mission in Montana and remains one of the Flathead Valley's most prominent landmarks.

In 1855, the Flatheads signed what came to be known as the Hellgate Treaty, which established the current reservation in the Jocko River Valley, north of Missoula. The treaty also promised a reservation in the Bitterroot Valley, but growing pressure from white settlers forced its residents onto the Jocko reservation in 1891. Loss of aboriginal lands in the Bitterroot Valley did not signal the end of encroachment by the U.S. government. In 1887, Congress passed legislation allowing the federal government to partition tribal holdings into 80- and 160-acre parcels. The effect was to destroy the Indians' communal way of life and force them to become individual farmers. With the natives each allotted their piece of land, remaining lands were deemed "surplus," and opened to non-native settlers. In the case of the Flathead Reservation, the Allotment Act was especially damaging to the Indians' land base because of the reservation's agricultural potential. Under the act, just over half of the land was opened to homesteading. As a result, the Flathead Reservation has a much larger non-Indian population than Montana's other reservations; in fact, the Salish and Kootenai Indians who live here are a minority within their own reservation. Of the nearly 21,000 people living on the reservation, fewer than one-fifth are enrolled members of the tribe. Because of the loss of so much of their land to homesteaders, the Salish and Kootenai tribes have been aggressive in controlling ownership of their remaining tribal lands, which include a rich body of timber and agricultural lands. In addition, they receive sizeable rent payments from the Montana Power Company for the operation of Kerr Dam near Polson. Of all seven Montana Indian reservations, the Flathead is wealthiest in terms of natural resources.

Bordered on the east by the imperial Mission Range and watered by Flathead Lake, the Flathead and Jocko rivers, the reservation is also rich in scenic and recreational assets, including the nation's first tribally established and managed wilderness. The **Mission Mountains Tribal Wilderness** is an 89,500-acre tract of airy peaks and alpine lakes that provide Flathead Indians with an important link to their ancestral heritage. It adjoins another 74,000-acre parcel managed by the Flathead National Forest as the **Mission Mountains Wilderness.** While these rugged lands are managed cooperatively, there are differences in management practices. Hunting in the tribal wilderness is reserved for tribal members only, and each summer a 12,000-acre portion of the tribal wilderness near 9,820-foot McDonald

Peak is closed to protect an estimated 25 grizzly bears that come to feed on cyclical swarms of ladybugs and cutworm moths. To help finance management of the wilderness, the tribe sells use permits to non-tribal members for a small fee. Permittees are entitled to hike, fish, and camp on tribal wilderness lands. No special permits are required for these activities on the federally designated wilderness, which lies east of the crest of the Mission Range.

The Flathead Reservation also encompasses an important piece of Western Americana—the **National Bison Range**—as well the Ninepipe and Pablo national waterfowl refuges. Established in 1908 with the progeny of bison that survived the mass extermination of buffalo from the plains in the previous century, the National Bison Range now supports a sizeable herd of 400 to 500 bison on 19,000 acres of natural grassland. Visitors can expect to see bison, as well as pronghorn, elk, deer, and bighorn sheep along an auto tour route that takes in sweeping views of the Mission Range. Newborn bison calves steal the show here in spring; in early October, visitors can witness the drama of an authentic buffalo roundup, when cowboy rangers thin the herd. Range headquarters are at Moiese, west of US 93, at the south end of the reservation.

Less dramatic but no less significant is the **Ninepipe National Wildlife Refuge** between St. Ignatius and Ronan. Hundreds of glacial potholes and a large reservoir sustain more than 180 species of birds in this watery environment. Cormorants, herons, gulls, shorebirds, bald eagles, and pheasants round out the roster of birds, primarily waterfowl, that nest and rest here. A few miles north, between Pablo and Polson, the **Pablo National Wildlife Refuge** provides additional wetlands. Spring migration peaks from late March to early May, and fall populations approach 200,000 birds.

■ GLACIER NATIONAL PARK *map page 257*

The entire Glacier Park/Bob Marshall/Seeley Swan wild realm covers about three million largely unpopulated acres of adjoining public lands, an area roughly the size of Connecticut. The undisputed centerpiece is Glacier National Park, which crowns the North American continent with 1,500 square miles of exquisite ice-carved terrain. Here, serrated ridges and horn-shaped peaks reign over a jumble of

Sunrise highlights the mountains surrounding St. Mary's Lake in Glacier National Park.

turquoise lakes, waterfalls, cascades, river valleys, hanging gardens, and alpine meadows. Born of geologic and glacial violence, this random landscape couldn't be more perfect had it been designed and executed by Michelangelo. Like the ocean, its sheer scope has a way of putting humanity in its place. People are merely visitors here, unable to meet the rigors of a severe northern climate.

Harsh as it is in winter, Glacier Park is on its best behavior during the summer months. Each year, about 1.7 million pilgrims journey to this place still held sacred by Blackfeet Indians, whose reservation forms the park's eastern border. Travelers come from throughout the world to hike its trails, drive its magnificent **Going-to-the-Sun** highway—the park's amazing east-west route—or simply to drink in the pristine beauty of one of America's largest intact wild areas. Visitors commonly see mountain goats from roadside turnouts, and need take only a short hike to see bighorn sheep, white-tailed ptarmigan, and many of the other birds and mammals that live here. More than a thousand species of plants, many of them hardy alpine wildflowers, embroider the park in dazzling primary colors and pastels as they follow spring up the mountains all summer long.

NORTHWEST MONTANA AND THE FLATHEAD

One of Glacier Park's most popular views is of St. Mary's Lake and Wild Goose Island.

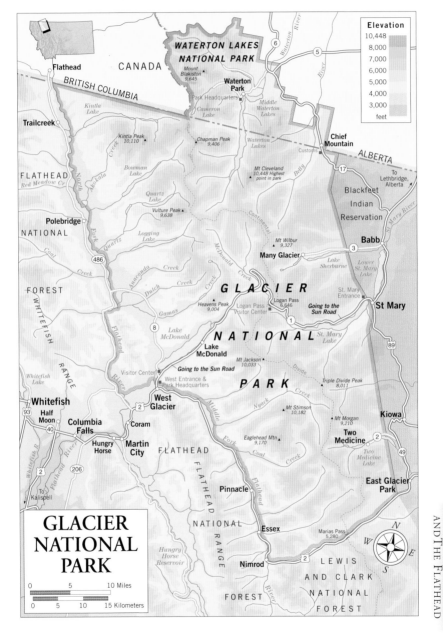

Elevation
10,448
8,000
7,000
6,000
5,000
4,000
3,000
feet

WATERTON LAKES NATIONAL PARK

CANADA

Flathead

BRITISH COLUMBIA

Mount Blakiston 9,645

Waterton Park

Park Headquarters

Cameron Lake

Middle Waterton Lakes

Chief Mountain

ALBERTA

Customs

To Lethbridge, Alberta

Trailcreek

Kintla Lake

FLATHEAD
Red Meadow Cr.

Kintla Peak 10,110

Chapman Peak 9,406

Waterton Lakes

Mt Cleveland 10,448 Highest point in park

Bowman Lake

Quartz Lake

Blackfeet

Indian

Reservation

Babb

Polebridge

Vulture Peak 9,638

NATIONAL

486

Logging Lake

Mt Wilbur 9,327

Many Glacier

Lake Sherburne

Lower St. Mary Lake

3

FOREST

WHITEFISH

GLACIER

Heavens Peak 9,004

Logan Pass Visitor Center

Logan Pass 6,646

St. Mary Entrance

Going to the Sun Road

St Mary

8

Lake McDonald

NATIONAL

St. Mary Lake

89

RANGE

Whitefish Lake

Visitor Center

Lake McDonald

Going to the Sun Road

Mt Jackson 10,033

PARK

Triple Divide Peak 8,011

Whitefish

West Entrance & Park Headquarters

West Glacier

Middle

Nyack

Mt Stimson 10,182

Mt Morgan 9,210

Kiowa

93

Half Moon

Columbia Falls

Coram

Two Medicine

2

40

Hungry Horse

Martin City

FLATHEAD

Eaglehead Mtn. 9,170

Two Medicine Lake

49

2

206

Fork

Coal

East Glacier Park

To Kalispell

Pinnacle

FLATHEAD

Creek

GLACIER
NATIONAL
PARK

NATIONAL

Essex

Marias Pass 5,280

LEWIS

0 5 10 Miles
0 5 10 15 Kilometers

Hungry Horse Reservoir

RANGE

Nimrod

2

AND CLARK

NATIONAL

FOREST

FOREST

THE CONTINENTAL DIVIDE

Known among the West's native peoples as the "backbone of the world," the Continental Divide runs along the crests of the Rocky Mountains from Canada to Mexico, literally dividing the waters of the North American continent. In Montana, it zigzags across the Rockies, entering the state from the north at Glacier National Park and exiting in Yellowstone National Park on the state's southern border. Waters running west of the Great Divide feed the Columbia River and drain into the Pacific Ocean; waters flowing east fill the Missouri-Mississippi Basin and drain into the Gulf of Mexico. And from one point in Montana—Glacier Park's Triple Divide Peak—water also flows north to Hudson Bay, making Montana the only state that replenishes three oceans.

While the image of the Continental Divide suggests a distinct, knife-like ridge that neatly splits the Atlantic and the Pacific, the topography varies greatly. On prominent peaks and ridges you can actually see the waters of two oceans dividing at your feet, but at other places along the divide it is hard to even pinpoint the ridge as it meanders across broad plateaus. Sometimes obvious, sometimes obscure, the Continental Divide is Montana's single most important topographical feature. More importantly, it is the birthplace of the nation's waterways.

HIKING THE DIVIDE

The **Continental Divide National Scenic Trail** was established by Congress in 1968, making this lofty spine accessible to hikers, horseback riders, and in some cases, motorized travelers. Roughly 800 miles of the entire 3,100-mile-long trail lie along or near the ridgetops of Montana's Rocky Mountains. Passing through some of North America's most scenic backcountry, the trail crosses Glacier and Yellowstone national parks, in addition to 10 national forests with designated wilderness areas, including the Bob Marshall, Great Bear, Scapegoat, and Anaconda Pintler. Historic attractions along the trail include several ghost towns and two mountain passes crossed by Lewis and Clark on their 1804–06 search for an inland water route to the Pacific Ocean. In southwestern Montana, the trail passes high above Big Hole National Battlefield, site of the 1877 clash between the U.S. Army and the Nez Perce Indians, and Red Rock Lakes National Wildlife Refuge, a national sanctuary for trumpeter swans.

The trail has yet to be fully constructed and marked in Montana. Temporary routes have been established pending completion of the final route. Anyone considering a Continental Divide trek should contact the U.S. Forest Service before setting out.

With more than 730 miles of trails in Glacier, there are at least five lifetimes of memorable hikes in this national park. They range from day hikes into secluded lakes and living glaciers to extended treks across snowfields and cloud-covered mountain passes. One popular day hike in the west side of the park takes visitors from McDonald Lake to Avalanche Lake; another farther east leads to Hidden Lake from the Logan Pass Visitor Center atop the Continental Divide. The landscape of Glacier will leave a lasting imprint on the minds and in the hearts of visitors who absorb its vistas in a way that only hiking allows.

♦ Going-to-the-Sun Road

This serpentine, 52-mile-long road quickens the hearts of motorists as it climbs more than 3,000 feet from lush, lake-lined valley floors on either side of the park to its windswept summit at Logan Pass on the Continental Divide. Along the way, it sidesteps gushing waterfalls, winds through glaciated valleys, and traverses an imposing, knife-like ridge called the Garden Wall before topping out at just over 6,600 feet above sea level. Begun in 1916 and completed in 1932, the "Sun" road is an engineering masterpiece that deserves the attention of unhurried motorists.

In direct competition with the Canadian Pacific Railway, which was promoting Banff National Park in Alberta, and the Northern Pacific in Yellowstone National

continues page 262

Many of Glacier's historic chalets no longer exist. However, the park still has magnificent, rugged lodges, plus inns and campgrounds. (courtesy, Montana Historical Society)

LODGING NEAR GLACIER NATIONAL PARK

Columbia Falls

Bad Rock Country B&B.
4 mi. south of town off Hwy. 206;
888-892-2829
Guestrooms in the main house and in four rustic-yet-modern log cabins complete with pine furniture and fireplaces. Hot tub, bucolic setting, gracious hosts, and breakfast fit for a king—One of Montana's best.

Plum Creek House B&B.
985 Vans Ave.; 800-682-1429
Posh fully equipped rooms overlooking the Flathead River with views of Glacier National Park; hearty farm breakfasts.

Essex

Izaak Walton Inn.
US 2; 406-888-5700
Historic inn near Glacier National Park specializing in cross-country skiing; dining car restaurant.

Glacier Park/West Glacier

Glacier Park, Inc.
West Glacier, MT 59936;
602-207-6000
The central lodging office for Glacier and Waterton National Parks. Choose from a range of accommodations (and rates) including motor inns, hotels, cabins, and lodges. The popular Many Glacier Hotel and Glacier Park Lodge may also be booked through this office.

Glacier Park Lodge.
West Glacier; 406-226-9311
One of the great park hotels of the West; with high ceilings, magnificent views. The train pulls up to the door.

Glacier Wilderness Resort.
West Glacier; 406-888-5664
Luxury log homes near Glacier Park offering a variety of options.

Mountain Timbers B&B.
West Glacier;
406-387-5830 or 800-841-3835
Beautiful hand-hewn log lodge just seven miles from park. Rustic splendor with modern amenities. Hiking and cross-country skiing trails right out the door.

Polebridge

North Fork Hostel & Square Peg Ranch.
406-888-5241
On the western edge of Glacier National Park. Charming: no electricity, but hot showers and kitchen facilities are available, also canoes and horses for rent. Bring food, towels, flashlight, and sleeping bags.

Whitefish

Bay Point on the Lake.
300 Bay Point Dr.;
406-862-2331 or 888-BAY POINT
Luxury condominiums on Whitefish Lake, near Glacier National Park and The Big Mountain ski area.

Hidden Moose Lodge.
1735 Lakeshore Dr.;
406-862-6516 or 888-733-6667
This elegant alpine-style lodge is warmly appointed with a cozy common area and eight rooms with private baths and decks. Close to town and the slopes.

Bear grass, a common wildflower at Glacier National Park, blooms only once every seven years.

Park, the Great Northern Railway marketed Glacier as the "Switzerland of America," and built hotels and chalets to fulfill the slogan's image. The vaulted ceilings, heavy beams, and pillars of Glacier Park Lodge and Many Glacier Hotel evince the exuberance of an earlier era. Other lodges, cabins, and campgrounds are located throughout the park and are generally open from June to Labor Day, with some remaining open until mid- or late-September. There are additional rooms and campgrounds outside the park.

Adjoining Glacier on the north is Canada's **Waterton Lakes National Park.** In 1932, the governments of Canada and the United States established the world's first international park—**Glacier-Waterton International Peace Park**—to commemorate the friendship and good will between the two nations. Smaller than Glacier, Waterton boasts the same magnificent scenery, activities, and services. The primary route between the two parks is Chief Mountain International Highway along the extreme northeast edge of Glacier. Both the Chief Mountain and Going-to-the-Sun highways are closed to winter travel. Glacier Park officials and area businesses are currently trying to find the least painful way of closing large portions of Going-to-the-Sun during the summer for much-needed repairs.

■ BOB MARSHALL COUNTRY   *map page 249, D/E-3/4/5*

Glacier shares its southern border with a massive wildlife sanctuary and roadless retreat actually consisting of three federally designated wilderness areas: the **Great Bear, Bob Marshall,** and **Scapegoat Wilderness Areas.** The entire 1.5-million-acre expanse is known as Bob Marshall Country in memory of the young forester and adventurer whose vision of preservation led him to found the Wilderness Society more than 50 years ago. Known affectionately by its many friends and visitors simply as the Bob, this is one of America's oldest, largest, and best-known preserves, regarded among foresters and conservationists as the "flagship" of the nation's wilderness fleet.

Encompassing entire river drainages and mountain ranges, 2,400 square miles in all, Bob Marshall Country embodies the spirit of the Wilderness Act of 1964. It is truly a place "where man himself is a visitor who does not remain." Rather, this is the domain of some of North America's largest, most majestic big-game animals. Together with Glacier National Park, the Bob forms a critically important wildlife corridor for the once-dominant, now-threatened grizzly bear. An estimated 250 to 350 of the great bears roam freely throughout this Northern Rockies refuge.

Bighorn sheep graze the eastern slopes of the wilderness, while mountain goats take to higher ground, along the mountain crests. Several elk herds, with animals numbering in the thousands, make the Bob a hallowed place for hunters. More than 50 outfitters work the Bob, guiding clients on fall hunts as well as summer horsepack trips.

The Bob appeals equally to land lovers and to water bugs. Besides hiking, hunting, and horseback riding, there are rapids to be ridden and pools to be probed for cutthroat trout. The South and Middle forks of the Flathead River penetrate the core of the Bob. Together with the North Fork, which flows along the western edge of Glacier National Park, they form the nation's longest wild and scenic river system. The Middle Fork promises some of the most challenging whitewater in Montana, with rapids made immortal by names like "Jaws" and "Screamin' Right-Hand Turn." Several rafting companies in the Flathead offer guided trips ranging from half-day whitewater trips and evening dinner floats to extended camp-float, fly-fishing, and combination horsepack/float trips on wilderness rivers.

A trip to the Bob can be a life-changing experience. Because of its sheer size, you can hike or ride horseback for miles and for days, exploring new country each day and living by your wits with a fishing rod, a map, and a compass. At night, you can explore the mysteries of the universe beneath a starry sky and wonder, with friends around a campfire, what it's all about.

■ SEELEY SWAN VALLEY   *map page 249, D-4*

Lying immediately west of the Bob is an informal wilderness known as the Seeley Swan Valley. Flanked by the imposing walls and peaks of the Mission and Swan mountain ranges, this densely forested valley stretches 90 miles from Clearwater Junction at the intersection of State Highways 200 and 83, into the heart of the Flathead Valley at Bigfork. Montana State Highway 83, the so-called **Seeley Swan Highway,** is a scenic alternative to the Flathead's more heavily traveled US 93.

Along the floor of the Seeley Swan, the Clearwater and Swan Rivers link a chain of lakes that mirror snow-capped peaks and thick stands of larch, fir, aspen, and birch. When the valley fills up with snow and the lakes glaze over with ice, the boaters, campers, and canoeists of summer give way to ice fishermen, snowmobilers, and cross-country skiers. Year-round, this quiet land of mountains and rivers

(following pages) Looking toward Glacier's snow-capped Mount Grinnell from Granite Park Chalet.

and forest-clad lakes provides sanctuary for a diversity of wildlife ranging from the elusive loon to the grizzly bear. White-tailed deer are so abundant they pose a hazard to motorists traveling Montana State Highway 83 in the early morning and at dusk.

The water corridors around Seeley Lake sustain the largest population of nesting common loons in the Western lower 48 states. Loons and a lot more can be seen on the Clearwater Chain-of-Lakes driving tour, which extends about 18 miles from Salmon Lake to Rainy Lake at the south end of Montana State Highway 83. Have the binoculars ready because there are several designated viewing areas just off the highway at Salmon, Seeley, Alva, and Rainy Lakes. North of Seeley Lake, the Clearwater Canoe Trail is an easy, four-mile float through an outdoor auditorium specializing in loon music.

Outside the small communities of Seeley Lake, Condon, and Swan Lake, the valley consists almost entirely of public land. Campgrounds, motels, and rustic resorts dot the larger lakes of the Seeley Swan. Miles of trails take day hikers to picnics beside waterfalls, and backcountry travelers to remote wilderness destinations in the Missions and the Bob Marshall.

■ JEWEL BASIN   *map page 248, C-3*

The Jewel Basin is just that—a peaceful pocket of lakes for hikers only. Visitors limited by time or apprehension about backcountry travel can enjoy a condensed wilderness experience in this special management area of the Flathead National Forest between Kalispell and Hungry Horse Dam. Thirty-five miles of trails connect most of the area's 27 alpine lakes, putting them within a two- to three-hour hike of the parking lot. The view from 7,528-foot-high **Mount Aeneus** has been described as one of the best 360-degree panoramas in western Montana, with sweeping vistas of Glacier Park, the peaks of the Bob Marshall Wilderness, the Swan and the Mission Ranges, as well as the lake-studded interior of the Jewel Basin. Most of the lakes are concentrated on the west side of the basin and hold the promise of pan-size cutthroat and rainbow trout.

Prime time in the Jewel Basin is the same as it is for other mountain treks in Montana—the window of opportunity from July into September, when last winter's snow is gone and next year's has yet to arrive. Visitors are advised that Montana's seasonal window can be slammed shut any month of the year by sudden storms.

■ NORTHWEST CORNER

In all respects but one, northwestern Montana is the antithesis of the Big Open. Perhaps more than any two regions, they represent the physical diversity of the state. Unlike the thirsty, windswept plains of eastern Montana, the northwest woods fill up with snow each winter, yielding roughly double the moisture of the Big Open. In Montana, the difference between 13 and 26 inches is the difference between a ranch economy and a timber economy. Here, the trees grow so thick that there isn't space to graze a cow.

Nearly everyone who explored this region, using the 600-mile-long **Kootenai River** as a highway, had something to say about the dense forests that grew here and their potential value to an expanding frontier. But it was David Thompson, the first non-native explorer to chart these woods and waters, who nailed down the one feature northwestern Montana shares with the Big Open. In his journals, he noted that the area's isolation left its timber "without the possibility of being brought to market."

Railroads eventually made it possible to market the timber, but the area's population still lives a world apart from "mainland" Montana. Not really on the way to anywhere, the Northwest Corner is in Montana but not of it. Residents are oriented not so much to Kalispell, the hub of the nearby Flathead Valley, but to Spokane, Washington, a good 150 miles from Libby, this region's largest community. Like the Big Open, the Northwest Corner remains a remote and undiscovered destination.

But here the similarity ends. To a rancher from the plains, this region's tall, dense forests are cause for anxiety as they close in around him and block his customary 180-degree view of the sky. But to a native of these parts, the deep, dark woods are like a cozy down comforter. To be in their midst is to be snug and secure. These woods are like no other woods in Montana. They are taller, thicker, and far more diversified than the fir and pine forests that grow east of the Rockies. Like the coastal forests to the west, these woods are a fusion of plant species. Cedar, hemlock, pine, fir, larch, and spruce—15 species of conifers in all—grow side by side above a thick understory of shrubs, ferns, berries, and wildflowers.

■ LOGGING

For most of its recorded history, this area has relied on the cyclical fortunes of the timber industry for its economic well-being. Before the turn of the century, settlers were clearing wooded areas and hauling trees to the Kootenai or one of its tributaries, where they awaited massive spring log drives that sent the harvest downriver to mills in Idaho. The arrival of railroads transformed logging from a local practice into an industry, and shortly thereafter the federal government created the National Forest Reserves, forerunner of today's Forest Service, to manage the resource. Besides providing a ready market for railroad ties and bridge timbers, the railroads revitalized local markets by luring more settlers out West, and they opened national markets. They also provided mills with a steady supply of timber, making milling a profitable, year-round enterprise.

Northwest Montana's first sawmill was built in 1889 near Eureka. Since then, millions of logs have been transformed at local mills into billions of board feet of finished lumber, house logs, plywood, pulp, and paper products. Evidence of the logger's trade is everywhere, from the extensive clearcuts and logging roads that scar hillsides to the giant logging trucks that rumble down narrow mountain roads, and the ubiquitous green signs posted outside homes and businesses proclaiming the owner's allegiance to the timber industry.

There is good reason for all those green signs. This industry is in trouble, not just here but in all the timber-producing states. Over-cutting, compounded by a soft market, national concern for endangered species, and protracted debates over wilderness and forest management practices have created a critical shortage of raw timber. In the mills, technology and mechanization have eliminated many good-paying jobs. Today, the mill at Libby has been replaced with a heavily automated plywood plant. While a former editor of Libby's *Western News* proclaimed early in the century that "without question, lumbering is Lincoln County's greatest industry and will continue to be so," the future of northwestern Montana's principal industry is very much in question.

■ MINING

Hardrock mining is another fickle industry in the region. Ever since gold was discovered along Libby Creek in 1860, miners have been lured by the prospect of major deposits in these mountains. By 1900, mining camps had sprung up near

Wild mountain streams and deep, dark forests are typical of the state's northwest corner.

Loggers, loners, and lions know that Yaak River country is just this side of heaven.

Troy, Libby, and the in Yaak River Valley. But this is hardrock country, and for many years mining fell off as removing precious metals from the ore bodies in this area. New technology has revived the hardrock industry throughout western Montana, however, and the mining industry has set its sights on copper and silver deposits that lie beneath the Cabinet Mountains Wilderness. The Sterling Mining Company proposes one of the nation's largest underground mines near the town of Noxon, on the west side of the mountains. The huge Rock Creek Mine was formerly owned by ASARCO. Conservationists in Montana and Idaho have fought mineral development in this pristine wilderness since the late 1970s.

■ LIBBY   *map page 248, B-2*

One of the worst mining disasters in the nation's history only recently came to light in this sleepy town in Montana's extreme northwest corner. It took an investigative reporter from the *Seattle Post-Intelligencer* to uncover the cause of nearly 200 deaths in Libby due to asbestos poisoning from the now closed Zonolite vermiculite mine owned by the W. R. Grace Co. (the same firm made infamous by Jonathan Harr's *A Civil Action,* an account of the aftermath of cancer-causing industrial wastes deposited in the water table of Woburn, Massachusetts). There is plenty of blame to go around for Libby's dark secret. Company and government records show that not only did Grace know about the risk of the highly toxic form of vermiculite it was mining; so did state and federal health officials. And, in fact, so did Libby residents who feared the loss of good-paying jobs should the situation be known. So toxic is the substance that the wives and children of miners are still dying slow deaths caused by asbestosis and lung cancer.

Earlier in the century, the Lincoln County seat of Libby was a company town that owed its existence to a Wisconsin lumberman, Julius Neils, who purchased an existing mill in Libby in 1910 and eventually transformed it into the largest single lumber enterprise in Montana. In addition to the mill, the J. Neils Lumber Company owned timberlands, logging equipment, and railroads. The mill has since changed hands many times, and is an on-again-off-again component of the Libby area economy.

◆ HERITAGE FESTIVALS

Nevertheless, this community of 2,600 is proud of its roots and celebrates its cultural and ethnic heritage every year at well-attended festivals.

Logger Days

Lumberjack traditions are the focus during July's Logger Days, every July, the oldest festival of its kind in Montana. Unlike the eastern Montana rodeo circuit—where working cowboys and cowgirls cover up their lean bodies with cowboy hats, boots, and chaps, Libby Logger Days is an exhibition of biceps, beards, and billed caps. Professional loggers compete for the Montana Lumberjack Championship and "Bull of the Woods" title using chainsaws, crosscut saws, and axes.

Nordicfest

This celebration of the community's Scandinavian and northern European heritage draws thousands of visitors in September.

Crafts, quilts, antiques, "Norse-west" melodrama, a Norwegian fjord horse show, and food booths and meals featuring Scandinavian specialties highlight this three-day festival. Visitors are also attracted at this time of year to the stunning show of fall color that ignites the wooded landscape.

Hillsides covered with aspen and western larch form the monochromatic canvas which in fall becomes an impressionist painting, a wash of points and strokes in every gradation of color from green to gold to crimson. What distinguishes fall foliage here from autumn shows east of the Rockies is the predominance of the western larch, or tamarack, a conifer that sheds its lacy web of needles after its seasonal blaze of color has smoldered and died.

■ BULL RIVER VALLEY   *map page 248, A-2*

Two of the prime spots to view fall colors are the Bull and Yaak River Valleys. The Bull River waters a largely unsettled valley south of Troy. Bordered on both sides by the peaks of the Cabinet Mountains, the Bull River Valley encompasses public and private forest lands between US 2 and Montana State Highway 200. The Bull River Road (Montana State Highway 56) ushers travelers to backcountry lakes and campgrounds, as well as to a noble grove of giant western red cedars and to Montana's westernmost wilderness.

◆ ROSS CREEK CEDAR GROVE

The Ross Creek Cedar Grove, just west of Bull Lake, is a 100-acre preserve of old-growth cedars, some of which measure eight feet wide and soar to 175 feet. A short, self-guided nature trail with interpretive signs takes visitors through this enchanted woods, a fairy tale illustration complete with dangling ferns, crooked and bulbous trees snaking upward through the filtered light, and naturally hollowed out cedar trunks big enough to house an elf or a goblin.

◆ CABINET MOUNTAINS WILDERNESS   *map page 248, A/B-3*

On the east side of the road lies the 94,000-acre Cabinet Mountains Wilderness. This federally protected wilderness extends along the crest of the Cabinet Mountains, whose peaks appear higher than their actual elevation because they rise from the lowest corner of the state. Within viewing distance of 8,712-foot-high Snowshoe Peak (the Cabinets' highest summit), the Kootenai River leaves Montana at a mere 1,820 feet above sea level. Snow lies several feet deep in these mountains, providing more than 100 inches of runoff. The result is a tangle of trees, delicate ferns, and berry bushes. A network of trails penetrates this temperate jungle, taking hikers from the edge of the wilderness to its interior alpine lakes and ridgetops. Visitors come primarily for the fishing, berry-picking, and wildlife watching. A remnant population of grizzly bears inhabits the Cabinets, but more abundant are elk, deer, mountain goats, and bighorn sheep. This long, narrow forest preserve can be reached from Libby and US 2 on the east side as well as from the Bull River Road on the west.

■ THE YAAK   *map page 248, A-1*

The **Yaak River Valley,** to the north, is a wilderness without the capital W. If northwest Montana is remote, then this northwesternmost valley, known among Yaakers simply as the Yaak, is the end of the line. A paved road north of Troy follows not only the colorful fall trees but the colorful history of the valley nearly to the Canadian border. Abandoned homesteads, mining camps, logging roads, and clearcuts interrupt but never obscure the transcendent beauty of the Yaak River and the surrounding Purcell Mountains. Besides a few stray grizzly bears, caribou, and the usual complement of elk, deer, moose, mountain lions, and black bears, the Yaak is inhabited by loners, loggers, and a handful of urban migrants who believe they have died and gone to heaven. The social and commercial hub of the valley is the town of Yaak, which consists of the Dirty Shame Saloon and the Yaak Mercantile, a one-stop, one-room supply depot that stocks gas, propane, and limited groceries, swaps paperbacks, rents pipe dies and cable pulleys, takes phone messages, and dispenses hunting and fishing information.

■ LIBBY DAM   *map page 248, B-2*

From Yaak, motorists can follow Montana State Highway 508 back to Libby, or continue east along a paved forest road to Dodge Summit, then drop down to giant **Lake Koocanusa** at the base of the Purcells. The lake, whose name is an amalgam of Kootenai, Canada, and U.S.A, was created by the impoundment of the Kootenai River, a major tributary of the Columbia River. The massive project, begun in 1966 and completed in 1973, was carried out under the terms of an international treaty signed by the United States and Canada to achieve flood control, navigation, irrigation, and power generation on the river they share. In addition, the construction of Libby Dam, just 20 minutes from the town of Libby, created a brand new recreation area. Stretching 90 miles north of the dam, Lake Koocanusa crosses the international border about halfway up the lake. Montana's longest and highest bridge spans the lake near Rexford. Numerous campgrounds, boat ramps, and recreation areas surround the reservoir, while a visitor center, observation deck, and lounge can be found at the dam.

YAAK RIVER VALLEY: BEAUTY AND THE BEAST

I can't tell you when the blinders of art, only art, first lifted: at what precise point I looked beyond the immediate visual reaction of what was being done to the country—the surgical incisions of the clearcuts, the scalpings—and felt the unease, or dis-ease, deeply enough to begin acting, or trying to act, against it. I'm not sure at which point I allowed the pain of it to be absorbed by me deeply enough so that I had no choice but to react against it. The clearcuts were never attractive, but for at least a year or two they did not touch me or harm me, nor my belief in peace, the way they do now—as does the threat of those clearcuts yet to come.

There had to be some point, though—some moment, some place, where something in me reached saturation—where I could not accept the sight of it anymore, and the knowledge of what the roads and clearcuts were doing to the ecology of the valley as well as to the economy of man. Undoubtedly this feeling of pain, this saturation, came at some point after I had gone through a full cycle of the four seasons; perhaps after I had gone through them a couple of times. I moved through the woods on hikes and hunts, open-minded—I had heard that the clearcuts were sometimes beneficial for the production of summer browse for deer (never mind that the deer populations might rise beyond the limitations of their winter range). There still seemed to be plenty of diversity in the forest types I saw, and the roadless cores—the sanctuaries—still seemed intact.

That was just over a decade ago. I'm not sure when I began to realize that they—the timber industry—wanted it all: or if not all of it immediately, then access to all of it, forever. Or as the occasional bumper sticker declared, "Wilderness = Land of No Use."

Each season, I picked up the feel and taste of cycles. My blood began to learn new rhythms. My body became increasingly fluent in the language of cycles: splitting wood on cold mornings, cleaning a grouse in the evening—the solace, and ceremony, of plucking the feathers. Noticing where elk foraged in summer and where they foraged in winter. Noticing where the bears fed and what they ate. Watching the pulse of different creeks and the Yaak River itself—skinny in autumn, icy but poised in winter—wild, joyful and enormous in spring, then steady and clear on into summer, with caddis flies and mayflies rising from it every evening, and the giant spruce and fir trees shadowing it, keeping it cool and alive...

Small cycles radiated into larger ones. I kept following them—noticing different ones each day—and continue to. I became more comfortable moving through the woods—slipping between alder, climbing under and over the latticework of lodgepole blowdown, crossing streams on slippery cedar logs, climbing the rock cliffs, descending the avalanche chutes into the parklike stands of old growth larch, their needles brilliant gold in the autumn, and brilliant gold underfoot, as if moving across a land padded with gold, an inch of black soil atop the rocky rubble-traces of glaciers; sometimes two inches of soil, sometimes three, but then rock, with the soil so thin underfoot that you did not have to be a scientist to understand that one shot was all most of this place was ever going to have at grace—that it had taken some of these trees, these forests, five hundred years to achieve climax, five hundred years and three inches, and that once you swept them clean, the soil would go with them, and for a long time there would be only emptiness, rather than grace—that then there would be only the echo of grace.

I hiked around, just watching and listening. Making up my own mind. Noticing the difference between logged and unlogged areas. Not all logged areas had that confusion of spirit or loss of grace; some of them retained, or reshaped, the grace of the woods (or rather, the grace of the woods altered itself and still flowed around and through those areas that had been logged with care and respect).

But even those areas compared in no way with the untouched areas—the incredible vitality of cycles still ongoing in the deep places of the valley—the last untouched corners.

I realized that the point at which what was being done to the valley began to hurt me deeply was the time I first began to feel that I was starting to fit: that the landscape and I were engaged in a relationship. That I was being reshaped and refashioned, to better fit it in spirit and desire. That I was neither fighting this nor resisting it. As it became my home, the wounds that were being inflicted upon it—the insults—became my own.

—Rick Bass, *The Book of Yaak*, 1996

Like most dams, this one sparked considerable debate over the loss of wildlife habitat, alteration of streamflow, and erosion of the local tax base caused by the flooding of productive lands. New recreation and wildlife sites have appeased some of the critics, but many residents still mourn the shackling of a great wild river. On the lighter side, the project revealed insight into the Montana mindset the day former President Gerald Ford came to town to dedicate Libby Dam. Local lore has it that the President's bodyguards were alarmed by all the guns they saw, mounted on gunracks in nearly every pickup in town. Instructed to remove all these firearms, the local sheriff is said to have responded with a laugh that said, "You gotta be kidding." Apparently he satisfied visiting law-enforcement personnel with a quick lesson in local culture, explaining that in Montana, hunting is a religion and guns are a birthright.

■ KOOTENAI COUNTRY   *map page 248, A/B-1*

When Montanans aren't hunting or fishing, they're likely to be scouting their next hunting or fishing trip. In the Northwest Corner, the possibilities are unlimited, not just for sporting expeditions but simply for enjoying the outdoors. Covering 2.25 million acres—an area nearly three times the size of Rhode Island—the Kootenai National Forest *is* northwestern Montana. In addition to the Kootenai River, Lake Koocanusa, and the Cabinet Mountains Wilderness, the forest encompasses several smaller rivers, more than 100 lakes, and two special management areas in addition to the Ross Creek Cedars.

◆ SCENIC AREAS

The **Northwest Peaks Scenic Area** is a rugged 19,000-acre landscape of high peaks and deep valleys that nearly touches both Canada and Idaho. With few trails and unpredictable weather, it appeals to adventurers seeking a primitive experience.

Ten Lakes Scenic Area, to the east, is for the rest of us. Sculpted by glaciers, this cavernous valley of high lake basins, streams, waterfalls, forests, and wildflowers has long been considered a candidate for federal wilderness protection. Hiking and horseback trails crisscross its 15,700-acre interior, with public campgrounds at a couple of trailheads. The best approach is from U.S. Route 93, between Fortine and Eureka. Both of these scenic areas are gorgeous and empty.

◆ RIVER VALLEYS

While nearly all of northwestern Montana is shaded by trees, it is bordered on the north and south by two open, river-fed valleys that support limited agriculture. On the north, the **Tobacco Valley** takes its name from the crop once cultivated here by Kootenai Indians. **Eureka,** its major community, is now more famous for its Christmas trees.

To the south, **Thompson Falls** sits on the Clark Fork River and relies on a mix of logging, agriculture, and recreation. This corner of the state also supports Montana's only Amish community. Founded in 1985 by a small group of Amish migrants from the Midwest, the colony has since split in two, with one community staying in Rexford and the other living near Libby. The primary source of revenue for both is a log-home business.

STEINBECK'S MONTANA

I am in love with Montana. For other states I have admiration, respect, recognition, even some affection, but with Montana it is love, and it's difficult to analyze love when you're in it.... It seems to me that Montana is a great splash of grandeur. The scale is huge but not overpowering. The land is rich with grass and color, and the mountains are the kind I would create if mountains were ever put on my agenda. Montana seems to me to be what a small boy would think Texas is like from hearing Texans. Here for the first time I heard a definite regional accent unaffected by TV-ese, a slow-paced warm speech. It seemed to me that the frantic bustle of America was not in Montana. Its people did not seem afraid of shadows in a John Birch Society sense. The calm of the mountains and the rolling grasslands had got into the inhabitants. It was hunting season when I drove through the state. The men I talked to seemed to me not moved to a riot of seasonal slaughter but simply to be going out to kill edible meat. Again my attitude may be informed by love, but it seemed to me that the towns were places to live in rather than nervous hives. People had time to pause in their occupations to undertake the passing art of neighborliness.

—John Steinbeck, *Travels with Charley: In Search of America,* 1962

S C E N I C   R O A D S

IN A STATE AS GRAND AND DIVERSE as Montana, nearly every highway has scenic appeal. Depending on your preference for plains or mountains, gravel or blacktop, however, some are more inviting than others. When traveling on backroads through western Montana's forests, it's always a good idea to have a forest map in addition to the state highway map When driving on eastern Montana's back roads, it's important to keep your eye on weather conditions since even the slightest rain can turn the clay-like soil to gumbo and stop you in your tracks. Unpaved roads should be regarded as seasonal routes, best traveled in summer and early fall. The numbers in front of the following road descriptions are keyed to the Scenic Roads map on page 258.

A country road north of Helena.

■ EASTERN MONTANA

① **MT 200 from Lewistown to Sidney** *(paved):*
Take to the open road through the heart of the Big Open. This trip is a meditation on sage and sky; for the sheer love of driving, it can't be beat. (270 miles).

② **Crooked Creek, Hell Creek, and Pines Roads** *(gravel):*
These scenic routes through badlands and breaks provide rugged, all-weather access to giant Fort Peck Lake and the C. M. Russell Wildlife Refuge, with few people and lots of watchable wildlife. All lead to recreation areas on the lake. Crooked Creek Road runs north from Winnett (40 miles); Hell Creek Road is north of Jordan (30 miles); and Pines Road runs southwest from MT 24, north of the town of Fort Peck (25 miles).

③ **Makoshika State Park** *(gravel/unimproved):*
In this badlands park are close to 10 miles of scenic roads with to overlooks, vistas, and nature trails. Travelers should check weather and road conditions before proceeding beyond Tower Junction toward Artists Point or the Sand Creek Overlook.

SCENIC ROADS

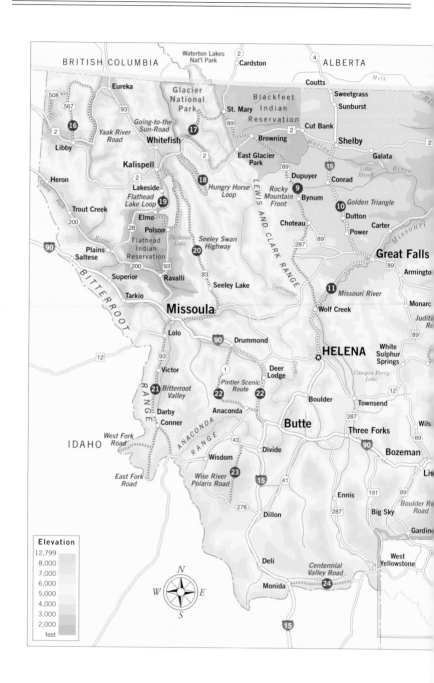

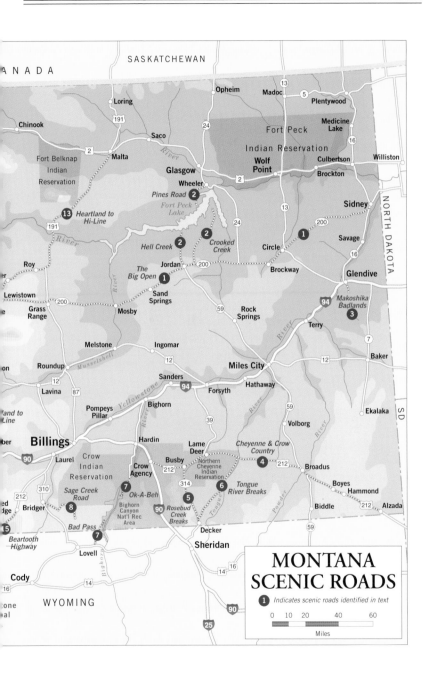

CANADA
SASKATCHEWAN

Loring
Opheim
Madoc
Plentywood
13
5

Chinook
191
Saco
Medicine Lake
16

Fort Belknap Indian Reservation
2
Malta
River
Fort Peck Indian Reservation
Wolf Point
Culbertson
Williston

Glasgow
Wheeler
2
Brockton
NORTH DAKOTA

13
Heartland to Hi-Line
Pines Road
2
Sidney

191
River
Hell Creek
2
Fort Peck Lake
2
Crooked Creek
Circle
200
Savage

Roy
The Big Open
Jordan
1
200
Brockway
94
Makoshika Badlands
3
Glendive

Lewistown
Sand Springs
59
Rock Springs
Terry
7

Grass Range
200
Mosby
Baker

Melstone
Ingomar
12
Miles City
12

Roundup
Musselshell
Sanders
94
Forsyth
Hathaway

Lavina
12
87
Yellowstone
Bighorn
39
59
Volborg
Ekalaka
SD

Billings
90
Hardin
Lame Deer
Cheyenne & Crow Country
4
212
Broadus

Laurel
Crow Indian Reservation
Crow Agency
7
Busby
212
Northern Cheyenne Indian Reservation
6
Tongue River Breaks
Boyes
Hammond

310
Sage Creek Road
Ok-A-Beh
314
5
212
Biddle
212
Alzada

Bridger
8
Bighorn Canyon Nat'l Rec Area
90
Rosebud Creek Breaks
Powder River
59

15
Bad Pass
7
Decker

Beartooth Highway
Lovell
Sheridan

Cody
14
14
16

Yellowstone
WYOMING
90
25

MONTANA SCENIC ROADS

1 *Indicates scenic roads identified in text*

0 10 20   40   60

Miles

SCENIC ROADS

④ **US 212 between Alzada and Crow Agency** *(paved):*
Rough breaks and badlands, ponderosa pine forests, abundant wildlife, rivers that flower the plains, two Indian reservations, and the Little Bighorn Battlefield National Monument are all part of the view along southeastern Montana's major east-west artery. 165 miles.

⑤ **Route 314 between Busby and Decker** *(paved):*
Red cliffs, wildlife, and the Rosebud Creek breaks are all part of the immediate view, while the Rosebud Mountains rise in the west. About 35 miles.

⑥ **Tongue River Breaks** *(gravel):*
Follow the Tongue River from Ashland to Birney, then down to the Tongue River Reservoir on a road that follows the river (after you pass the Diamond Cross Ranch, be on the lookout for a sign to the Tongue River Dam; follow the sign). You will drive through the austerely beautiful Tongue River Canyon, with views of coulees and breaks, red scoria rock, and weathered pines. Camping, boating, and good fishing for walleye, crappie, and bass at the reservoir. About 45 miles.

⑦ **Ok-A-Beh and Bad Pass roads at Bighorn Canyon National Recreation** *(paved):*
Ok-A-Beh (between Fort Smith and the Ok-A-Beh boat ramp) takes motorists through a short-grass prairie with expansive views of the Bighorn Mountains and Bighorn River Valley (11 miles). At the south end of the canyon (entered via Lovell, Wyoming), the Bad Pass Road connects Horseshoe Bend and Barry's Landing. The best view of the canyon is along this road at Devil Canyon Overlook (17 miles).

Hell Creek Road in eastern Montana (above) and Going-to-the-Sun-Road (above opposite).

⑧ **Pryor Mountains/Sage Creek Road** *(gravel):*
A lovely, lightly traveled route into the Pryors south of Billings. There's lots to explore in this remote, highland junction of desert and ice, including numerous ice caves and a wild horse range. It's easy to get lost, so be sure to have a Custer National Forest map About 30 miles from the US 310 turnoff south of Bridger to the Big Ice Cave.

■ CENTRAL MONTANA

⑨ **Rocky Mountain Front** *(paved):*
Follow US Routes 89/287 from Glacier National Park to Wolf Creek. This is a dramatic landscape where the mountains meet the plains (about 140 miles).

⑩ **Interstate 15, between Shelby and Great Falls** *(paved):*
In late summer, precede the harvest through the heart of Montana's Golden Triangle. Rippling waves of grain break over oceans of ripening wheat fields (85 miles).

⑪ **Interstate 15, between Great Falls and Helena** *(paved):*
Follow the Missouri through Charlie Russell country as the suns sets over Square Butte, painting a picture as brilliant as any painted by Russell himself. A paved recreation road between Cascade and Wolf Creek has river access and views of the river and the rock sculpture of Wolf Creek Canyon (90 miles, total; recreation road, 35 miles).

⑫ **Judith River Valley** *(gravel):*
Follow this back road along the Judith and the South Fork of the Judith through the grass-rich valley where Charlie Russell first lived in Montana. It's working cattle and dude-ranch country along the eastern edge of the Little Belts (about 50 miles).

⑬ **US 191 between Big Timber and Malta** *(paved):*
View central Montana's "island" mountain ranges—the Crazies, the Snowies, the Judith Mountains and the Little Rockies—as you drive through the farm and ranch country between Big Timber and Lewistown, and the breaks and badlands of the Missouri River farther north (235 miles). Inviting side trips (on mostly unpaved roads) include the ice caves and waterfalls in the Big Snowy Mountains, Judith Mountain ghost towns north of Lewistown, Slippery Ann Wildlife Viewing Area at the western edge of the C. M. Russell National Wildlife Refuge, the historic mining town of Zortman in the Little Rockies, and Mission Canyon at the south end of the Fort Belknap Indian Reservation.

⑭ **Boulder River Valley south of Big Timber** *(pavement/gravel):*
Follow Route 298 past some of Montana's most beautiful ranches along a corridor that leads to the Absaroka-Beartooth Wilderness. The road turns from pavement to gravel to dirt before ending at a wilderness trailhead, with fishing, camping, and hiking along the way (about 45 miles).

⑮ **Beartooth Highway/US 212** *(paved):*
Renowned as one of North America's most beautiful drives, the Beartooth begins at Red Lodge and climbs the glacially carved walls of Rock Creek Canyon en route to Yellowstone National Park. Switchbacks and hairpin turns twist higher and higher until the highway levels off at nearly 11,000 feet. This breathtaking route is generally open from late May to mid-October (68 slow miles).

■ WESTERN MONTANA

⑯ **Yaak River Road** *(paved):*
Route 508, north of Troy, follows the Yaak River through the Kootenai National Forest, with views of the Purcell Mountains. At Yaak, turn south on 508 to get back to Libby (loop is about 100 miles), or continue east on Route 92 to Rexford. There, you can cross Lake Koocanusa to Montana State Highway 37 or travel south on Forest Road 228 along the west side of the lake (loop is about 150 miles).

⑰ **Going-to-the-Sun Road** *(paved):*
This is Glacier National Park's magnificent east-west highway, starting at either St. Mary or West Glacier and crossing the Continental Divide at Logan Pass. It's normally open from early June into October. Summer crowds and scenic turnoffs make this a slow trip (55 miles).

⑱ **Hungry Horse Loop** *(gravel):*
Make a full circuit around 34-mile-long Hungry Horse Reservoir, along the west edge of the Great Bear Wilderness. There are plenty of campgrounds, boat launches, trailheads, and great views all the way around (115 miles, takes about six hours).

⑲ **Flathead Lake Loop** *(paved):*
Montana State Highways 35, 82, and US 93 form a scenic loop around Flathead Lake, with views of the lake and the Swan Range, plus access to state parks and campgrounds (about 85 miles).

⑳ **Seeley Swan Highway** *(paved):*
Montana State Highway 83 follows a chain of lakes through dense forests, with views of the Mission and the Swan ranges. Access to campgrounds, lakes, hiking trails, and fishing spots (91 miles).

㉑ **Bitterroot Valley, US 93** *(paved):*
This is a busy highway that follows the Bitterroot Valley and provides magnificent views of the Bitterroot Range and the Sapphire Mountains; between Florence and Hamilton, the East Side Highway (County Road 269) is a leisurely alternative, with access to the Lee Metcalf Wilderness. At the south end of the valley, the secondary East Fork and West Fork roads provide scenic access to fishing, hiking, and camping.

㉒ **Pintler Scenic Route** (paved):
Montana State Highway 1, between Drummond and Anaconda, follows Flint Creek to Georgetown Lake, with views of the Flint Creek Range and the Anaconda Pintler Wilderness, and access to fishing, camping, and ghost towns (55 miles). Interstate 90, east of Anaconda, forms a loop back to Drummond, via Deer Lodge and the Grant-Kohrs Ranch National Historic Site.

㉓ **Wise River-Polaris Road** *(pavement/gravel):*
This is an enjoyable back road through the Pioneer Mountains, recently designated a National Scenic Byway. Besides great views of the East and West Pioneers, it offers access to camping, hiking, and fishing, the ghost town of Coolidge, and a rockhounder's playground called Crystal Park. Most easily traveled in the summer, but also popular with snowmobilers and skiers in the winter (40 miles).

㉔ **Centennial Valley Road** *(gravel):*
This is a rough road to paradise, best traveled in summer. It lies west of Yellowstone National Park, between the Centennial Mountains and Red Rock Lakes National Wildlife Refuge. The refuge is home to the rare trumpeter swan and a tremendous diversity of waterfowl, shorebirds, songbirds, and raptors. Elk, moose, antelope, and other wildlife abound in the surrounding, sparsely settled valley (about 55 miles).

TRANSPORTATION

STATEWIDE TRAVEL
INFORMATION

Listings

■ AREA CODE

The area code for all of Montana is 406. Use it when dialing in-state as well as when dialing from outside.

■ TRANSPORTATION

◆ BY AIR

Because Montana is so far removed from the nation's major air routes, it is about as expensive to fly from Denver to Montana's capital city of Helena as it is to fly from Los Angeles to New York. Nonetheless, there are plenty of flights in and out of Montana. Three of the nation's major airlines—Northwest, Delta, and United serve the principal cities, with commuter lines making connections from smaller towns. Montana's largest commercial airports, ranked in order of passenger traffic, are Billings, Bozeman, Missoula, Kalispell, Great Falls, Helena, and Butte. West Yellowstone has commercial air service in the summer, and the smaller towns of Miles City, Glendive, Sidney, Wolf Point, Glasgow, Havre, and Lewistown are served year-round by commuter flights.

◆ BY CAR

Most of Montana's visitors arrive by car on interstate highways. Two east-west interstate highways (Interstates 90 and 94) converge in Billings, while Butte lies at the junction of Montana's major north-south and east-west routes (Interstates 15 and 90). State highways and secondary roads provide access to Montana's smaller towns and hidden places, while gravel roads reach deep into Montana's vast backcountry and open spaces. The deeper they go, the better they get. Visitors should take note that eastern Montana is notorious for a soil condition that turns clay into greasy grabby gumbo and renders travel difficult to impossible after even the slightest rain. It is always a good idea in this part of the state to check on weather and road conditions before leaving the pavement. There are so few people out here that if you get lost or stuck, you may be on your own for quite awhile.

Highway rest areas appear sporadically along the interstates, but there aren't enough of them to satisfy most motorists, especially in winter, when many are closed. The Montana Highway Department does a fine job of maintaining roads in good driving condition year-round. Sudden storms occasionally block highways in winter, but not for long. Nevertheless, smart winter motorists are prepared for the worst. Although few motorists carry all of these items, the ultimate winter survival kit would include snow tires or chains, a shovel and window scraper, flares or a reflector, a blanket or sleeping bag, a first-aid kit, sand, gravel or traction mats, a flashlight with extra batteries, matches, a lighter or candle, paper, non-perishable foods, and a tow chain or rope.

Because distances are long and traffic is light, Montanans are notoriously fast drivers. Montana gained national notoriety in the 1990s when the State Legislature abolished all speed limits. Thrill seekers around the nation came to test their wits and their wheels on the "Montabahn" for several years until legislators came to their senses and reinstituted numerical speed limits on Montana roadways.

◆ BY RAIL

Amtrak's Empire Builder parallels U.S. 2 across northern Montana, en route between St. Paul and Seattle. The passenger train makes daily stops at 11 stations along the Hi-Line. At East and West Glacier, it drops summer visitors off at Glacier National Park, and at Whitefish, it delivers skiers to The Big Mountain winter resort. Call Amtrak at 800-872-7245.

◆ BY BUS

Greyhound Lines provides east-west service along Interstates 90 and 94, with stops in all major cities, including Glendive, Miles City, Billings, Livingston, Bozeman, Butte, and Missoula. Greyhound also travels U.S. 191 between Bozeman and Idaho Falls, with a stop in West Yellowstone. A local bus company, Rimrock Trailways, provides passenger service to Anaconda, Dillon, Helena, Billings, Bozeman, Missoula, Great Falls, Kalispell, Havre, Lewistown, Shelby, and Cut Bank. Kaarst Stage of Bozeman provides seasonal service from Bozeman and Livingston to Yellowstone Park, and a Wyoming bus line, Powder River Transportation, travels Interstate 90 south of Billings through Hardin.

(above) Sheep wagons are still commonly seen across Montana; this one has been retired to the Sod Buster Museum in Windham.

(opposite) An old gas pump stands outside the Utica Museum in central Montana.

■ SEASONS

Travel Seasons. Montana has two distinct travel seasons and two shoulder seasons. Winter travel is growing each year, but the vast majority of Montana's visitors still prefer to explore Montana in the trusted comfort zone of summer.

High Season. Warm-weather travel reaches its peak during July and August, Montana's hottest, driest period. Skies are clear, roads are dry, fishing, hiking, and camping are in full swing, and summer events are back to back.

Autumn. An initial jolt of cold weather, usually in early September, scares most visitors away. But residents know the best time of year is at hand. Warm, bright days and crisp nights linger into October, even early November. Summer crowds have subsided, aspen and larch kindle Montana's fall colors, the air is exhilarating, and the fishing is prime.

Spring. The other side of autumn is spring, which is received as a tonic by residents, but is too cool and wet for most visitors. Rivers are high, backroads and trails are still snowed in, and spring storms are frequent.

Winter Cold. Montana often makes the national news with record low temperatures from a couple of notorious weather stations near Glacier and Yellowstone national parks. As a result, Montana has an undeserved reputation as an icebox. Unlike many areas of the nation, however, where winter settles in for keeps, Montana's cold spells are frequently interrupted by Chinook winds and mild periods. Its dry climate also makes Montana milder than most Midwestern states. While temperatures can be extreme in Montana, humidity is low, so the weather is never oppressively hot or cold. The coldest sub-zero day in Montana is never as cold as the coldest winter day in Minneapolis or Chicago.

Summer Heat. The hottest summer day in Montana is never suffocating like a summer day in Washington, D.C. Humidity rarely reaches 50 percent, and generally ranges between 20 and 30 percent.

Rainfall. Average annual rainfall is 15 inches (38 cm), varying from less than 10 inches (25 cm) on the plains to more than 50 inches (125 cm) in the mountains. Average daytime temperatures vary from 0° F (-16° C) in January to 85° F (29° C) in July.

Weather Patterns. Montana's weather patterns are generally more extreme in the east than they are in the west. Winters are colder and summers are hotter on the plains than they are in the mountains, where a milder, Pacific weather system prevails.

■ VISITOR INFORMATION

Whatever the season, Montana's dress code is informal. Wardrobes run from shorts and slacks in summer to wool pants, flannel shirts, and sweaters in winter. Jeans are always in season and jackets or sweaters are never out of reach. Contrary to modern folklore, not every Montanan wears cowboy boots. Visitors are often amused, however, by the high proportion of Montana businessmen who combine boots and ties. Most sports practitioners wouldn't leave home without their favorite fly rod, touring bike, or kayak. All of those toys and more can be put to good use in Montana. But if you're traveling far or just getting started, most sporting goods stores around the state will rent the equipment you need to sample the great outdoors. From backpacks to skis, mountain bikes to horses, all can be had on a rental basis.

Montana has a growing number of distinctive homes that take in guests. To accommodate this growth, the Montana **Bed & Breakfast Association** has been formed to help keep standards up. Call 800-453-8870 for a free directory. While they are a good central resource for finding accommodations, many non-association B&B's offer excellent lodging opportunities.

State Visitor Agencies

Montana Arts Council.
316 N. Park, Helena, MT 59620;
406-444-6430

Montana Board of Outfitters.
111 N. Jackson St., Helena, MT 59620;
406-444-3738

Montana Department of Fish, Wildlife & Parks.
1420 E. Sixth Ave., Helena, MT 59620;
406-444-2535

Montana Department of Transportation.
2701 Prospect Ave., Helena, MT
59620; 406-444-6200

Montana Historical Society.
225 N. Roberts St., Helena, MT 59620;
406-444-2694

Montana Outfitters & Guides Association.
Box 1248, Helena, MT 59624;
406-449-3578

Statewide Weather Reports.
406-453-2081

Road Reports.
800-226-7623

Travel Montana.
1424 Ninth Ave., Helena, MT 59620;
800-VISIT MT or www.visitmt.com
This is the foremost source for comprehensive statewide tourist information.

Lodging Services

www.elderhostel.org
Group travel and educational
opportunities for seniors.

Montana Bed & Breakfast Association.
800-453-8870; www.mtbba.com

Montana Ranch Vacation Association.
406-328-6883.

Montana Dude Ranch Association.
www.montanadra.com

www.montanalewisandclark.org
The definitive word on Lewis and Clark
Bicentennial Observance activities and
events in Montana.

www.discoveringmontana.com
A comprehensive website about
Montana, including visitor information.

National Parks and Forests

Beaverhead Dearlodge National Forests.
420 Barrett St., Dillon 59725;
406-683-3900

Bitterroot National Forest.
1801 N. First St., Missoula 59840;
406-363-3131

Custer National Forest.
2602 First Ave. N., Billings 59103;
406-657-6361

Flathead National Forest.
1935 Third Ave. E., Kalispell 59901;
406-755-5401

Gallatin National Forest.
Federal Building, Bozeman 59715;
406-587-6701

Glacier National Park.
West Glacier 59936;
406-888-7800

Helena National Forest.
2880 Skyway Dr. (near airport), Helena
59601; 406-449-5201

Kootenai National Forest.
506 US 2 W., Libby 59923;
406-293-6211

Lewis and Clark National Forest.
1101 15th St. N., Great Falls 59403;
406-791-7700

Lolo National Forest.
Fort Missoula, Missoula 59801;
406-329-3750

U.S. Bureau of Land Management.
Box 36800, Billings 59107;
406-255-2938

U.S.D.A. Forest Service.
Northern Region; 200 E. Broadway,
Missoula 59807; 406-329-3511

Yellowstone National Park.
Yellowstone National Park, WY 82190;
307-344-7381

RECOMMENDED READING

■ HISTORY

Abbott, E. C., and Helena Huntington Smith. *We Pointed Them North: Recollections of a Cowpuncher.* Norman: University of Oklahoma Press, 1955. One of Montana's best storytellers recounts the glory days of the open range.

Alderson, Nannie T., and Helena Huntington Smith. *A Bride Goes West.* Lincoln: University of Nebraska Press, 1969. One of the finest records of a woman's life on the Montana frontier.

Ambrose, Stephen E., *Undaunted Courage.* New York: Simon & Schuster, 1996. The Lewis and Clark Expedition comes alive in the hands of this first-class historian.

DeVoto, Bernard, ed. *The Journals of Lewis and Clark.* (abr.) Boston: Houghton Mifflin, 1953. Meriwether Lewis and William Clark were better explorers than they were writers, but the journals they kept as they traveled up the Missouri and across the Northern Rockies are delightful reading for anyone following the same route, either by car or canoe.

Garcia, Andrew. *Tough Trip Through Paradise.* Sausalito, CA: Comstock Editions, 1976. A mountain man's lively account of life among the Indians.

Glasscock, C. B. *The War of the Copper Kings.* New York: Bobbs-Merrill, 1935. Much of Montana's history was written in the mining city of Butte, and no one has written a more colorful account than this one.

Malone, Michael, Richard Roeder, and William Lang. *Montana: A History of Two Centuries.* Seattle: University of Washington Press, 1991. Standard text on Montana history.

Russell, Charles M. *Trails Plowed Under.* New York: Doubleday, 1937. Colorful yarns about the West by the famed cowboy artist.

■ NATIVE AMERICANS

Brown, Mark H. The Flight of the Nez Perce. Lincoln: University of Nebraska Press, 1982. The definitive work on the Nez Perce War of 1877.

Bryan, William L., Jr. *Montana Indians: Yesterday and Today.* Helena: American Geographic Publishing, 1985. Words and photographs illustrate the diversity, cultural traditions, and contemporary issues of Montana's Indian tribes.

Bullchild, Percy. *The Sun Came Down.* New York: Harper & Row, 1985. A collection of Blackfeet Indian stories acclaimed as one of the finest ever published of traditional Native American literature.

Deloria, Vine, Jr. *Custer Died for Your Sins: An Indian Manifesto.* Norman: University of Oklahoma Press, 1985. Witty, incisive polemic about this nation's dismal relationship with its native inhabitants.

Farr, William E. *The Reservation Blackfeet, 1882–1945: A Photographic History of Cultural Survival.* Seattle: University of Washington Press, 1986. Graphically illustrates the impact of Euro-American civilization on native culture.

■ REMINISCENCES & ESSAYS

Bass, Rick. *The Book of Yaak* and *Winter.* New York: Houghton Mifflin, 1996. Passionate pleas of preservation and eloquent exaltations on the wonders of the Yaak River Valley, a remote corner of the state criss-crossed with clearcuts and pristine open spaces.

Doig, Ivan. *This House of Sky: Landscapes of a Western Mind.* Orlando: Harcourt Brace, 1978. A gifted Montana writer explores his connections to the land and the people who shaped his values.

Duncan, Dayton. *Out West.* New York: Penguin Viking, 1987. Follow the same route Lewis and Clark did through the eyes of a modern explorer.

Frazier, Ian. *Great Plains.* New York: Farrar, Straus & Giroux, 1989. From Custer and Crazy Horse to MX missiles, Frazier gives his readers a new look at America's heartland.

Kittredge, William, ed. *Montana Spaces.* New York: Lyons & Burford, 1988. Original essays about the land and the people of Montana by some of the West's finest writers.

Kittredge, William, and Annick Smith, eds. *The Last Best Place.* Seattle: University of Washington Press, 1988. The best in history, poetry, and literature, all wrapped up in one five-pound volume.

Maclean, Norman. *A River Runs Through It and Other Stories.* Chicago: University of Chicago Press, 1976. Humor and tragedy blend in this American classic about living and fishing in the Blackfoot River country of Montana.

McFadden, Cyra. *Rain or Shine.* New York: Alfred A. Knopf, 1986. The daughter of a famous Montana rodeo announcer and dancer-turned-trick rider recounts her childhood on the rodeo circuit.

Newby, Rick, and Suzanne Hunger, eds. *Writing Montana. Literature under the Big Sky.* Helena: Montana Center for the Book, 1996. Twenty-seven essayists examine Montana's literary tradition.

Stegner, Wallace. *Wolf Willow.* Lincoln: University of Nebraska Press, 1980. One of the West's great writers explores his boyhood on the plains of southern Saskatchewan, just north of the Montana border.

■ POETRY

Hugo, Richard. *The Lady in Kicking Horse Reservoir.* New York: Norton, 1973. Before his death in 1982, this poet was mentor to many of Montana's leading writers as director of the University of Montana's creative writing program.

Keeler, Greg. *American Falls.* Confluence Press, 1987. Fishing is the metaphor for this poetry by a delightfully offbeat professor-writer-musician-angler.

McRae, Wallace. *It's Just Grass and Water.* Oxalis, 1986. One of Montana's favorite cowboy poets talks of life on the range.

Zarzyski, Paul. *Roughstock Sonnets.* Kansas City: Lowell Press, 1989. Refreshing and contemporary twist on cowboy poetry.

■ FICTION

Doig, Ivan. *Dancing at the Rascal Fair.* New York: Atheneum, 1987. A chronicle of the American experience, beginning in Scotland in 1889 and ending three decades later on the Rocky Mountain frontier. *Bucking the Sun.* New York: Simon & Schuster, 1996. A novel built against the backdrop of the construction of Fort Peck Dam.

Dorris, Michael. *A Yellow Raft in Blue Water.* New York: Warner Books, 1988. A sensitive and spellbinding portrait of three generations of contemporary Indian women.

Guthrie, A. B., Jr. *The Big Sky.* Boston: Houghton Mifflin, 1947. The best known of several historical novels by Montana's Pulitzer prize winner.

Johnson, Dorothy. *A Man Called Horse,* and *The Hanging Tree.* New York: Ballantine, 1953, 1957 (respectively). Two of the late Montana author's short stories that became motion pictures.

Rolvaag, O. E. *Giants in the Earth.* New York: Harper & Row, 1965. You will taste the dust and dread the wind by the time you finish this classic about the homestead experience.

Walker, Mildred. *Winter Wheat.* New York: Harcourt Brace, 1944. A girl grows up in the dryland wheat country of central Montana.

Welch, James. *Fools Crow.* New York: Viking Penguin, 1986. A fictional account of the impact of white civilization on a band of Blackfeet Indians.

■ GLACIER AND YELLOWSTONE NATIONAL PARKS

For a complete list of field guides, general books, and maps, contact:

Glacier Natural History Association. Box 327, West Glacier, MT 59936; (406) 888-5756

Yellowstone Natural History Association. Box 117, Yellowstone National Park, WY 82190; (307) 344-7381

I N D E X

COMPASS AMERICAN GUIDES

Alaska
(3rd edition)
$21.00 ($32.00 Can)
0-679-00838-1

Arizona
(5th edition)
$19.95 ($29.95 Can)
0-679-00432-7

Boston
(3rd edition)
$21.00 ($32.00 Can)
0-676-90132-8

Chicago
(3rd edition)
$21.00 ($32.00 Can)
0-679-00841-1

Coastal California
(2nd edition)
$21.00 ($32.00 Can)
0-679-00439-4

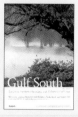
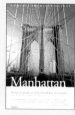

Colorado
(5th edition)
$19.95 ($29.95 Can)
0-679-00435-1

Florida
(1st edition)
$19.95 ($27.95 Can)
0-679-03392-0

Georgia
(2nd edition)
$21.95 ($32.95 Can)
0-676-90137-9

Gulf South
(1st edition)
$21.00 ($32.00 Can)
0-679-00533-1

Hawaii
(5th edition)
$21.00 ($32.00 Can)
0-679-00839-X

Idaho
(2nd edition)
$21.00 ($32.00 Can)
0-679-00231-6

Kentucky
(1st edition)
$21.00 ($32.00 Can)
0-679-00537-4

Las Vegas
(7th edition)
$21.00 ($32.00 Can)
0-676-90138-7

Maine
(3rd edition)
$19.95 ($29.95 Can)
0-679-00436-X

Manhattan
(3rd edition)
$19.95 ($29.95 Can)
0-679-00228-6

Michigan
(1st edition)
$21.00 ($32.00 Can)
0-679-00534-X

Minnesota
(2nd edition)
$19.95 ($29.95 Can)
0-679-00437-8

Nevada
(1st edition)
$21.00 ($32.00 Can)
0-679-00535-8

New Mexico
(4th edition)
$21.00 ($32.00 Can)
0-679-00438-6

New Orleans
(4th edition)
$21.00 ($32.00 Can)
0-679-00647-8